THE MISSIONARY SPIRIT

The American Society of Missiology Series, published in collaboration with Orbis Books, seeks to publish scholarly works of high merit and wide interest on numerous aspects of missiology—the study of Christian mission in its historical, social, and theological dimensions. Able presentations on new and creative approaches to the practice and understanding of mission will receive close attention from the ASM Series Committee.

American Society of Missiology Series, No. 61

THE MISSIONARY SPIRIT

Evangelism and Social Action in Pentecostal Missiology

Jerry M. Ireland

ORBIS BOOKS
Maryknoll, New York 10545

Founded in 1970, Orbis Books endeavors to publish works that enlighten the mind, nourish the spirit, and challenge the conscience. The publishing arm of the Maryknoll Fathers and Brothers, Orbis seeks to explore the global dimensions of the Christian faith and mission, to invite dialogue with diverse cultures and religious traditions, and to serve the cause of reconciliation and peace. The books published reflect the views of their authors and do not represent the official position of the Maryknoll Society. To learn more about Orbis Books, please visit our website at www.orbisbooks.com.

Copyright © 2021 by Jerry M. Ireland.

Published by Orbis Books, Box 302, Maryknoll, NY 10545-0302.

All rights reserved.

All scripture quotations are from the NASB95 Bible unless otherwise noted.

No part of this publication may be reproduced or transmitted in any form or by any means, electronic or mechanical, including photocopying, recording, or any information storage or retrieval system, without prior permission in writing from the publisher.

Queries regarding rights and permissions should be addressed to: Orbis Books, P.O. Box 302, Maryknoll, NY 10545-0302.

Manufactured in the United States of America.
Manuscript editing and typesetting by Joan Weber Laflamme.

Library of Congress Cataloging-in-Publication Data

Names: Ireland, Jerry M., author.
Title: The missionary spirit : evangelism and social action in Pentecostal missiology / Jerry M. Ireland.
Description: Maryknoll, NY : Orbis Books, [2021] | Series: American society of missiology; no. 61 | Includes bibliographical references and index.
Identifiers: LCCN 2021005441 (print) | LCCN 2021005442 (ebook) | ISBN 9781626984295 (trade paperback) | ISBN 9781608338924 (epub)
Subjects: LCSH: Pentecostal churches—Missions. | Pentecostal churches—Doctrines.
Classification: LCC BV2565 .I74 2021 (print) | LCC BV2565 (ebook) | DDC 266/.994—dc23
LC record available at https://lccn.loc.gov/2021005441
LC ebook record available at https://lccn.loc.gov/2021005442

*Dedicated to
my daughter, Charis*

Contents

Preface to the American Society of Missiology Series   xi

Foreword by Dick Brogden   xiii

Acknowledgments   xvii

Introduction   xix
    A Nuanced Approach   xxiii
    Potential Objections to Pentecostal
        Prioritism   xxvii
    The Missionary Spirit   xxxii
    Definitions: *Missio Dei*, Mission, and
        Missions   xxxiii

1. **"How Shall They Hear?"**
   The Priority of Proclamation in Pentecostal Perspective   1
    What Is Pentecostalism?   2
    A Spirit-empowered Missionary Movement   5
    Pentecostalism and the Drift to Holism   6
    Pentecostalism and the Nations   12
    The Spirit and the Nations   19
    A Missionary and Pentecostal Ecclesiology   22
    Pentecostalism, Missions, and Ecclesial
        Priorities   24

2. **The Missionary Nature of Tongues in the Book of Acts**   29
    Proposal for a Narrow View of Pentecostal
        Missions   31
    Pentecostal Holism   33

The Spirit and the Nations in Acts   43
Glossolalia and the Nations   44
The Enduring Evidence of a Global Mission   47

3. Language, Missions, and *Glossolalia* in Patristic Thought   55
The New Testament Data   61
Montanism and Tertullian   64
Greek Fathers   70
   Irenaeus   71
   Origen   74
   Chrysostom   76
Language, Otherness, and the Value of
   Glossolalia   79

4. From Solidarity to Sodality
Compassionate Mission and the Local Church   85
Winter's Modality and Sodality Structures   86
Evaluating the Modality-Sodality Distinction   89
Modalities, Sodalities, and Indigenous Mission
   Movements   95
Second Stage Missions   96
Solidarity in the Pauline Epistles   99
Solidarity and the Spirit   104

5. A Pentecostal Approach to Discipleship in Missions   109
Compassion and the Kingdom of God   111
The Primary and Secondary Aspects of Witness   114
Compassion and the Church   121
Christian Unity and the Holy Spirit   125
The Goal of Compassionate Discipleship:
   Practicing Solidarity   128
Solidarity and the People of God:
   The Priority of Community   129

6. From *Ubuntu* to *Koinonia*
   *The Spirit-formed Community and Indigenous
      African Compassion*   135
   NGOs and Compassion in Africa   136
   Christian Faith-Based Organizations (FBOs)   139
   Development and Pentecostal Churches   141
   Ubuntu: Community in African Culture   143
   Koinonia and the Redemption of *Ubuntu*   144
   Koinonia in Paul   147
   Grace Generation Movement in Togo   149

7. The Secularizing and Anti-Secularizing Potential
   of African Pentecostalism   153
   Secularism and African Pentecostalism   154
   Missional Pentecostalism   158
   Prosperity Pentecostalism   165
   Clarifying Terms   169

Epilogue: Concluding Thoughts on the Missionary Spirit   173

Selected Bibliography   179

Index   189

The American Society of Missiology Series   199

Preface to the American Society of Missiology Series

The purpose of the American Society of Missiology Series is to publish—without regard for disciplinary, national, or denominational boundaries—scholarly works of high quality and wide interest on missiological themes from the entire spectrum of scholarly pursuits relevant to Christian mission, which is always the focus of books in the Series.

By mission is meant the effort to effect passage over the boundary between faith in Jesus Christ and its absence. In this understanding of mission, the basic functions of Christian proclamation, dialogue, witness, service, worship, liberation, and nurture are of special concern. And in that context questions arise, including, how does the transition from one cultural context to another influence the shape and interaction between these dynamic functions, especially in regard to the cultural and religious plurality that comprises the global context of Christian life and mission.

The promotion of scholarly dialogue among missiologists, and among missiologists and scholars in other fields of inquiry, may involve the publication of views that some missiologists cannot accept, and with which members of the Editorial Committee themselves do not agree. Manuscripts published in the Series, accordingly, reflect the opinions of their authors and are not understood to represent the position of the American Society of Missiology or of the Editorial Committee. Selection is guided by such criteria as intrinsic worth, readability, coherence, and accessibility to a range of interested persons and not merely to experts or specialists.

The ASM Series, in collaboration with Orbis Books, seeks to publish scholarly works of high merit and wide interest on numerous aspects of missiology—the scholarly study of mission. Able presentations on new and creative approaches to the practice and understanding of mission will receive close attention.

ASM Series Committee Chair: Dr. Robert Hunt
ASM Publisher: Dr. Darrel Whiteman

Foreword

Prophetic voices are typically allowed only the occasional sweet lullaby. As with Jeremiah in the Old Testament, God's prophets plead with the Lord, sometimes whining, asking him to be more agreeable and less stringent. On bad days prophets curse the day they were born, preferring just to go to heaven where there is, presumably, no dissent needed (though we shouldn't be surprised upon arrival if Luther is still trying to reform something). In the meantime, prophets do have many good days as the fire smolders within and on occasion erupts through a raised voice, poised pen, or finger-tapping correction that pushes back against the current of popular thinking, hammering the word of God home.

Jerry Ireland is one such prophetic voice, and he has just erupted through the challenging work and words you now hold in your hands. Jerry is unique in that he is both erudite and energized, academic and animated. He can hammer with the best of them, yet he does so with precision and skill. The fire that burns within Jerry is only partially veiled by his intelligence. To be exposed to his thinking is to be both cut and cauterized in a surgically loving and gentle way. This work is best read by picturing his bright eyes smiling and by remembering that he hits you in the head because he cares about God's heart.

God's heart is indeed for the integrated person's body, mind, and soul to live eternally with God free from sin, death, sickness, pain, or tears. God's heart is that these integrated persons will dwell in God's presence, representing every tribe, tongue, people, and nation. God's heart is that in this period of redemptive history, we the church should focus on the soul so that mind and body can be eternally whole. God's commissions in scripture prioritize our attention on the evangelism of unreached peoples and the discipleship of the found through faith communities that we call the church. And therein is the rub: the concept of prioritizing the saving of the souls, specifically unreached souls, through the verbal preaching and proclamation of the gospel and the gathering of these redeemed from every nation into indigenous churches. This concept has been often challenged, with mounting academic protests claiming that to prioritize proclamation is to undermine compassionate ministry.

In this timely book, Jerry stands amid the tidal wave of thinking regarding holistic mission as a rock unmoved. In Pentecostal missiology and beyond there is a shying away from affirming the priority of the saving of souls, discipleship, and the planting of churches through the verbal proclamation of the gospel. Jerry makes a scriptural and scholarly case for the prioritization of evangelism, discipleship, and church planting (all components of one core aim) by means of verbal proclamation in the power of the Holy Spirit. With sound scriptural exegesis, critical historical analysis, and informed research and reading, Jerry is unembarrassed to say that we the church must prioritize the saving of souls even amid the necessity of caring for minds and bodies. Jerry posits, and in my view proves, that biblically it is our required obedience to prioritize the saving and discipling of souls through the verbal proclamation of the gospel and that this in no way devalues ministry to mind and body. Prioritization will in fact enhance our holism, not undermine it. If we will prioritize preaching, teaching, discipling, and the planting of indigenous churches, those churches are the best organism and organization for the full-orbed representation of God in the world.

Representing Christ fully does indeed require that we engage the lost with love, truth, and power. Love is life on life, giving and serving and being poured out for others. Truth is the proclaimed word of God, the preaching and teaching and discipling that was the modus operandi of both Jesus and the apostles. Power is the dynamic work of the Holy Spirit in dreams, miracles, healings, and power encounters. All three of these aspects (love, truth, and power) interact in gospel ministry even while the insertion point is arbitrary. Bluntly presented, prioritizing the truth of the gospel through proclamation points out that faith still comes by hearing the word of God. Neither the cup of water nor the sign and wonder are salvific. You can indeed be saved without human love or divine healing—but you cannot be saved if you have not been born of the Spirit that alone results from hearing and believing the truth of what God has done in Christ. The gospel is still about Christ and his finished work on the cross. The gospel is still true though all of us be liars.

For the last three decades my wife, Jennifer, and I have experienced what Jerry definitively declares in this book. We have prioritized proclamation and seen how it has fueled, enhanced, and guided holism. We have prioritized preaching the gospel, making disciples, and planting indigenous churches. We have then encouraged these indigenous churches to be God's ambassadors in society and culture, attacking evil wherever they find it, representing the King everywhere and always by all means. We have learned that the two great redemptive structures of God's mission (the mission agency and the church) have different, while related, functions. The missionary agency and agent are purposed to preach Christ where Christ is not known, make disciples, and plant churches. The means of that preaching and evangelism may include a range of compassionate and social means—but the goal is ever the indigenous church. The indigenous church made up of local believers, then, is the engine that represents the King in all his glory and love to all sectors of our broken world. We have seen that prioritizing proclamation in order to evangelize, disciple, and plant indigenous churches empowered and propelled those churches to launch focused ministries that included education, relief, development, training, athletics, compassion, literacy, sanitation, and a range of other social projects. We have lived out the reality that prioritizing proclamation and soul-saving energizes holism, rather than diluting it.

Though we have lived prioritizing the proclamation of the gospel and testify to its potency, we were never able to articulate it well, stammering away with polemic passion yet without the considerate dexterity this complex issue requires. Then along came our beloved friend Jerry. His book contains the required blend of biblical interpretation, historical review, academic reflection, pragmatic application, and compassionate motive that we have struggled to represent and articulate. Reading this work has ignited my spirit and inspired my mind all over again as the truths articulated here are timeless and timely. I recommend them to you without reservation and with my hearty agreement and support.

DICK BROGDEN
Co-Founder of the Live Dead Movement

Acknowledgments

I have lots of folks to thank for this book. First, I want to thank those who have disagreed with me on the relationship between evangelism and social action, especially my dear friends Johan Mostert and JoAnn Butrin. They both take slightly different perspectives on this issue, but to my delight, these differences have never hampered our friendship in any way. Their thoughtful rejoinders have also helped me sharpen my argument and made this book better than it would have otherwise been. More important, their passion for serving the poor and marginalized often reminds me of the need for theology to find genuine expression in the life of the church. Any good theology must, in the end, be a practical theology.

Second, I must thank my lovely wife, Paula. She has been my constant champion, spurring me on when I felt like giving up and, more important, daily showing me the love of Christ in tangible ways. She has always been for me the embodiment of evangelistic and compassionate faith.

Third, I especially need to thank my daughter, Charis, who has perhaps paid the highest price in the writing of this book because she paid in time that might have been spent with her. I only pray the sacrifice, hers and mine, will bear fruit for the kingdom and that it will have in the end been worth it all. She often puts a smile on my face and reminds me that the real work of the kingdom is not always or even mostly in the ivory towers of academia but in the midst of a pile of Legos and Barbie dolls.

Finally, I want to thank my students at the University of Valley Forge for their thoughtful questions, passion for the mission of God, and commitment to the church. They have helped me in many ways to think more practically about theological truths and daily fill me with hope for the future of the church and God's mission. I suspect it will not be long before they show us all a better way. Their impact on me and this text cannot be overstated.

Introduction

The global explosion of Pentecostalism owes much of its success to an urgent evangelism that has defined the movement since its birth in the early twentieth century.[1] However, as many have noted, Pentecostals were slow to develop the theological foundations for their missionary work because this was always secondary to missionary praxis. In reality, Pentecostal mission history tells a slightly more complex story. Pentecostal mission theology from early on centered on the twin themes of an urgency for world evangelism and a Spirit-led indigeneity. That is, its early missiology was not without theological grounding but from the beginning was interwoven with practical concerns related to evangelism and church planting. Today, Pentecostal missiology has largely moved away from this narrower view of mission in order to adopt a broader perspective.

Alice E. Luce's series of essays in *The Pentecostal Evangel* in 1921 represented an important early step in defining the essence of Pentecostal missiology.[2] Luce herself had been influenced by Roland Allen's *Missionary Methods*, first published in 1912 (though

---

[1] Allan Anderson, *Spreading Fires: The Missionary Nature of Early Pentecostalism* (Maryknoll, NY: Orbis Books, 2007), 3.

[2] Luce, a pioneer in correspondence education, had first been a British missionary to India before becoming a missionary to Spanish-speaking Americans. Alice Luce, "Paul's Missionary Methods," *The Pentecostal Evangel* (January 8, 22, and February 5, 1921); Edith L. Blumhofer, *Restoring the Faith: The Assemblies of God, Pentecostalism, and American Culture* (Champagne: University of Illinois Press, 1993), 245; Edith L. Blumhofer, *The Assemblies of God: A Chapter in the Story of American Pentecostalism*, vol. 1 (Springfield, MO: Gospel Publishing House, 1989), 316.

she admits to recalling the book but not the name of its author). The writings of both Luce and Allen would prove influential in the work of Melvin Hodges—an Assemblies of God missionary to Latin America and one of the most important early missiologists to come from within Pentecostalism. His work *The Indigenous Church*, first published in 1953, would lay the theoretical foundation for Assemblies of God World Missions, in which he served for decades to come.[3] Hodges's work emphasized church planting and evangelism as the heart of missionary enterprise. For Hodges, the goal of missions was "to establish a strong church patterned after the New Testament example."[4] And, in accord with Roland Allen, Hodges declared that "in order to have a New Testament church, we must follow New Testament methods."[5] At the center of that method was a profound trust in the Holy Spirit's ability to form local, indigenous expressions of the church, but only if missionaries would increasingly step into the background and eventually remove themselves from the process once local leadership was in place.[6]

It would not be until the 1991 publication of the highly influential work *Called and Empowered*, edited by Murray Dempster, Douglas Peterson, and Byron Klaus (all of whom had close ties to Pentecostal missionary efforts in Latin America), that the groundwork laid by Hodges would begin to shift.[7] The impact that *Called and Empowered* made on Pentecostal missiology cannot be overstated. This text has given rise to a plethora of Pentecostal missiologies seeking to move beyond what some consider the naivete

---

[3] Gary B. McGee, "The Legacy of Melvin L. Hodges," *International Bulletin of Missionary Research* 22, no. 1 (1998): 20–24; Veli-Matti Kärkkäinen, "The Pentecostal Understanding of Mission," in *Pentecostal Mission and Global Christianity*, ed. Wansuk Ma et al. (Oxford, UK: Regnum, 2014), 29–30.

[4] Melvin Hodges, *The Indigenous Church* (1953; repr. Springfield, MO: Gospel Publishing House, 2009), 22.

[5] Ibid.

[6] Roland Allen, *Missionary Methods: St. Paul's or Ours* (Cambridge, UK: Lutterworth, 2006), 149–50.

[7] Kärkkäinen, "The Pentecostal Understanding of Mission," 30.

of the early movement and to do so by advocating variously for liberationist motifs, holistic paradigms, and greater appreciation for religious plurality.[8] These important works that have followed and built on *Called and Empowered* include those by Amos Yong, Julie Ma and Wansuk Ma, and Andy Lord especially.[9] Not only have these shifts taken place in academia, but the fundamentals of these various holistic perspectives have filtered their way into many expressions of Pentecostal missiology. For example, the Pentecostal World Fellowship, a cooperative of Pentecostal denominations from thirty-three countries, as of January 2020 has adopted a broadly holistic approach to mission that appears to embody many of the concerns expressed in these new Pentecostal missiologies.[10] In other words, these developments have moved beyond theory and now can be considered central to the practice of Pentecostal missions in a number of places around the globe.

My central thesis in this book is that these shifts represent a turning away from the inherent genius intuited by early Pentecostal missionaries who held tightly to the priority of proclamation even as they engaged in social action in a multiplicity of ways. They did so neither because early Pentecostals were oblivious to the need and importance of social justice nor blind to the liberating work of Christ or the holistic nature of salvation; neither were they ignorant of the need for genuine dialogue with those of other faiths. Instead, they held these things in tension with an abiding

---

[8] Murray Dempster et al., *Called and Empowered: Global Mission in Pentecostal Perspective* (Grand Rapids, MI: Baker Academic, 1991).

[9] See especially Amos Yong, *The Missiological Spirit: Christian Mission Theology in the Third Millennium Global Context* (Eugene, OR: Cascade, 2014); Amos Yong, *Mission after Pentecost* (Grand Rapids, MI: Baker Academic, 2019); Andrew Lord, *Network Church: A Pentecostal Ecclesiology Shaped by Mission* (Leiden, The Netherlands: Brill, 2012); Andrew Lord, *Spirit-Shaped Mission: A Holistic Charismatic Theology* (Bletchley, UK: Paternoster, 2005); Julie C. Ma and Wansuk Ma, *Mission in the Spirit: Towards a Pentecostal/Charismatic Missiology* (Eugene, OR: Wipf and Stock, 2010); Ma et al., *Pentecostal Mission and Global Christianity*.

[10] Pentecostal World Fellowship, "Pentecostal Development Partner's Summit," January 2020.

commitment to the fact that evangelism was the first-order work of the church because it alone constituted the church's unique role in the world. And so even as early Pentecostals engaged in compassionate missions in places like West Africa, Latin America, and India through clinics, orphanages, and education programs, they did so always with one eye fixed firmly on the eschatological horizon of scripture, longing for a world made right and whole through the advent of Christ at which time would also come the judgment of the world. Their concern to see lost humanity escape the coming eschatological judgment provided the urgency that characterized the movement. Beyond that, early Pentecostals began to realize that the best version of any local church would emerge only if missionaries focused on training and equipping by stepping increasingly into the background, so that the Spirit would lead local believers to develop local expressions of the church. This belief, as already indicated, was deeply rooted in the notions of indigeneity promoted by Allen, Luce, and Hodges. In other words, a truly Pentecostal approach to missionary activity was embodied in these early theologies of missions emphasizing evangelism and church planting because they also emphasized that both of these efforts were ultimately the work of the Spirit.

My argument here centers on a key misstep among those who seek to move beyond this early and effective paradigm, a misstep that assumes, along with much of contemporary missiology, that missions must be broad or narrow but cannot be both. In the current literature the narrow sense of missions is often relegated (at least implicitly) to the narrow-minded.[11] This is evident in the constant calls (with which I will engage throughout this book) for newer, better, more mature paradigms of Pentecostal mission and in the general assessment that missionaries have only recently awakened to the holistic implications of the gospel. This is of course absurd, for the very notion of the Pentecostal "Full Gospel"

---

[11] Throughout this text I use the term *mission* primarily to refer to all that God is doing in the world, or to the broad sense of mission; and I use the term *missions* to refer specifically to cross-cultural evangelism and church planting.

that emphasized physical healing alongside spiritual renewal was deeply rooted in a holistic understanding of salvation. The practical wisdom that caused Pentecostal missionary outreach to flourish was precisely that it knew that each paradigm—the broad and the narrow senses of missions—had its place, and that eternal matters always outweighed temporal ones.

A NUANCED APPROACH

It seems fitting to me that I should preface my discussion of Pentecostal missions with a testimony of the sort that once was a sustaining force of Pentecostalism. I came to Christ in my early thirties through the ministry of Teen Challenge—a discipleship ministry that has been historically loosely associated with the Assemblies of God and that aims to help those struggling with addictions. It was not until a decade or so later, when I had become a missionary with the Assemblies of God, that I discovered that within Pentecostalism there existed a rift between advocates of social concern and those who prioritized evangelistic and church planting efforts. My initial reaction was one of dismay. Of course we should preach the gospel *and* we should help those who are suffering. Why would anyone question either of these notions?

But as I began to study the issue academically, my position began to shift, and I came to value and appreciate the need for theological precision in articulating how evangelism and social concern should relate to one another. Early on in my career as a missionary, I stood firmly in the holism camp. In fact, I began my doctoral dissertation with the goal of defending that position and showing inconsistencies in the theology of Carl F. H. Henry on the subject of precisely how evangelism and social concern relate.[12] Henry, known especially for his treatise *The Uneasy Conscience of Modern Fundamentalism*, chastised fundamentalism (a movement

---

[12] Jerry M. Ireland, *Evangelism and Social Concern in the Theology of Carl F. H. Henry* (Eugene, OR: Pickwick, 2015).

to which he had close ties) for its knee-jerk reaction to liberal theology and abandonment of social action.[13]

In that study I discovered insights that I had not previously considered, and my efforts to denounce Henry soon morphed into a defense of his positions because I found his arguments exegetically compelling. Granted, Carl Henry is not usually the first person who comes to mind when one thinks of Pentecostal theology, for obvious reasons. Nonetheless, what I discovered in Henry was a robust challenge to the broad sense of mission that denied any notion of priority. Henry, unlike nearly everyone else writing on the subject, was able to hold on to the priority of proclamation even as he advocated for the *necessity* of evangelical social action. Specifically, Henry's argument for the priority of evangelism rested on his revelational epistemology, which centered on the dual axiom's of God's existence (the ontological axiom) and divine revelation (the epistemological axiom). One might sum up Henry's approach with a bit of a Socratic exercise, by first asking, "Why do we know anything at all about God?" and answering, "We know because God has revealed Godself through grace for the salvation of lost humanity everywhere." That is, divine revelation has at its core not the betterment of society but the salvation of those separated from Christ. But in our efforts to proclaim that salvation, the way we live and treat others matters, especially when it comes to the neediest among us. Henry thus laid the groundwork for my search for other theological resources that aided in holding together the broad and narrow sense of missions.[14] But I sensed something else was missing.

As I have shifted my study of evangelism and social action to explore Pentecostal approaches to mission, I have discovered a

---

[13] Carl F. H. Henry, *The Uneasy Conscience of Modern Fundamentalism* (1947; repr. Grand Rapids, MI: Eerdmans, 2003).

[14] For a summary article on my research, see Jerry M. Ireland, "Carl F. H. Henry's Regenerational Model of Evangelism and Social Concern and the Promise of an Evangelical Consensus," in *Controversies in Mission: Theology, People, and Practice of Mission in the 21st Century*, ed. Rochelle Cathcart Scheuermann and Edward L. Smither (Pasadena, CA: William Carey Library, 2016).

pervasive tendency toward oversimplification when it comes to the task of defining mission(s). By that I mean that the question of whether the church's mission should be holistic or if it should prioritize proclamation and evangelism has often been reduced to a series of either/or scenarios that fail to take into account the complexities of mission according to scripture. Mission, we are told, is either holistic, or it is governed by false dichotomies based on Enlightenment paradigms. We either care about people's present lives, or we care only about their eternal lives. Mission is either transformational and liberating in terms of addressing social injustice, or it is truncated and neocolonial. Salvation either includes the social sphere, or it gives too much credence to Western individualism. I find all of these claims to be far too simplistic and lacking attention to the key concepts described above.

In this book I address those problematic claims and attempt to articulate a more nuanced position that takes into account the fullness of the biblical witness; manages to uphold the importance of social justice even while prioritizing evangelism, especially among the nations; and cares simultaneously about the present and the future. Specifically, in Chapter 1 I examine the historic priority of proclamation in early Pentecostalism in light of the current drift to holism. I observe that holistic paradigms often leave cross-cultural witness unarticulated and ambiguous—a perspective I find problematic given the way in which God's people in both the Old and New Testaments are defined according to their role among the nations. I explore in Chapter 2 the way that *glossolalia* (speaking in tongues) in the book of Acts relates to God's concern for the nations and the cross-cultural trajectory inherent in Pentecostal ecclesiology and missiology. I do this by building on Michael Goheen's important work emphasizing proclamation to the nations as the "ultimate horizon of missions" and arguing that this strengthens the need for maintaining the narrow sense of missions concerning the church's cross-cultural work.[15]

---

[15] Michael Goheen, *A Light to the Nations: The Missional Church and the Biblical Story* (Grand Rapids, MI: Baker Academic, 2011), 199.

In Chapter 3 I turn to Greek and Latin fathers of the church to explore whether or not they connected *glossolalia* to the church's missionary mandate. If indeed early Pentecostals were correct in seeing a connection between tongues and the church's cross-cultural mission, then one would hope that such a perspective had some historic roots in the church, given that theological novelties should always be looked upon with suspicion. To search out this question, I build on an important study by Yuliya Minets regarding linguistic otherness in the Greco-Roman world and find surprising evidence among these church fathers connecting tongues to mission that lends credibility to the notion of tongues as evidence of the Spirit's work through the church concerning the nations. Furthermore, this missional link to tongues may also offer an alternative to the demise of tongues speech, often attributed to the rise of Montanism.

In Chapter 4 I explore the notions of mission and missions in light of Ralph Winter's modality-sodality paradigm and argue that there is a place for both the narrow and broad senses of missions. In Chapter 5 I develop this further as I look to how Pentecostals have emphasized discipling for compassion in a cross-cultural context, how this fits best within a priority perspective, and how it offers the greatest hope for long-term impact. Chapter 6 focuses on compassionate discipleship in Africa by exploring well-documented ways that nongovernmental organizations (NGOs) and faith-based organizations (FBOs) can subvert indigenous expressions of compassion and how Pentecostal churches have succeeded in this arena where others have failed. I assess both the African concept of *ubuntu* and Western individualism in light of the biblical concept of *koinonia*. This chapter concludes with a story of indigenous compassion from Togo, West Africa, that demonstrates the unique potential of Spirit-led, local expressions of compassion and why these are to be preferred over missionary-led forms.

Chapter 7 examines two strands of Pentecostalism that lie at opposite ends of the spectrum, namely, what I describe as *prosperity Pentecostalism* and *missional Pentecostalism* and how these each have the potential to either foster or refute secularization, respectively. I conclude in the Epilogue with a brief summary of main ideas and some thoughts on their application.

POTENTIAL OBJECTIONS TO PENTECOSTAL PRIORITISM

I anticipate several objections to this project. First, the idea of holism has become so embedded in contemporary thought regarding the church's mission that it is rarely questioned anymore. Therefore, one often has to go back a decade or two to find significant academic works that continue to wrestle with the issue in any substantive way. In fact, most writers nowadays feel content to simply assume a holistic model without defending it in more than a passing manner. My priority perspective will surely cause some to accuse me of looking too far into the past or worse, of being hopelessly stuck there. Steven Studebaker, for example, has said that "despite their recent appearance in the history of Christianity, Pentecostals are particularly prone to romanticizing the past."[16]

But looking to the past in order to recover that which drove the success of Pentecostalism early on lies at the very center of this effort. It constitutes a quite intentional and necessary part of my methodology. New does not always mean better, and I contend that the strand of Pentecostal missions that was embedded in its early praxis and that still continues at the pragmatic level among many (most?) classical traditions represents an enduring paradigm for Pentecostal missiology in that it is grounded in the nature of God as a sending God and in the church whose identity is determined by the actions of God, first and foremost. In other words, despite their unsophisticated beginnings, early Pentecostals "stumbled by the Spirit" on something important. Plus, as I will show, I think the holistic models have some major theological and practical flaws that are remedied by a return to Pentecostalism's

---

[16] Steven M. Studebaker, *Defining Issues in Pentecostalism: Classical and Emergent* (Eugene, OR: Pickwick, 2008), 5.

roots. I see my efforts therefore as in no way romanticizing the past but rather as more fully appreciating the historical grounding of Christian theology. Christianity is after all a faith deeply rooted in historical events, the interpretation of which by the early church established the bedrock of all future doctrine (Eph 2:20). My goal is to reground Pentecostal missiology in the enduring principles that governed the apostolic church and that gained widespread acceptance in twentieth-century Pentecostal missions.

Another objection I anticipate is that I have not engaged significantly with the work of Amos Yong, arguably one of Pentecostalism's most prominent missiologists. But Yong's work focuses largely on theologies of religion, interreligious dialogue, and postmodern critiques of colonial and neocolonial missionary approaches, especially those that embody some form of exclusivism.[17] While these relate somewhat tangentially to the issue of how evangelism and compassion fit within a Pentecostal missiology, to my knowledge Yong has not written extensively on the issue of whether Pentecostal missions should be holistic or if it should embody certain priorities. That said, I am fairly certain he would fall within the former camp. And this likely owes to reasons I have just stated—that for many within this space such a discussion is passé and a settled issue. In fact, Yong nearly says as much when in his proposal for "a way forward" he likens Christian mission to a modernist project that has failed to embrace the many "posts" of the contemporary world (postcolonial, post-Enlightenment, and post-Christendom).[18]

That said, I have found helpful Yong's analysis of the history of classical Pentecostal missiology from Charles Parham's *xenolalic* understanding of tongues as speaking in known languages one had not learned and the lasting influence of both Parham and William Seymour on the evangelistic and missional thrust of Pentecostalism. I especially appreciate his concluding analysis that classical Pentecostalism "was motivated first and foremost

---

[17] See especially Yong, *The Missiological Spirit* and *Mission after Pentecost*.

[18] Yong, *Mission after Pentecost*, 5.

by the practical exigencies of fulfilling the Great Commission."[19] I agree. What I fail to grasp is why Pentecostal missiologists seem in such a hurry to jettison a past that, though not without occasional problems related to neocolonialism, paternalism, and the like, has effectively planted thriving, indigenous, Pentecostal churches around the world, often at great cost to the missionaries who went.[20] I am indeed all for some of the things that Yong champions, especially more dialogue on the listening end for us Westerners as it concerns religious otherness. I am just not as convinced as he appears to be of the failure of missionaries in the classical tradition on this front and am fairly certain that the success of Pentecostal missions up until now has partially rested on the ability and willingness of practitioners to engage in dialogue and learn the language and culture of those to whom they went to share the gospel. I must confess, then, to being at a loss to know what Yong means when he refers to classical missions as a "moribund enterprise."[21] For example, when Yong talks about the need for and reality of post-Enlightenment and post-mission missions, he seems to assume that the primary reason mission sending from Western nations in the nineteenth and twentieth centuries was one directional (or as is sometimes said, "from the West to the rest"), was because of a perceived cultural superiority embodied explicitly or implicitly by those who went and by those who sent them. I would argue in contrast, though, that the one-directional nature of missions in its early years flowed from the often accurate assumption that the unregenerate in the West at least *could* access the gospel if they so desired, whereas those in foreign lands often could not.[22] Pentecostal missionaries were keenly aware of this. Thus the notion of missions *to* the West rightly seemed absurd, not because the West was perceived as a bastion of all things good and holy, but because in the West one could practically walk one hundred yards in any direction in any

---

[19] Yong, *The Missiological Spirit*, 98–99.
[20] Cf. Kärkkäinen, "The Pentecostal Understanding of Mission," 26.
[21] Yong, *Mission after Pentecost*, 20.
[22] Ibid., 2–5.

large city and find a Bible-believing church. Knowing that this was patently not the case in many places around the globe, and that those in foreign lands could not walk one hundred miles in any direction and find a church, missionaries of the early Pentecostal movement spanned out across the globe with great fervor and commitment to take the gospel to where it was not yet known. It was thus a known lack of access to Christ, not cultural superiority, that drove early Pentecostal missionaries.

Yet another objection that will likely be leveled against this text is that I have not taken fully into account Luke's teaching in his Gospel regarding social justice. Much has been made of Luke's Gospel as it relates to the church's compassionate mandate, and Luke 4:18–19 especially has been a favorite passage for liberation theologies and their holistic offspring.[23] But central to my project here is that while I concur with the scholarly consensus that views Luke-Acts as consecutive volumes of the same work, this should not lead us to conclude that they are essentially homogenous and deal with the same material or only ever make the same points.[24] Instead, I propose that the very existence of Luke's two volumes, his Gospel and Acts, supports my central argument for the distinction between the modality of the local church and the sodality of the mission band. In other words, whereas the Gospel

---

[23] For a brief overview of various approaches to Luke 4:16ff., see Ron Sider, *Good News and Good Works: A Theology for the Whole Gospel* (Grand Rapids, MI: Baker, 1993; Kindle edition), 50–51.

[24] Luke Timothy Johnson argues for the unity of the two volumes and rejects attempts to "re-segment" them from one another. I agree and suggest that the two be held together, but that key differences be recognized in content, theme, and emphases; Luke Timothy Johnson, *Prophetic Jesus, Prophetic Church: The Challenge of Luke-Acts to Contemporary Christians* (Grand Rapids, MI: Eerdmans, 2011), 2–4. Paul Borgman argues that the canonical separation of Acts from the Gospel of Luke has contributed to the problematic tendency to read them apart, and I think he is right. My goal, though, is not to contribute to reading them apart, but rather reading them together in their own right. See Paul Borgman, *The Way According to Luke: Hearing the Whole Story of Luke-Acts* (Grand Rapids, MI: Eerdmans, 2006), ix–xi.

of Luke deals with the formation of disciples and by extension especially deals with what will become the prerogative of the local church (modalities), Acts is concerned with local churches only as it relates to their missionary function (sodalities).[25] Otherwise, one is left with an inexorable dilemma. If Luke and Acts are so tightly connected that we should expect nothing new theologically in volume two, then we must ask, where precisely do these social justice themes for which volume one is so famed ever appear in volume two? The mysterious answer is they do not. Nowhere in Acts is the church shown engaging in any kind of social justice work outside the church, and when the subject comes up internally, it is expeditiously dealt with in order to avoid any hindrances to the church's evangelistic mandate under way.[26] This is precisely the story of Acts 6 and the choosing of the seven to the diaconate in response to the needs of widows in the church (Acts 6:1–7). As Roland Allen observes of this passage, the way Luke deals with this incident is quite bizarre "unless his concern were not almost wholly with evangelization."[27] And the result of this speedy and decisive action? "The Word of God kept on spreading" (v. 7). Again, as Allen observes, we are told nothing of almost any of the main characters in Acts except as it relates to their missionary calling. This holds true for Stephen, Philip, Barnabas, Paul, John Mark, Silas, Timothy, and Apollos. "Thus

---

[25] Hans Conzelmann observes of Lukan theology that "the period of Jesus and the period of the church are represented as two distinct, but systematically interrelated epochs." Conzelmann, *The Theology of St. Luke* (Philadelphia: Fortress, 1961), 14.

[26] Richard B. Hays, who argues for a liberation motif in Luke-Acts, also notes that "the book of Acts gives no evidence of the apostles seeking to reform political structures outside the church, either through protest or by seizing power. Instead, Luke tells the story of the formation of a new human community—the church—in which goods are shared and wrongs are put right." Hays, *The Moral Vision of the New Testament: A Contemporary Introduction to New Testament Ethics* (New York: HarperCollins, 1996), 135.

[27] Roland Allen, *The Ministry of the Spirit: Selected Writings of Roland Allen* (London, UK: World Dominion, 1960), 16.

it is plain that, if we consider Acts as a book of Christian biography, we must consider it as a work of *missionary* biography" (emphasis added).[28] And so in the same way that Pentecostals have produced successful arguments to let Luke be Luke and Paul be Paul in relation to the Spirit's work, so too must we let Luke's Gospel be his Gospel and Acts be Acts as they relate to different aspects of the church's mandate—namely, her local and global mandates—even as we uphold the continuity between the two. In doing this we discover a Lukan basis for both compassionate outreach, especially for those most disenfranchised, like the shepherds present in the birth narrative, and for cross-cultural missions in the narrow sense of evangelism and church planting that refuses to get side tracked even by such a dominant biblical theme as the care of widows, because such a task belongs to the modality, not the sodality. That is, this is the task of the local church, not the missionary.

THE MISSIONARY SPIRIT

A central issue I see in contemporary Pentecostal missiologies relates to the question of what the church should expect of the Spirit in each new age. Should we expect a complete revisioning of what missions is and means (as most suggest), or should we expect (as I contend) mainly that the Spirit helps us reapply the ancient paradigm of missions as cross-cultural witness through new Spirit-inspired strategies and practices? Most of this book can be considered an elaboration of this central theme.

Central to the argument in this text is that the Holy Spirit is *the* missionary Spirit.[29] That is, missions—defined as reconciling all nations to Christ—constitutes an ontological aspect of the Spirit's very nature and being. Missions exists as a function of the church because it first exists ontologically in God's own nature. Again, Roland Allen proves instructive when he argues that

---

[28] Ibid., 14–15.
[29] Ibid., 21.

the Spirit which inspires and directs a certain action must necessarily be a Spirit whose nature is such that this action is agreeable to Him and expresses His mind. The history of the spread of the gospel must, then, be a revelation of the mind of the Spirit; the zeal of the apostles must be a revelation of the nature of the Spirit which inspired them to such action.[30]

Furthermore, the Spirit in Acts is everywhere portrayed in relation to the certainty of those whom the Spirit fills. No one "has the Spirit" unknowingly or unwittingly in the book of Acts, contrary to popular tendencies to speculate about the Spirit's presence and work within non-Christian religions. "Did you receive the Holy Spirit when you believed?" (Acts 19:2) must always be understood to mean the cognitive awareness of the Spirit as well as the Spirit's relationship to Christ and consequently the concern for the nations demanded of the believer as a direct product of the indwelling Spirit. As John V. Taylor writes, "There can be no mission until eyes have been opened to see the living Christ."[31] It is the Spirit that opens eyes and the Spirit that closes them (Rom 11:8). By this I do not mean to limit the freedom of the Spirit, for indeed, the wind of the Spirit blows where the Spirit wishes. Rather, I am suggesting that God has ordained the church as the primary agent of the kingdom and the main realm of the Spirit's activity.

DEFINITIONS: *MISSIO DEI*, MISSION, AND MISSIONS

Normally this would be a good place to define key terms related to this volume, especially what is meant by the word *Pentecostal* and equally what is meant by *mission(s)*. But the meaning of these terms cannot be established by mere assertion either in isolation of the vast bodies of literature related to both issues or from the practical realities that have governed these expressions. Therefore,

---

[30] Ibid., 20.
[31] John V. Taylor, *The Go-Between God: The Holy Spirit and Christian Mission* (London: SCM Press, 1975), 20.

fuller definitions of both will emerge as a result of the study. That is, I hope to show that the intertwined nature of Pentecostalism and missions as understood within the early classical tradition has certain characteristics related to the ontology of God and the church that can be defended as enduring elements. That said, it may be helpful to set this all in the broader evangelical discussion of the *missio Dei* from which has flowed the mission/missions distinction that constitutes so central a piece to my thesis.

As already indicated, much of the confusion in contemporary missiologies can be traced to a lack of clarity over the manifold terms that are now commonplace in discussions about the church's role in society and the world. Key terms such as *mission* (singular), *missions* (plural), *missional,* and *missio Dei* are variously employed with reference to that which the church is called to be and do, often in relation to cultural linguistic otherness as well as to various forms of social activism. A brief overview of the history of these terms will prove helpful.

In many ways the term *missio Dei* (the mission of God) constitutes the most apt starting place for a conversation on Pentecostal missiology because the concept has been widely used of contemporary missionary endeavor with conflicting definitions. David Bosch helpfully delineates the relationship between *missio Dei* terminology and the *mission/missions* distinction in the introduction to his magnum opus, *Transforming Mission:*

> We have to distinguish between mission (singular) and missions (plural). The first refers primarily to the *missio Dei* (God's mission), that is, God's self-revelation as the One who loves the world, God's involvement in and with the world, and in which the church is privileged to participate. *Missio Dei* enunciates the good news that God is a God-for-people.[32]

The modern proliferation of talk about the *missio Dei* can be traced to the 1952 International Missionary Conference of the

---

[32] David Bosch, *Transforming Mission* (Maryknoll, NY: Orbis Books, 1991), 10.

World Council of Churches (WCC) in Willingen, Amsterdam. Willingen was the fifth such conference of the WCC following the first in Edinburgh in 1910. Though some have claimed that a trinitarian understanding of mission preceded that conference in a series of lectures Karl Barth gave in 1932, John Flett has shown this to be fallacious. "In reality, Barth never once used the term *missio Dei*, never wrote the phrase 'God is a missionary God,' and never articulated a Trinitarian position of the kind expressed at Willingen."[33] Though speakers such as Karl Hartenstein, undoubtedly influenced by Barth's broader theology of the Trinity, helped advance an understanding of *missio Dei* that located missions primarily in the actions of God, the conference itself and its legacy most directly bequeathed to the church a theology of *missio Dei*.[34] Barth had undoubtedly been an influence on Hartenstein, but perhaps not as directly influencing his theology of missions as is often asserted.

The Willingen conference played a pivotal role in the emergence of contemporary *missio Dei* lexicography. As Johannes Verkuyl observes, "At Willingen, a Copernican revolution happened, at least as regards terminology."[35] It is true that the history of this idea often has been traced to Augustine of Hippo, who in his refutation of the Arians emphasized the sending of the eternal Son as *missio*.[36]

---

[33] John Flett, *The Witness of God: The Trinity, Missio Dei, Karl Barth, and the Nature of Christian Community* (Grand Rapids, MI: Eerdmans, 2010), 18. Even Bosch, though, makes the claim that Barth "became one of the first theologians to articulate mission as an activity of God himself." Bosch, *Transforming Mission*, 389.

[34] See Karl Hartenstein, "The Theology of the Word and Missions," *International Review of Mission* 20, no. 2 (1931): 210–17.

[35] Johannes Verkuyl, *Contemporary Missiology: An Introduction* (Grand Rapids, MI: Eerdmans, 1978), 3.

[36] Edward W. Poitras, "St Augustine and the Missio Dei: A Reflection on Mission at the Close of the Twentieth Century," *Mission Studies* 16, no. 2 (1999): 28–46. See John Flett's excellent discussion of the theological issues associated with Augustine's work in De Trinitatae in Flett, *The Witness of God*, 18.

Even so, the use of these terms has diverged widely, and they carry different and important implications within various ecclesiological traditions.[37] Overall though, the goal and result of *missio Dei* thinking was to center mission, however defined, as originating in the activity of God rather than in the activities of the church. But even from Willingen there emerged not a single understanding of *missio Dei* but at least three distinct proposals, none of which was ultimately agreed upon.[38] The consequences of this within the ecumenical movement was twofold in that it, first, led to understanding mission as being broader than that which the church was called to be and do, and second, moved away from any understanding of mission in geographic terms. Instead, mission came to be seen as all that God was doing in the world, both within the church and without, and could not therefore be confined to cross-cultural church planting without limiting the sovereignty of God.[39]

In reflecting on these historical developments, Bishop Stephen Neill writes, "The age of missions ended. The age of mission began."[40] To this David Bosch adds, "It follows that we have to distinguish between mission and missions. We cannot without ado claim that what we do is identical to the *missio Dei*; our missionary activities are only authentic insofar as they reflect participation in the mission of God."[41] It is not hard to see then how these kinds of missiologies emerged as disconnected from the local church and moved away from a primary focus on evangelism and church planting. This was particularly embodied in the theology of Johannes C. Hoekendijk, who helped define mission "more and more comprehensively."[42] Writing in the 1950s and 1960s during the

---

[37] Bosch, *Transforming Mission*, 392.

[38] Henning Wrogemann, *Theologies of Mission, Intercultural Theology*, vol. 2 (Downers Grove: IVP Academic, 2018), 69.

[39] Ibid., 68–69.

[40] Stephen Neill, *A History of Christian Missions* (1964; repr. New York: Penguin, 1990), 477.

[41] Bosch, *Transforming Mission*, 391.

[42] Wrogemann, *Theologies of Mission*, 72.

era of "decolonization" and national independence in places like Africa along with rising secularism in Europe, Hoekendijk talked about mission as the "shalomization of the world" and set forth the tripartite features of the *missio hominum* (the human aspect of the *missio Dei*) as *kerygma*, *koinonia*, and *diakonia*. These later proved foundational to the missions theology advocated by Murray Dempster and others in *Called and Empowered* (though without any specific reference to Hoekendijk).

It is worth reiterating that much of this was rooted not in the search for more solid theological foundations for missions but rather in a growing antipathy in the middle of the twentieth century toward the church itself. In this, problems such as paternalism and colonialism that indeed sometimes went hand-in-hand with missionary endeavor led to the search for a missionary paradigm that was at home among the anti-ecclesiological and anti-universal claims that were then emerging and in contrast to a firm commitment to the church and to the unique claims of Christ that had been a central feature of Christian missions since apostolic times. Thus, while some continue to see this broadened definition of mission as contextualized to the needs and realities of the twentieth century, on closer inspection it turns out instead to be merely an odd mix of Enlightenment-based plurality and postmodern uncertainty dressed up as progress.

In the chapters that follow I unfold a proposal for a distinctly Pentecostal missiology, defined in the narrow sense, that therefore speaks primarily to the work of cross-cultural evangelism and church planting. As such, I consider this project to be in no way comprehensive. Rather, it should be seen as merely the contours and skeleton of a narrowly defined Pentecostal missiology that attempts to ground itself in the nature of God and in the church God begets and that attempts to contextualize the apostolic model of missions intuited by early Pentecostals in the context of the twenty-first century by demonstrating its ongoing relevance and fruitfulness. Furthermore, I aim to reclaim the mission/missions distinction not as the old form no longer tenable and the new made vague and nonthreatening, but as paradigms for the local church in its own context and the missionary band engaged in cross-cultural evangelism and church planting. In short, I hope to show that the missionary Spirit that bore along the apostolic witness and early Pentecostal movement remains the guiding Power that propels God's people to the nations with the good news of Christ.

1

"How Shall They Hear?"

THE PRIORITY OF PROCLAMATION IN PENTECOSTAL PERSPECTIVE

At Lausanne II in Manila in 1989 Peter Kuzmic declared that "the answer to the question of world evangelization, 'How shall they hear?' is inextricably linked to and conditioned by the answer to the related question, 'What shall they see?'"[1] And indeed, Kuzmic is exactly right. The evangelistic mandate of the church will be aided or hindered by the moral and ethical disposition of the church. However, to say that these two aspects of the church's mandate are inextricably linked tells us nothing of the precise relationship between the two, nor does it say anything about priorities. In fact, such a statement has the subtle tendency to move the church away from the very notion of priorities. Yet Pentecostal missions have historically operated from a perspective that gave prime place to the church's cross-cultural evangelistic mandate. Modern Pentecostalism, though, has turned away from the priority of proclamation toward a more holistic approach. I believe this represents a reduction of

---

[1] Peter Kuzmic, "The Gospel and Salvation II: How to Teach the Truth of the Gospel," in *Proclaim Christ until He Comes: Calling the Whole Church to Take the Whole Gospel to the Whole World*, ed. J. D. Douglas (Minneapolis, MN: World Wide Publications, 1989), 199.

Pentecostalism's historic roots and theological grounding in the activity of the Spirit that fundamentally creates the church to be missionary by its very nature.

WHAT IS PENTECOSTALISM?

Throughout this chapter I explore the suggestion that Pentecostalism can best be understood as a Spirit-empowered missionary movement.[2] In this I am not unaware of the contemporary definitions of Pentecostalism that include classical Pentecostalism, indigenous Pentecostalism, neo-Pentecostalism, charismatics, and progressive Pentecostalism.[3] But my focus is mainly on the classical Pentecostalism that arose in the early twentieth century out of an eschatological urgency that manifested a passion for the lost and perishing, and the realization that reaching these souls would take a mighty move of the Spirit, a blowing of the divine wind across the nations.[4] That is, the experience of the Holy Spirit and the practice of spiritual gifts were catalysts for what would become a worldwide missions movement. This Spirit-empowered, missionary zeal characterized the church in its earliest stages of expansion in the first century and characterized many, if not all,

---

[2] Paul Pomerville, *The Third Force in Missions* (1985; repr. Peabody, MA: Hendrickson, 2016), 95.

[3] Donald and Tesunao Yamamori Miller, *Global Pentecostalism: The New Face of Christian Social Engagement* (Berkeley and Los Angeles: University of California, 2007), 26–30. I find Andy Lord's distinction between Pentecostalism as referring to the movement more broadly and Pentecostal to specifically indicate classical Pentecostalism to be helpful, even though linguistically *Pentecostal* does not always work as well as *Pentecostalism*. Andy Lord, *Network Church: A Pentecostal Ecclesiology Shaped by Mission* (Leiden, The Netherlands: Brill, 2012), 5–6.

[4] L. Grant McClung Jr., "'Try to Get People Saved': Revisiting the the Paradigm of Urgent Pentecostal Missiology," in *The Globalization of Pentecostalism: A Religion Made to Travel*, ed. Murray Dempster, Byron D. Klaus, and Douglas Petersen (Oxford, UK: Regnum, 1999), 36.

of the global Pentecostal revivals like those at Azusa Street[5] and elsewhere.[6]

In this, I am intentionally moving away from more common contemporary definitions of Pentecostalism, such as that of Allan Anderson, who defines the term broadly to include all that emphasizes the gifts of the Spirit.[7] Anderson's admirable concern is to be as inclusive as possible regarding the various strands that self-identify as Pentecostal around the globe and to move away from neocolonial interpretations of history. Therefore, he believes that the common thread running through these theologically and historically diverse movements is that of spiritual gifts. While historical realities certainly have great value in understanding a diverse movement such as Pentecostalism, I prefer theological definitions because they state the ideal, not necessarily the actual. Theological definitions declare what the church ought to be rather than what the church is, because they seek after what the Spirit has said through the medium of special revelation.[8] It is therefore important, as Donald Dayton has argued, to move beyond the various manifestations and praxis of Pentecostalism

---

[5] A historic revival meeting that began on Azusa Street in Los Angeles, California, in 1906, led by William J. Seymour, is commonly believed to be the beginning of what is today called Pentecostalism.

[6] Andrew M. Lord, "The Voluntary Principle in Pentecostal Missiology," *Journal of Pentecostal Theology* 8, no. 17 (2000): 87. See also Allan Anderson, *Spreading Fires: The Missionary Nature of Early Pentecostalism* (Maryknoll, NY: Orbis Books, 2007).

[7] Allan Anderson, *An Introduction to Pentecostalism*, 2nd ed. (Cambridge, UK: Cambridge University Press, 2014), 6. See also Archer's discussion regarding definitions of Pentecostalism in Kenneth Archer, *The Gospel Revisited: Towards a Pentecostal Theology of Word and Witness* (Eugene, OR: Pickwick, 2011), xv–xx. Archer argues similarly in noting that Anderson does not allow, for example, the means to distinguish between the noun *Pentecostal* and the adjective *charismatic*—which might aptly be applied to any number of other theological distinctive groups such as Calvinism, Lutheranism, and Catholicism.

[8] Michael F. Bird, *Evangelical Theology: A Biblical and Systematic Introduction* (Grand Rapids, MI: Zondervan, 2013), 64.

and focus on theological underpinnings.[9] While Anderson's emic definition is not without value, especially in its ability to capture the diversity of global movements that self-identify with Pentecostalism, I prefer to focus in this study on etic definitions that seek to identify the theological bases for Pentecostal missiology.[10] As such, I share William Faupel's conviction that Pentecostalism was born of millenarian expectancy.[11]

An end-times urgency for world evangelism gave Pentecostalism key elements of its early identity. Plus, missions should be understood not only as something the church does but also as something the church is. The church, before it was anything else, was mobile, and it was mobile because it was missionary.[12] This is the very idea behind Martin Kähler's famous axiom that missions is the mother of theology. Indeed, the church owes its very existence to missions. The church exists because God is a missionary God, because the nations are in rebellion, and because the Christ sent from heaven sends his church to carry on his work. As Jürgen Moltmann says, "Mission does not come from the church; it is from mission and in the light of mission that the church has to be understood."[13]

---

[9] Donald Dayton, *Theological Roots of Pentecostalism* (Metuchen, NJ: The Scarecrow Press, 1987), 16.

[10] In this, I am arguing in ways similar to McClung Jr., who says that "the primary missiological issues of the 1990s and beyond will not be methodological, but theological. L. Grant McClung Jr., "Pentecostal/Charismatic Perspectives on a Missiology for the Twenty-First Century," *Pneuma* 16, no. 1 (1994): 14.

[11] D. William Faupel, *The Everlasting Gospel* (Blandford Forum, UK: Deo, 2009).

[12] Egbert Egberts, *La Tente De Dieu Dans Le Désert Des Hommes* (Cleon D'Andran: Éditions Excelsis, 1997), 100. See also Blauw, who argues for the missionary nature of the church in Johannes Blauw, *The Missionary Nature of the Church* (New York: McGraw-Hill, 1962).

[13] Jürgen Moltmann, *The Church in the Power of the Spirit: A Contribution to Messianic Ecclesiology*, trans. Margaret Kohl (Minneapolis, MN: Fortress Press, 1993), 1. Logos edition.

A SPIRIT-EMPOWERED MISSIONARY MOVEMENT

At the Second General Council of the Assemblies of God in Chicago in 1914, leaders committed themselves and the movement to "the greatest evangelization the world had ever seen."[14] This concern for greater effectiveness in global missions was in fact one of the primary reasons that delegates gathered in Hot Springs, Arkansas, earlier in May of that same year. This was not a vain declaration based on prideful self-confidence; it was rooted in the belief, based on firsthand experience, that God's Spirit was again being poured out in the churches, and this was taken as a clear sign of Jesus's imminent return. Early Pentecostals based this theology of a "latter rain" on a missiological and eschatological understanding of the former rain poured out in the book of Acts and on hints in the prophetic writing of a latter rain that would empower the church for global witness and usher in the end times.[15] This outpouring of the Spirit created a heightened concern about global missions as an outflow of the many revivals taking place around the world. In this, it can and has been said that Pentecostalism is synonymous with missions. To be Pentecostal is to be missionary.[16] As Anderson says, "The present proliferation of Pentecostalism and indeed its inherent character result from the fact that this was fundamentally a missionary movement of the

---

[14] Combined Minutes of the General Council of the Assemblies of God, Hot Springs, AR, and Chicago, IL, 1914.

[15] On the Latter Rain movement, see Dayton, *Theological Roots of Pentecostalism*, 26–28. Also see Archer, who observes that "the purpose of the latter rain outpouring was to bring the Church to perfection and unity, while empowering the individual Christian with supernatural power in order to be a witness in these last days. Archer, *The Gospel Revisited*, 31. Anderson also notes that worldwide revivals contributed to the belief in a global revival that would result in "unprecedented missionary activity around the globe." Anderson, *Spreading Fires*, 31.

[16] McClung, "'Try to Get People Saved,'" 31.

Spirit from the start."[17] This sentiment echoes that of one early leader in the Assemblies of God, John W. Welch, who said that the fellowship was never intended to be an institution, but only a missionary agency.[18]

PENTECOSTALISM AND THE DRIFT TO HOLISM

Early Pentecostal missions were characterized by a clear prioritization of world evangelization even though they often included various types of compassionate outreach.[19] In recent years, though, this emphases on cross-cultural proclamation as the essence of missions has evaporated, owing in part to the mission as transformation/holistic mission movement emerging from the various Lausanne congresses that have taken place between 1974 and 2010. Much of this shift comes from increased attention to and broad acceptance among evangelicals at large regarding the kingdom of God as inaugurated eschatology and can be traced to the developments at the World Council of Churches conference at Willingen regarding the *missio Dei* described earlier.[20]

Paul Pomerville addressed this issue in *The Third Force in Missions*. In doing so, Pomerville defended the historic Pentecostal understanding of missions in the narrow sense as referring to the proclamation of the gospel among the unreached.[21] As Pomerville has observed, evangelical advocates of the broad sense of mission

---

[17] Anderson, *Spreading Fires*, 5. Also see John V. York, who argues that "the agenda of the Spirit [is] the agenda of the people of God moving in the power of God to accomplish the mission of God (missio Dei)." John V. York, *Missions in the Age of the Spirit* (Springfield, MO: Logion, 2000), 186. See also Veli-Matti Kärkkäinen, "Mission in Pentecostal Theology," *International Review of Mission* 107, no. 1 (2018): 11.

[18] John W. Welch, "A Missionary Movement," in *The Pentecostal Evangel* (Springfield, MO: Gospel Publishing House, November 13, 1920), 8.

[19] Anderson, *Spreading Fires*, 212–15.

[20] Julie C. Ma and Wansuk Ma, *Mission in the Spirit: Towards a Pentecostal/Charismatic Missiology* (Eugene, OR: Wipf and Stock, 2010), 7.

[21] Paul Pomerville, *The Third Force in Missions* (1985; rev. ed., Peabody, MA: Hendrickson 2016), 222–25.

often emphasize the equal standing of the church's evangelistic and cultural mandate as the result of a kingdom rubric rooted in dispensational theology. However, such perspectives neglect the particular way in which the Third Person of the Trinity works uniquely through the church and denies "the very age of the Spirit itself."[22] Specifically, these approaches tend to minimize the way in which the Spirit works, namely, by indwelling the Christian community in miraculous power in accompanying gospel proclamation.[23] In this approach Pentecostalism offers a corrective to a Western cultural corruption of the gospel that moved away from the experiential aspects of the faith to a more rationalistic approach. As a result, and speaking more directly of ecumenical developments and their influence on evangelicals, "the limitless use of *missio Dei*, under the confessed purpose of attaining a holistic mission, appears to function as a smokescreen for an obvious bias for pursuing humanization in some conciliar mission theologies."[24] Not only ecumenical movements but also evangelical treatments of the kingdom of God such as the seminal work of George Eldon Ladd have noticeably been lacking in emphasis on the Spirit's role as it concerns the kingdom.[25] This also proved to be a missing piece in my study of Carl Henry. Contemporary Pentecostals at many points seem to have uncritically adopted this broadly evangelical kingdom perspective.

Lately, however, the notion of priority has given way to what Murray Dempster described as a "coming of age," as Pentecostal missions increasingly tend to set proclamation of the gospel and social concern on even footing.[26] Dempster's argument consists largely of setting both within a kingdom rubric wherein the

---

[22] Ibid., xviii.

[23] Ibid., 97–105.

[24] Paul Pomerville, "Pentecostalism and Missions," PhD dissertation, Fuller Theological Seminary, 1982, 317.

[25] Ibid.

[26] Murray W. Dempster, "Evangelism, Social Concern, and the Kingdom of God," in *Called and Empowered: Global Mission in Pentecostal Perspective*, ed. Murray W. Dempster et al. (Peabody, MA: Hendrickson, 1991), 22.

kingdom of God becomes the great homogenizer, as all kingdom activities are considered equally important.[27] In this, the concept of missions as witness is interpreted broadly according to what Dempster calls the threefold ministry of the church, focusing on its *kerygmatic, koinoniac,* and *diakonic* functions.[28] While Dempster is correct to argue for a missiology that integrates the elements of *kerygma* (proclamation), *koinonia* (community), and *diakonia* (service), there is nothing about integration per se that necessitates equality among the various components. It is quite possible for things to be conceptually bound together and yet differ in importance. Moreover, not only are there other important activities of the church that Dempster fails to mention, such as prayer and worship, but more important, even if these other elements were included, it would be possible for a church to do all of them and still not be engaged in cross-cultural missions. In other words, there is nothing explicit about any of those three functions that demands concern for the lost among the nations. As Alan Johnson has argued, "If there is indeed no difference between what I should be doing in my own local church in my own sociocultural setting and somewhere else, there is no compelling reason to cross geographic and cultural boundaries at all."[29] Even though Dempster argues that the "kerygmatic activity of the church aims to encourage individuals to become missionary agents of God's new order and life,"[30] the broad sense of missions that Dempster argues for could legitimately operate without explicit concern for the nations.

---

[27] Ibid.

[28] Ibid., 24. See also Henning Wrogemann's analysis of the missiology of Johannes Christian Hoekendijk as embodying essentially the same concerns, in Wrogemann, *Theologies of Mission,* vol. 2 of *Intercultural Theology,* trans. Karl E. Böhmer (Downers Grove, IL: IVP Academic, 2018), 73–91; C. Hoekendijk, *The Church Inside Out* (Philadelphia: Westminster, 1966).

[29] Alan Johnson, *Apostolic Function in 21st Century Missions* (Pasadena, CA: William Carey Library, 2009), 52.

[30] Dempster, "Evangelism, Social Concern, and the Kingdom of God," 26.

It is also worth noting that the exegetical boundaries for these terms are sometimes less static than Dempster's essay suggests. In Acts, for example, the term *diakonia* is used in relation to both table service (Acts 6:2) and service of the word, or proclamation (Acts 6:4). Apart from locating these terms in their canonical context, they inevitably become subject to reductionist interpretations. Darrell Guder proves helpful here, noting that "the danger of generalizing our terms in order to insure that everything is always being said can result in vagueness and platitudes that never define anything, and never challenge anyone."[31]

A litany of Pentecostal scholars have followed in Dempster's footsteps. For example, Peter Althouse builds on Dempster's paradigm but argues for a more distinctly trinitarian view of *missio Dei*. Althouse mistakenly claims this understanding of mission owes its lineage to Karl Barth, which as I noted in the Introduction is unsupportable.[32] While acknowledging that Pentecostals have generally prioritized proclamation, Althouse advocates for the broader sense and calls for greater attention to Jesus's so-called nonverbal communication.[33] Even this notion is suspect, however, given that we only know of such activities because they are verbally revealed in scripture. Not only this, but seldom does any nonverbal activity of Jesus in scripture appear apart from verbal interpretation through the lens of the gospel. That aside, this turn to a broad sense of mission represents a sharp departure from the historical understanding of Pentecostalism.

Similarly, Andrew Lord observes that this broadened definition of missions among Pentecostals results from detaching missionary enthusiasm from the "second coming" message that characterized early Pentecostal revivals. Lord considers this a good thing, and he rejects attempts by scholars such as Pomerville who have argued

---

[31] Darrell L. Guder, *Be My Witnesses* (Grand Rapids, MI: Eerdmans, 1985), 135.

[32] Peter Althouse, "Towards a Pentecostal Ecclesiology: Participation in the Missional Life of the Triune God," *Journal of Pentecostal Theology* 18, no. 2 (2009): 231.

[33] Ibid., 239.

for a return to the narrower sense of missions.[34] Finally, also endeavoring to develop a broad understanding of Pentecostal mission, Julie Ma and Wansuk Ma have made the case for "a deeper and wider" Pentecostal missiology that includes three spheres or "ripples" to be understood as concentric circles of missions with each one leading to and feeding the others.[35] Ma and Ma see these ripples not as simultaneous, however, but rather as progressive and thus a move away from the narrow sense of missions.[36] In all of these there has been a distinct and observable move among Pentecostal writers toward acceptance of missions in the broader sense. The tendency among contemporary Pentecostals is to speak of both the church's evangelistic mandate and its social or cultural mandate as kingdom activities of approximately equal importance.

The problem with such an approach is that it will inevitably lead to the neglect of gospel proclamation as the main thrust of missions. Pomerville's argument for continuing to define *missio Dei* in the narrow sense of gospel proclamation proceeds along the lines of addressing the kingdom homogenization described above and rejecting any understanding of the kingdom that fails to prioritize proclamation. Although Lord considers this "going back" to a narrow definition negatively, I see it as exactly the opposite and consider it a return to Pentecostalism's true identity. It is so in the sense that Pentecostalism has long understood God's activity in the world as a dynamic relationship between gospel proclamation and the ministry of the Spirit that accompanies, empowers, and works in and through the church's verbal preaching of the gospel.[37] This means that mission as the activity of God cannot be isolated from the people of God whom God has given his Spirit, fundamentally orienting God's people to their role among the nations. As Pomerville explains, there is therefore good reason for holding on to missions in the narrow sense:

---

[34] Andrew M. Lord, "The Voluntary Principle in Pentecostal Missiology," *Journal of Pentecostal Theology* 8, no. 17 (2000): 93.
[35] Ma and Ma, *Mission in the Spirit*, 10.
[36] Ibid., 25.
[37] Pomerville, *The Third Force in Missions*, 198–99.

After Pentecost, the redemptive activity of God is mediated primarily through the preaching of the gospel and the manifest power of the Holy Spirit in Jesus' name. The church empowered by the Spirit demonstrates the kingdom's presence and power by the preaching of the Gospel—Jesus' redemptive death for sin, which was confirmed by signs and wonders (Mark 16:15–17, 20). It is in this saving activity of God the Holy Spirit through the agency of the church, that the priority of mission is found. The priority of proclaiming the gospel, the Great Commission mission, dominates the church's mission in the book of Acts. Scripture does put emphasis on the evangelistic mandate, God's "special" mission.[38]

All of this raises the question of whether this shift to a broad understanding of mission really represents a coming of age for Pentecostalism, as Dempster says, or simply another subtle form of accommodation to the spirit of the age.[39] In this section I argue that it is the latter and that inattention to this matter sets Pentecostalism on a pathway to cultural accommodation that can only end—as so many other accommodations have throughout church history—with a church that has lost its prophetic voice. When the notion of priorities is sacrificed at the altar of the kingdom, the result is that, as Pomerville has observed, the church's mission becomes dictated by the world rather than by scripture and sound theology.[40] Human need rather than divine prognosis becomes the driving force in missions, and when that happens, there is no end to what might be classified as missions. This is because there is no end to human need or to human want parading around as need. The simple fact remains that the church does not exist as a cornucopia of solutions to a never-ending stream of human problems. Rather, it exists primarily for one problem;

---

[38] Ibid., 225.
[39] Ibid., 215.
[40] Ibid., 242.

that is, it serves as an agent of the kingdom to restore the broken relationship between God and humanity.

In deconstructing the modern tendency toward holism in Pentecostal missions, I attempt to strengthen Pomerville's argument by offering a Pentecostal missiology that underscores God's concern for the nations. In doing so I hope to continue Pentecostalism's historic understanding of the narrow sense of missions in a way that necessitates a concern for the nations as fundamental to Pentecostal ecclesiology.

PENTECOSTALISM AND THE NATIONS

Many pioneer Pentecostal missionaries misinterpreted the gift of tongues to be the ability to speak foreign languages without having to study in order to evangelize the nations as quickly as possible. Almost without fail, those who proceeded to foreign lands under this assumption met with disappointment. However, as Augustus Cerillo has observed, this does certainly highlight that missions and classical Pentecostalism were of one piece.[41]

While the orientation of God's people to the nations has been a frequent topic in texts on missiology, a Pentecostal missiology will be especially attentive to the role of the Spirit in this orientation. In doing so I wish to borrow a concept from Bishop Stephen Neill, who has argued that too often our definitions of the church have focused on the marks of the church, or what it does in any given context. But understanding the various functions of the church does not necessarily answer for us the question, *For what does the church fundamentally exist*? Neill's answer is helpful, as he notes that

> the one central purpose for which the church has been called into existence is that in this interim period, *zwischen den Zeiten*, between the epochs, as the Germans conveniently call

---

[41] Augustus Cerillo Jr., "Pentecostals and the City," in Dempster et al., *Called and Empowered*, 100. See also Anderson, *Spreading Fires*, 46.

it, it should preach the Gospel to every creature. Everything else—ministry, sacraments, doctrine, worship—is ancillary to this. A doctrine of the church must, therefore, be always forward looking, not only in the sense that it looks forward in hope to the final consummation of the ages, but in the sense that it takes account all the time of the unreached, the unaccomplished, the unattempted.[42]

This is precisely the problem with Dempster's functional ecclesiology described above. The church's missionary mandate must not only include the broad sense but also must have a vision for its unique role in God's desire to redeem a people from every tribe and nation, and even within that, there must be a particular emphasis on those who are most lost and who have the least access to the gospel.[43]

Early Pentecostal missiology was grounded in Pentecostal Christology. The designation of Jesus in Pentecostal thought as Savior, Spirit Baptizer, Healer, and coming King took root early on in the movement. This idea began to emerge from the Apostolic Faith Mission, "one of the oldest Pentecostal bodies," which talked about the foundation of the church in precisely these terms, with an additional fifth element: sanctification.[44] The fourfold pattern became more widespread, however, and was closely tied to Pentecostal emphases on the miraculous as a restoration of the apostolic faith. Pentecostals held to these on the basis of their belief in the immutability of God and in the conviction that all of these related to the church's evangelistic task.[45] As such, Pentecostal ecclesiology and missions were grounded in the nature of Christ and especially in his relation to the nations.

As Anderson has pointed out, early Pentecostal missionaries often based their passion for world evangelization on Jesus's

---

[42] Stephen Neill, *Creative Tension* (London: Edenburgh House, 1959), 112. See also Johnson, *Apostolic Function in 21st Century Missions*.

[43] See Johnson, *Apostolic Function in 21st Century Missions*, 51–102.

[44] Dayton, *Theological Roots of Pentecostalism*, 20.

[45] Ibid., 25–26.

command that "the gospel of the kingdom shall be preached in all the world for a witness unto all nations; and then the end shall come" (Mt 24:14).[46] But the narrower view of missions has tended to be grounded in the Great Commission text of Matthew 28:18–20.[47] A Pentecostal and missional understanding of this text, and one that will strengthen the case for the narrow sense of missions, can be found by examining Matthew's linking of the Great Commission to God's call of Abraham and the promise to bless the nations through him.

The message of the Bible centers on God's redemptive plan for all nations, and this should therefore constitute the proper center of the *missio Dei*. Even though Israel and the seed of Abraham were the avenues through which this plan would take shape, the outlook was always multinational and therefore cross-cultural. The call of Abraham in Genesis 12 unveils God's concern for the nations and promises to redemptively bless the nations through Abraham and his descendants.[48] Thus Israel's relation to the nations centers on its role as mediator of God's salvific words and deeds.[49] As Johannes Blauw observes, "The whole history of Israel is nothing but the continuation of God's dealings with the nations, and that therefore the history of Israel is only to be understood from the unsolved problem of the relation of God

---

[46] Anderson, *Spreading Fires*, 221.

[47] Ma and Ma, *Mission in the Spirit*, 5. See also Harry Boer's discussion "The Role of the Great Commission in Modern Missions," in Harry R. Boer, *Pentecost and Missions* (Grand Rapids, MI: Eerdmans, 1961), 15–27.

[48] Gordon D. Fee, "The Kingdom of God," in *Called and Empowered: Global Mission in Pentecostal Perspective*, ed. Murray W. Dempster, Byron D. Klaus, and Douglas Petersen (Peabody, MA: Hendrickson, 1991), 7. It is also noteworthy that Fee here emphasizes God's concern for the nations especially in terms of proclamation, an element that Dempster seems to overlook. Also see Galatians 3:8. As Guder says of Genesis 12, this passage is generally taken as the beginning of salvation history. Guder, *Be My Witnesses*, 8–9.

[49] John F. Walvoord, *The Nations in Prophecy* (Grand Rapids, MI: Zondervan, 1972), 42.

to the nations."[50] This problem finds resolution in the book of Revelation, owing to the messianic concern for gathering a people from every tribe and nation (Rev 5:9).

Genesis 12 and the call of Abraham to be an agent of God's blessing to the nations must be understood in light of Genesis 9 and 10. As Roger Hedlund observes, "The table of nations (Gen 10) suggests God's relationship to every human family, language and people."[51] In these chapters we see that the nations owe their very existence to both God's judgment and his subsequent offer of peace. The God who sends the flood also provides the rainbow. Scripture portrays the table of nations in Genesis 10 in terms of God's gracious offer of peace after the flood. The nations themselves stand as a sign of God's redemptive activity. As the redemptive work of God progresses throughout scripture, Israel serves centripetally as a light to the nations, as the nations are drawn to God through Israel's holy living. This role would one day be taken up by the Servant described by the prophet Isaiah (Is 49:6). Jesus, who fulfills Isaiah's messianic expectations, then sets the mandate for fulfilling this task of being a light to the nations squarely on the church (Mt 5:14), though now moving out to the nations rather than drawing them in.[52] All this means, as Blauw has noted, that Israel's history must be understood in relation to the nations and God's redemptive acts. He writes, "Israel has been called in her election by Yahweh to be preacher and example, prophet and priest for the nations."[53]

---

[50] Blauw, *The Missionary Nature of the Church*, 19.

[51] Roger E. Hedlund, *The Mission of the Church in the World* (Grand Rapids, MI: Baker, 1991), 25.

[52] Blauw, *The Missionary Nature of the Church*, 19–20; Guder, *Be My Witnesses*, 13. See also F. F. Bruce, *The Book of the Acts*, New International Commentary on the New Testament, Accordance electronic ed. (Grand Rapids, MI: Eerdmans, 1988), 36.

[53] Blauw, *The Missionary Nature of the Church*, 28. See also Jaroslav Pelikan, *The Light of the World: A Basic Image in Early Christian Thought* (New York: Harper Brothers, 1962); Richard Bauckham, *Bible and Mission: Christian Witness in a Postmodern World* (Grand Rapids, MI: Baker Academic, 2003), 13.

This theme occurs frequently in the psalms as the songs and worship of Israel remind God's people of their missional role. Their role as divine emissary was to set before the nations the standard by which God would judge the world (Ps 9:19). Their holy living and worship of YHWH cannot be understood in isolation but as an invitation to the nations to leave behind their idolatry and to gather together in the Holy City (Pss 22:27; 33:12; 46:10; 47:8; 67:2; 86:9). Not only was Israel to be a standing testimony to life made whole and complete through God's presence dwelling among them, but they were to declare this, and

> tell of His glory among the nations,
>   His wonderful deeds among all the peoples.
>   (Ps 96:3)

The fact that references to the nations occur so frequently in the psalms reminds Israel that her worship can never be detached from her mission and that her mission is preeminently centered on both God's judgment and promise.

This illuminative task regarding the revealed will of God for the nations as a central work of the Messiah and his followers is also well captured in Matthew's Gospel. Just as Israel's election was for the sake of the nations, so too was the founding of the church. Matthew has carefully framed his entire Gospel in dual references to the Abrahamic covenant in order to make this point. In Matthew 1:1 the author describes Jesus as "the son of David, the son of Abraham." In doing so, this Gospel sets the messianic role of Jesus in the context of God's covenant promises, first to Abraham and then to David. These twin references pull together the promise of not only a perpetual kingdom (1 Sam 7:12–16) but also one in which God's mercy will be extended to all the families on earth (Gen 12:1–3). Later, God explains this more fully by declaring that Abraham will be the father of a multitude of nations (Gen 17:4).[54] This shows not only that God's redemptive

---

[54] Victor P. Hamilton, *The Book of Genesis, Chapters 1—17*, New International Commentary on the Old Testament. Accordance electronic ed. (Grand Rapids, MI: Eerdmans, 1990), 464.

work from the beginning was global in scope and teleologically oriented to the redemption of all nations, but that Matthew goes to great lengths to set his entire Gospel, and thereby the church's mission, in this global trajectory.[55]

This is further evidenced in the closing verses of Matthew, which function in much the same way, as Jesus's disciples are sent out to make disciples of all nations (lit. *ethnicities*; Mt 28:18–20).[56] Thus in the opening verses and in the closing verses of Matthew, the messianic purpose becomes framed within the context of the movement of God's people to the nations. By framing this statement in twin references to the Abrahamic covenant, and thereby in God's concern to redemptively bless the nations, Matthew has forestalled any understanding of discipleship that does not center on concern for the nations through the use of this missional *inclusio* drawing his readers back to the Abrahamic covenant.

Many commentators have rightly observed of the Great Commission text in Matthew 28:18–20 that the command is not to "go" but to "make disciples." This is technically true. There is only one imperative in this passage and it is to make disciples. The "go" portion of the text functions as an assumption, a participle, and can be accurately translated "as you go." However, this does not tell the whole story. Going can be assumed in Matthew only because it is commanded in Genesis in the context of God's covenant with Abraham. By bookending this gospel in references to the Abrahamic covenant, the author has gone to great lengths to ensure that this point is not missed. Thus, however else we may define Christian missions, its central feature is the forward movement of God's people to the nations. This is especially significant given the Jewish audience of Matthew's Gospel, the predominantly Jewish focus of Jesus's own ministry (Mt 15:24), and the fact that the writer goes to great lengths to underscore the Messiah's

---

[55] Bauckham, *Bible and Mission*, 33. See also James LaGrand, *The Earliest Christian Mission to "All Nations" in the Light of Matthew's Gospel* (Grand Rapids, MI: Eerdmans, 1999), 172.

[56] Cf. R. T. France, *The Gospel of Matthew*, New International Commentary on the New Testament, Accordance electronic ed. (Grand Rapids, MI: Eerdmans, 2007), 35.

desire to gather the nations. As Blauw observes, the early position of "going forth" in the Great Commission "places emphasis on going, on travelling."[57] Just as it would not suffice for Jewish converts to Christianity to be content with reaching out to Judaism alone, neither will it suffice for the church to remain content with doing evangelism while neglecting God's concern for the nations. In short, "the making of disciples can happen only in a movement of the disciples of Christ towards all nations."[58] Thus concern for the nations and their redemption lies at the center of the discipleship process because it lies at the center of who God is.

This point is further made by consideration of Matthew 5:13–16, wherein the church is called to be salt of the earth and light of the world. This text, as with the aforementioned references to Abraham, orients Jesus's disciples to the nations that are perishing apart from the knowledge of God.[59] Indeed, some scholars have seen in this text a reference to the Jewish and Gentile missions of both Jesus and the church.[60] Salt was often a symbol in the Old Testament of God's covenant with Israel, whose primary nature and calling was as a witness to the nations.[61] Thus Jesus's iteration of this, following the Beatitudes, sets Christian ethical mooring in the context of mission. Christian ethics stands not just for shaping the conduct of individuals but for shaping the life and mission of the church. This reality then requires an ecclesiology that centers on the movement of God's people to the nations as this movement, according to Matthew's Gospel, lies at the heart of Christian discipleship. Thus, to be a follower of Jesus cannot be reduced to reciting a short prayer or adhering to a list

---

[57] Blauw, *The Missionary Nature of the Church*, 86.

[58] Ibid.

[59] Johannes Nissen, *New Testament and Mission* (Frankfurt: Peter Lang, 2007), 27.

[60] John Nolland, *The Gospel of Matthew: A Commentary on the Greek Text*, New International Greek Testament Commentary (Grand Rapids, MI; Eerdmans, 2005), 212–13.

[61] Num 18:19; 2 Chron 13:5; Don Garlington, "'The Salt of the Earth' in Covenantal Perspective," *JETS* 54, no. 4. (2011): 715–48.

The Priority of Proclamation in Pentecostal Perspective 19

of doctrines but instead involves being discipled to long for the redemption of all nations, just as God longs for and pursues this through God's covenant people.

What modern Pentecostal scholars miss, in their advocacy for a broader understanding of mission based on the central role of the kingdom of God in the ministry of Jesus, is that the many images of the kingdom, especially those found in Jesus's parables, focus on the kingdom of God as it relates to God's concern for the nations. As Blauw observes, concern for the nations as the preeminent focus of the kingdom is evident in images such as: gathering of the flock (Mt 25:31); the Temple (Mk 11:17); a city on a hill (Mt 5:14); the light on the stand (Mt 5:15); the stream of life (Jn 7:37); the inheritance (Mt 25:34); and the trees where the birds make their nests (Mt 13:32)—all of which point to God's desire to gather a people from every tribe and nation.[62] This has vital implications for understanding the church as missionary. As Blauw explains, "The church no longer merely anticipates, but remains the symbol of the hopes for the kingdom in the fullness of the nations. Mission comes into view when this hope takes the form of acts of *proclamation* on behalf of Christ."[63]

THE SPIRIT AND THE NATIONS

The trinitarian formula that forms part of the Great Commission is not without significance. Jesus in Matthew 28:18–20 not only sends his disciples on a global mission to make more disciples from all nations (*panta ta ethne*), instructing them in all that Jesus did and taught, but he also frames this otherwise impossible task in a surprising and important reference to the Holy Spirit. Andrew Overman says that Matthew's formula here reflects Daniel 7:13–14, where God the Father is described as the Ancient of Days and Jesus as the Son of Man. That passage declares that

---

[62] Blauw, *The Missionary Nature of the Church*, 70.
[63] Ibid.

> One like a Son of Man was coming,
> And He came up to the Ancient of Days
> And was presented before Him.
> And to Him was given dominion,
> Glory and a kingdom,
> That all the peoples, nations and *men of every
>   language*
> Might serve Him. (Dan 7:13–14)

Overman also notes that in the LXX version of Daniel 7, one finds the very same phrase referring to the nations (*panta ta ethne*). In borrowing from this passage in Daniel, Matthew sets the commission of the disciples on a worldwide mission to make disciples in Jesus's name. But it is the Spirit who baptized Jesus and in whom these disciples will also be baptized (Jn 3:11) that provides Matthew's unique understanding of these things. Thus, in relation to the mention of the Spirit in the Great Commission, one can only conclude that "the community believed that they enjoyed the continued presence and continued power and authority of Jesus through this spirit."[64] All of this means that authentic expressions of missions must first be grounded in the doctrine of the Trinity. On this the Willingen scholars were not wrong. But since the nations constitute the preeminent concern of God, so too must they become the main concern of God's people. It then follows that just as God is missionary in nature, it becomes inescapable that the church God begets and the disciples that form the church must also be missionary in nature. This seemingly impossible task finds impetus in the sending God of scripture, in the "sentness" of Jesus the Messiah, and in the Holy Spirit sent by the Father and the Son, who empowers the church to make disciples not just of local people, but globally as well. *Panta ta*

---

[64] Andrew J. Overman, *The Church and Community in Crisis: The Gospel According to Matthew* (Valley Forge, PA: Trinity, 1996), 409–10; France, *The Gospel of Matthew*, 1112–13. For an alternative view, see Robert Gundry, *Matthew: A Commentary on His Literary and Theological Art* (Grand Rapids, MI: Eerdmans, 1982), 595.

ethne serves to remind the church that it cannot be domesticated and remain a true church. It cannot be settled and shut off to the world and still remain connected to the missionary God it serves. Missions and concern for the nations lie at the very heart of what it means to be God's people.

This point is even clearer in Luke-Acts. Luke connects his version of the Great Commission (Lk 24:47–48) explicitly to the need for the Spirit's empowerment (Lk 24:49), but in the second part of his work he connects both to Christ's mandate for God's people to unceasingly push forward to take the gospel to the nations (Acts 1:8).[65] In Pentecostalism the Holy Spirit's work was often interpreted within an eschatological framework that served as a primary motivation for missions.[66] It is also worth noting that the first concrete result of the Spirit being poured out in the book of Acts is the proclamation of the gospel.[67] According to Blauw, proclamation of the gospel among the nations is possible only by (1) the voluntary sacrificial death of Jesus; (2) the resurrection of Jesus; and (3) the gift of the Holy Spirit equipping the church for witness.[68] It is the Spirit that calls forth, empowers, and sends the church on its global mission. The church's witness, according to the book of Acts, is not only global in nature, but more precisely oriented toward the bridging of cultural-linguistic barriers to take the gospel where it has not yet gone. Here we begin to understand what the Bible means by the word *nation*. As the church moves forward, we see confirming signs of the Spirit's work making those a people who were once not a people (1 Pet 2:10). Who are the nations? They are those not of true Israel, who previously had no knowledge of YHWH, of the God of Israel, but who have through the proclamation of the gospel and the efficaciousness of the Spirit are being welcomed home and brought back into the fold.

---

[65] Wonsuk Ma, "Full Circle Mission: A Possibility of Pentecostal Missiology," *Asian Journal of Pentecostal Studies* 8, no. 1 (2005): 15.

[66] Kärkkäinen, "Mission in Pentecostal Theology," 11.

[67] John V. Taylor, *The Go-Between God: The Holy Spirit and Christian Mission* (London: SCM Press, 1975), 17.

[68] Blauw, *The Missionary Nature of the Church*, 104–5.

To define missions as "to the uttermost parts" means nothing without this greater specificity. To a believer in Africa, a community in America's Bible Belt may legitimately qualify as the uttermost parts if the primary criterion is that of geographic distance. Missions does not mean simply sending Christians to foreign lands. Rather, Luke's own outline of the text provided in Acts 1:8 emphasizes not only the movement of Christ's witnesses to the nations, but also the restlessness of the gospel when it comes to the not-yet-reached.[69] The Holy Spirit is a border-crossing, idol-breaking, power-giving, reconciling Spirit constantly pushing the church forward toward to the not-yet-reached. The restlessness of the church flows from the restlessness of the Spirit that continues to empower God's people to proclaim the gospel of salvation to the nations. As Darrell Bock says of the Spirit in Acts, "The Spirit's coming showed the community that God had cleansed the Gentiles and called out from them a people for his name."[70] Because of this, the proclamation of the gospel made possible by the missionary Spirit of God constantly demands a fresh hearing among those most separated from the Truth. A church sensitive to the missional impulse of the Spirit will cling tenaciously to this reality.

A MISSIONARY AND PENTECOSTAL ECCLESIOLOGY

Much of the modern confusion about the church's missionary mandate can be traced to a failure to distinguish between missions and evangelism, and between missions and fraternal cooperation. Again, this problem is often framed by distinguishing between *missions* (plural) as referring narrowly to God's redemptive activity among the nations, and *mission* (singular) as broadly to

---

[69] As Bruce says, "It has often been pointed out that the geographical terms of verse 8 provide a sort of 'Index of Contents' for Acts." Bruce, *The Book of the Acts*, 36.

[70] Darrell L. Bock, *A Theology of Luke and Acts* (Grand Rapids, MI: Zondervan, 2012), 301.

all that God is doing in the world.[71] The general idea here is that God has one mission in the world (mission in the broad sense), but the church has many missions related to preaching the gospel and planting churches (missions in the narrow sense). Lesslie Newbigin proves instructive here in arguing for the narrow sense of missions as limited to successfully planting the church, even while admitting that successful church planting does not negate the need for that church to grow toward achieving its "total mission."[72] By distinguishing the narrow sense of mission from the broad sense, Newbigin rightly demarcates what Pomerville referred to as "the Great Commission mission" from the mission of the local church in context.

This idea was also expressed by Ralph Winter in his modality-sodality distinction, which differentiated the role of the church from that of the mission band.[73] Plus, Newbigin's argument provides a helpful guide in determining what activities are rightly to be considered missions, and what are better termed fraternal activity.[74] In this, one cannot but help hear echoes of Stephen Neill's famous axiom, "If everything is mission, nothing is mission."[75] Neill's concern pointed precisely to the issue to which I refer. "If everything the Church does is to be classified as 'mission,' we shall have to find another term for the Church's particular responsibility for 'the heathen,' those who have never heard the Name of Christ."[76] My contention is that much of what has been written by Pentecostals on the topic of *missio Dei* has conflated mission and missions and not given sufficient attention to the historical emphasis by classical Pentecostals on the biblical mandate to make Christ known among the nations.

---

[71] Pomerville, *The Third Force in Missions*, 208.

[72] Lesslie Newbigin, "Future of Missions and Missionaries," *Review and Expositor* 74, no. 2 (1977): 216.

[73] Ralph D. Winter, "Two Structures of God's Redemptive Mission," *Missiology* 2, no. 1 (1974).

[74] Newbigin, "Future of Missions and Missionaries."

[75] Neill, *Creative Tension*, 81.

[76] Ibid.

Advocates for missions in the broad sense often argue that missions is not the prerogative of the few but of every church member. As it is sometimes said, "Every person is a missionary and every place a mission field." As noble as this sounds, it is actually a formula that leads to a diminished emphasis on God's concern for the nations, as they ultimately drop out of purview as an object of particular concern both for God and the church. This does not mean though, as some claim, that an emphasis on the nations sets missionaries on a higher plane or superior status.[77] A true Pentecostal missiology will keep the nations central to the church's task, without minimizing that many within the church are also called to vital roles in a non-cross-cultural context. Of course, missions is the prerogative of the whole church. But the whole church does not engage in mission in the same way, just as the whole church does not relate to the task of preaching in the same way. Some prepare and deliver the message, even more hear and apply it. Even so, the many indirect ways that believers relate to the task of missions will find their greatest fulfillment in being connected to the church's global trajectory.

PENTECOSTALISM, MISSIONS, AND ECCLESIAL PRIORITIES

The greatest threat to biblical priorities is the idolatry of our opinions. And nothing more evidences the idolatry of our opinions than the tendency to find in the Bible exactly what we already believe. I suspect that something like this lies behind much of the present-day drift toward holism. Because priorities determine trajectory, this means that priorities must be in place in order for the church to remain oriented to the *missio Dei*, the mission

---

[77] I find Blomberg's idea that Jesus's point is that disciples should make other disciples "wherever they may be" to be problematic in that it seems to be a reaction to the overemphasis on the "going" in some forms of missionary recruitment. See Craig L. Blomberg, *Matthew*, The New American Commentary (Nashville, TN: Broadman, 1992), 431.

of God, as I have defined it here. Without priorities the church's mission becomes omnidirectional, with various functions of the church all competing against one another for attention and funding. I have previously noted the broad sense of missions as often consisting of the variations of the following components: centering on the idea of witness and focusing on the practices of *koinonia* (community), *diakonia* (service), and *kerygma* (proclamation). While these qualities *may* define what a healthy church looks like (and I think that is debatable if we include only these three), they become less helpful for understanding how a church comes to be, and thereby for establishing a missional trajectory.

In the "church as witness" model, *kerygma* refers not only to preaching the gospel to those outside the church, but also to instruction for those inside the church. *Diakonia* indicates service to both needy church members and to needy people in one's community. And *koinonia* relates not only to the community of saints, but also to the community in which the saints gather and reside. Yet the picture is still incomplete. The church-as-witness paradigm in reality describes a static church whose relationship to the world is nebulous because it lacks any explicit orientation to the nations such as that outlined above. Plus, to the extent that the church lacks any specific trajectory, it will likely become caught up in a myriad of activities that have little or no connection to the church's primary role of making God known among the nations. It is difficult to understand what is meant by the church as a "pilgrim people" if those people are not going anywhere. Therefore, I propose a missions ecclesiology that can be illustrated as follows:

A Person –> A Power –> A Proclamation –> and A People

I have adapted this in part from Everett Ferguson, who says that God first gave a person, then a proclamation, and then a people.[78] To this I have added "a power," as the church has no mission in and of itself, and indeed there can be no church outside the

---

[78] Everett Ferguson, *The Church of Christ: A Biblical Ecclesiology* (Grand Rapids, MI: Eerdmans, 1996), xvii.

operation of the Spirit. This model bears some resemblance to Howard Snyder's model of church-based evangelism, which he describes as follows:

Presence –> Proclamation –> Persuasion –> and Propagation[79]

The goal of all that the church does is the formation of a people set apart, called out of the world in order to take the gospel to those places where Jesus is not yet known (1 Pet 2:9). Importantly, this model emphasizes the dynamic relationship that has been a hallmark of Pentecostal missions between proclamation of the gospel and the power of the Spirit. It also captures the essence of the Great Commission, in that the church exists not for itself but as an agent of God's reconciling mission among the nations. It is only in the sense of God's desire to redeem the nations that the church can be said to exist for the sake of the world. Furthermore, this model represents trinitarian missions in the truest sense, because the church becomes the primary locus of the Father's redemptive activity through the Son and by the Holy Spirit. And it sets apart in a manner similar to that of the early church (Acts 13:1) those called to cross-cultural witness and sends them out to accomplish that task. All that the church does is oriented toward this ultimate goal.

The point in all of this is simply to set forth in basic terms the notions that (1) Pentecostalism and missions defined as cross-cultural evangelism have historically been synonymous; and (2) missions defined narrowly in terms of making Christ known among the nations finds its grounding in the triune God who is a missionary God. Further, God's missionary nature flows from a desire to redeem the nations, a theme that lies at the heart of biblical revelation from Genesis to Revelation. Any efforts to redefine missions in broader terms thus becomes guilty of attempting to create a god in our own image, an image increasingly uncomfortable with God's universal claims over the nations. The misstep

---

[79] Howard A. Snyder, "The Kingdom Mandate," chap. 6 in *Community of the King* (Downers Grove, IL: InterVarsity, 1977). Kindle edition.

of the Willingen scholars was not in grounding missions in who God is—on this they were absolutely right. Their problem was in not giving sufficient attention to how God has revealed Godself *for the redemption of the nations*. The god of ecumenism's *missio Dei* appears not primarily as redeemer and coming king, but more like a custodian and caretaker of the palace whose primary concern is to keep things from falling apart. Early Pentecostal missionaries who went to foreign lands proclaiming the whole gospel clung tenaciously to the scriptural affirmation that God can be known only through God's own revelation in Christ and in the Bible. They grounded their missiology in their Christology, wherein Christ is Savior, Spirit-Baptizer, Healer, and coming King. And they understood that all else that the church was called to be and do flowed into the church's evangelistic mandate, apart from which the nations are eternally lost.

2

The Missionary Nature of Tongues in the Book of Acts[1]

> When the social betterment of the populace has been the principal objective of mission, the tendency usually has been toward developing institutions such as schools, hospitals and agriculture projects. These are all worthy projects and the social betterment of a populace is the desire of every Christian. However, according to the New Testament plan these are byproducts rather than the heart of the missionary program. When we fail to see this, we build strong institutions but usually the church remains weak.
> —MELVIN HODGES[2]

Mission, then, cannot adequately be defined in terms of Christian effort to meet human need. This is equally true even when we include men's so-called spiritual needs. The weakness in any such definition is not that it tends to leave out the spiritual dimension of man but that it tends to leave

---

[1] An earlier version of this chapter appeared as Jerry M. Ireland, "The Missionary Nature of Tongues in the Book of Acts," *PentecoStudies* 18, no. 2 (2019): 200–23. Reprinted with permission.

[2] Melvin Hodges, *Growing Young Churches* (Chicago: Moody Bible Institute, 1970), 13.

out the action of God. And it is this alone which gives Christian mission its permanent and unchanging raison d'être.
—JOHN V. TAYLOR[3]

By now I have made it fairly clear that contemporary Pentecostal scholars by and large advocate a holistic (or broad) approach to mission based especially on broad understandings of the kingdom of God, but also on broad interpretations of the gospel and broad definitions of soteriology.[4] In doing so, advocates for these positions sometimes erase the already-blurred lines between missiology and other related but distinct doctrines, especially ecclesiology. Furthermore, this fairly recent trend among Pentecostals toward the broad sense of mission diverges widely from a previous generation of Pentecostal practitioners who both emphasized the priority of proclamation (also called the narrow sense of missions) and simultaneously engaged with issues of justice and liberation.[5]

---

[3] John V. Taylor, *For All the World* (Philadelphia: Westminster, 1966), 11.

[4] On broad interpretations of the kingdom of God, see Murray W. Dempster, "Evangelism, Social Concern, and the Kingdom of God," in *Called and Empowered: Global Mission in Pentecostal Perspective*, ed. Murray W. Dempster et al. (Peabody, MA: Hendrickson, 1991). One notable resource that develops all three of these themes from various authors representing the "conservative, evangelical, Pentecostal, charismatic wing of the church" is the edited volume *Holistic Mission: God's Plan for God's People*, ed. Brian Woolnough and Wonsuk Ma, Regnum Edinburgh 2010 Series (Eugene, OR: Wipf and Stock, 2010). See also Andy Lord, *Network Church: A Pentecostal Ecclesiology Shaped by Mission* (Leiden, The Netherlands: Brill, 2012), 11.

[5] See Mittelstadt's observation regarding Murray Dempster's role in inaugurating a Pentecostal emphasis on social justice "as missions," and the way in which this perspective is at odds with those like Robert Menzies who emphasize the proclamational function of the church in Luke-Acts: Martin William Mittelstadt, *Reading Luke-Acts in the Pentecostal Tradition* (Cleveland, TN: CPT, 2010), 116–18. See also Klaus Bockmuehl, *Evangelicals and Social Ethics* (Downers Grove, IL: InterVarsity, 1975), 42; Charles E. Self, "Toward the Centennial: Times of Transformation," in Gary B. McGee, *People of the Spirit: The Assemblies of God* (Springfield, MO: Gospel Publishing House, 2014), 513.

The primary argument in this chapter is that Luke in the book of Acts presents tongues speech (*glossolalia*) as the key to his missiology, one that orients the church to the nations and emphasizes its proclamational role. The idea that the relationship of God's people to the nations constitutes a fundamental aspect of their identity is nothing new. But the role of tongues in the book of Acts has not been sufficiently developed along these lines, nor have the implications for this been appreciated regarding the nature and meaning of missions. Specifically, Luke utilizes tongues speech in order to convey the ultimate trajectory of the church, namely, a concern for the nations. Understanding this trajectory helps temper narrowly individualistic interpretations of tongues as merely initial physical evidence, as well as holistic mission paradigms that often fail to articulate this key characteristic of God's people.

PROPOSAL FOR A NARROW VIEW OF PENTECOSTAL MISSIONS[6]

In this chapter I explore the missionary nature of tongues in Acts vis-à-vis these divergent approaches and argue that the Spirit especially orients the church to the nations.[7] This emphasis occurs as Luke presents *glossolalia* as the enduring evidence of the forward movement of the gospel to the nations. In this, and in contradistinction to most contemporary Pentecostals, I argue for the importance of the narrow view of mission based on occurrences of *glossolalia* in the book of Acts interpreted according to Luke's literary structure and based on Luke's explicit references to

---

[6] While I agree with the consensus that Luke-Acts represents a two-volume work by the same author, I also think that it must be admitted that there are emphases in Acts that are not present in Luke's Gospel. Among these are the role of the Spirit and the expansion of the church. For example, there are twice as many references to the Spirit in Acts as in Luke's Gospel, and this must be taken into account in a literary approach to the texts.

[7] Harry R. Boer, *Pentecost and Missions* (Grand Rapids, MI: Eerdmans, 1961), 135.

Israel as the basis for his ecclesiology. John V. Taylor's quotation above rightly grounds Pentecostal missiology in the unchanging nature of God. Because God does not change, and because mission is first and foremost God's mission, then missions does not change either. However, such an understanding of mission does not require the broad view of mission as some have suggested.[8] Melvin Hodges was right in declaring, "The idea that Christianity would have one application in apostolic times, but that we must look for a new application of the gospel to meet the social ills of the world, is false."[9]

Oddly, the book of Acts does not emphasize Jesus's disciples engaging in mission because they felt compelled by the Great Commission. However, the church in Acts is described over and over as a church that cultivates the Spirit's presence. When the Spirit moves, the church moves, often through the catalysts of persecution and suffering.[10] When the Spirit fell in the upper room, the church went out onto the streets of Jerusalem and Peter preached to a crowd of three thousand people (Acts 2). Later, the church moved out of Jerusalem to Judea and Samaria, not out of obedience to the command of Jesus, but because the Spirit moved even in the midst of the persecution and the martyrdom of Stephen (Acts 8:1).

Not until Acts 10 and the conversion of Cornelius did the breach finally take place, as the gospel is symbolically taken beyond Israel through the conversion of a Roman soldier. Yet

---

[8] See especially Paul Pomerville's discussion of the way in which Pentecostalism uniquely contributes to this question by affirming both that missions is God's mission but also that a Pentecostal understanding of the kingdom of God leads to a narrow view of missions. Paul Pomerville, *The Third Force in Missions* (1985; repr. Peabody, MA: Hendrickson, 2016), 210–16.

[9] Melvin Hodges, *A Theology of the Church and Its Mission: A Pentecostal Perspective* (Springfield, MO: Gospel Publishing House, 1977), 111.

[10] See especially Martin William Mittelstadt, *The Spirit and Suffering in Luke-Acts: Implications for a Pentecostal Pneumatology* (New York: T & T Clark, 2004).

again, this happens not because Peter feels compelled by the Great Commission, but because the apostolic church was a Spirit-filled church and when the Spirit moved the church moved. Thus, Taylor rightly observes, "Missions is often described as if it were the planned extension of an old building. But in fact it has usually been more like an unexpected explosion."[11] I would add that such explosions happen in churches that are attuned to the missionary impulse of the Spirit.

PENTECOSTAL HOLISM

Holistic mission among evangelicals at large can be traced especially to the Lausanne movement that began in 1974, wherein missiologists from the Global South borrowed from the language and categories of liberation theology in order to articulate a soteriology that went beyond individual salvation to a broader, more "holistic" understanding of the term.[12] As already noted, this line of thinking has become standard among Pentecostals especially since the publication of the edited volume *Called and Empowered*, in which writers such as Murray Dempster argue for an understanding of the church's mission according to a "mission as witness" paradigm based on a broad view of the kingdom of God.[13] Dempster defines mission according to the various activities of the church, especially *kerygma, diakonia*, and *koinonia*. This approach to mission continues to dominate discussions of Pentecostal missiology, as is evident in more recent works, including *Pentecostal Mission and Global Christianity*, edited by Wonsuk Ma, Veli-Matti Kärkkäinen, and J. Kwabena Asamoah-Gyadu.[14]

---

[11] John V. Taylor, *The Go-Between God: The Holy Spirit and Christian Mission* (London: SCM Press, 1975), 53.

[12] Chris Sugden, "Mission as Transformation—Its Journey since Lausanne I," in Woolnough and Ma, *Holistic Mission*, 31–36.

[13] Dempster, "Evangelism, Social Concern, and the Kingdom of God," 22–43.

[14] Wonsuk Ma et al., eds., *Pentecostal Mission and Global Christianity*, Regnum Edinburgh Centenary Series (Oxford, UK: Regnum, 2014).

Frank Macchia's take on initial evidence represents an earlier work that tracks along similar lines and is especially relevant to the present discussion given his argument's basis in Acts 10 and ensuing discussion of tongues speech. In his discussion of "shifting paradigms" in Pentecostal theology, Macchia observes a liberation motif as the foundational axiom of a contemporary Pentecostal theology. For instance, he describes, in relation to ongoing dialogue between Pentecostals and evangelicals, his hope for "a contextual and liberating theology" along with "liberating praxis" as a function of the "liberation story of Jesus."[15] In observing that Pentecostal theology itself was born of a paradigm shift from an inward focus on holiness to an external focus on empowerment for global witness, Macchia suggests the need to "broaden and deepen the theological understanding of how tongues symbolize an experience with God that continually urges the people of God to move beyond the confines of private piety or even church fellowship to the global issues of justice, peace, and the redemption of the world."[16] Macchia builds his argument for this perspective in part on the notion of solidarity expressed in Acts, first among the disciples with Diaspora Jews, and later with "hated Gentiles" in Acts 10:46.[17] He then proposes the need for a paradigm shift as it relates to how Pentecostals understand the gift of tongues:

> The early Pentecostals felt the urgency of the moment when they spoke in tongues as a miraculous sign of the gospel of Christ for all peoples. Contemporary Pentecostals must rediscover that sense of urgency, believing that tongues connect individual Christians and churches with the need for global justice, reconciliation, and redemption.[18]

---

[15] Frank D. Macchia, "The Struggle for Global Witness: Shifting Paradigms in Pentecostal Theology," in *The Globalization of Pentecostalism: A Religion Made to Travel*, ed. Murray W. Dempster et al. (Carlisle, UK: Regnum, 1999), 13.
[16] Ibid., 17–18.
[17] Ibid., 18.
[18] Ibid.

Finally, Macchia locates this perspective within a broad interpretation of the kingdom of God: "After all, if the healing of the body is the foretaste of the final resurrection of the body, why not consider the work of the Spirit in social transformation to be a foretaste of the kingdom of God?"[19]

A more recent take on the broad sense of mission by Pentecostals can be found in the work of Julie C. Ma and Wonsuk Ma in their 2010 book, *Mission in the Spirit*.[20] Ma and Ma argue for a Pentecostal holistic mission based on a creationist motif, intentionally moving beyond Luke-Acts for their missional ecclesiology.[21] I will have more to say on this later, but I believe this move away from Acts, as the most overtly missionary book the church possesses, to be somewhat misguided. Nonetheless, they look especially to the work of the Spirit in creation—as creator, sustainer of life, and divine presence in humanity. In each of these movements Ma and Ma examine the role of the Spirit both in creation and re-creation to locate their position within God's historically situated and restorative activity. In this, they do not reject the early Pentecostal emphasis on saving souls, but they see their broader paradigm as its natural evolution:

> For this reason, the Pentecostals' traditional emphasis on "saving [human] souls" is the right focus. In fact, its empowerment theology has prepared the "saved souls" to be empowered witnesses to the ends of the earth (Acts 1:8). The instrumentality of human agents is further brought forward by the critical role of the prophet in restoring the dry bones (Ezek. 37). This also challenges Pentecostals to view the entirety of human life as a "mission field." Especially important is human suffering as a critical missional agenda. Suffering is the sign of anti-creation, and God's people are

---

[19] Ibid., 23.
[20] Julie C. Ma and Wonsuk Ma, *Mission in the Spirit: Towards a Pentecostal and Charismatic Missiology* (Eugene, OR: Wipf and Stock, 2010).
[21] Ibid., 18.

called not only to care for those who suffer, but also to fight the roots of human suffering.[22]

One of the more constructive approaches to Pentecostal theology along holistic lines comes from Andy Lord in his *Spirit-Shaped Mission* and its later expansion, *Network Church*.[23] Lord argues in the former that greater attention by Pentecostals to ecclesiology has necessitated a turn to the broader sense of mission, even while acknowledging that Pentecostal missionary activity has historically prioritized proclamation/evangelism by linking it to eschatology. Lord aligns himself with Dempster by noting that a broad interpretation of the kingdom of God "seems the best way forward in understanding holistic mission."[24] From there, Lord presents an especially intriguing argument for holistic mission that maintains its eschatological emphasis but shifts what is meant by this—arguing for a nonlinear approach to time and thereby to the kingdom. He further argues for mission as a movement of the Spirit between the "universal" (creation, eschatological kingdom) and the "particular" (individuals, communities). As such, he denies that there can be a singular understanding of mission. "Participation in the mission of the Spirit will be unique for each individual and community as they respond to God and their situation."[25]

Finally, Wolfgang Vondey's *Pentecostal Theology* also proposes a Pentecostal theological method centering on the day of Pentecost "as the core symbol" and built around the narrative of the fivefold gospel—but set, like all other arguments for a holistic mission, within a broad understanding of the kingdom of God.[26]

---

[22] Ibid., 26.

[23] Andrew M. Lord, *Spirit-Shaped Mission: A Holistic Charismatic Theology* (Bletchley, UK: Paternoster, 2005); Lord, *Network Church*.

[24] Lord, *Spirit-Shaped Mission*, 51.

[25] Ibid., 137.

[26] Wolfgang Vondey, *Pentecostal Theology: Living the Full Gospel* (London: T & T Clark, 2018), 1–10. See especially Vondey's comment that "Pentecostalism can be identified by the day of Pentecost as the concern for an immediate encounter with God through the Spirit of

Regarding mission and Pentecostalism's unique emphasis, namely Spirit baptism, Vondey rightly observes the Western tendency to overly individualize tongues speech and Spirit empowerment.[27] He then argues for a sacramental understanding of Spirit baptism in which mission and the church's apostolic mandate broadly include both the "called-ness" and "sent-ness" of the church—its going out from God and returning to God in "faith, witness, worship, and service."[28]

All of the perspectives surveyed so far help demonstrate that holistic perspectives dominate Pentecostal missionary thinking, and in my view represent a subtle shift of the sort warned about by Stephen Neill when he famously declared, "If everything is mission, nothing is mission."[29] More to the point, though, one can practice mission in all of the ways described above—engaging in acts of global justice (Macchia); witnessing though proclamation, service, and community (Dempster); addressing human suffering (Ma and Ma); or, as Vondey concludes, being active in faith, witness, worship, and service—and yet still have no explicit concern for the movement of the gospel to those places among the nations where Christ is not known.[30]

Any understanding of the nature and purpose of the church (ecclesiology), and the church's relationship to the nations (missiology) must prioritize the primary resources from which the writers of the New Testament drew in elaborating these themes, namely, the role and nature of Israel. Ma and Ma's turn away from Acts represents a prime example of the problems that ensue when ecclesiology becomes divorced from its grounding in God's

---

Christ manifested in discernable signs and wonders as evidence of God's transforming and redeeming presence directing all of life towards the kingdom of God," 4.

[27] Ibid., 219, 239.

[28] Ibid., 243.

[29] Stephen Neill, *Creative Tension* (London: Edinburgh House, 1959), 81.

[30] On the demise of the Great Commission in missional thinking, see Pomerville, *The Third Force in Missions*, 196–217.

purposes for Israel.[31] Ma and Ma's argument not only raises the question of whether biblical anthropology (the Spirit of God in human beings) and the doctrine of creation (God's Spirit active in creation) constitute valid sources for ecclesiology and missiology, but also why the best and most historically grounded sources for these doctrines are passed over. Paul Borgman, for example, argues for the grounding of mission in Acts in the nature and calling of Israel, on the grounds that Jesus constitutes the center of volume 1 (Luke's Gospel) and Israel that of volume 2 (Acts).[32]

In addition, the basis for understanding ecclesiology as by-products of the nature and purpose of Israel should be obvious given Jesus's choosing of twelve disciples to reflect the twelve tribes of the newly reconstituted Israel, and on Luke's record of Jesus sending out the seventy (or seventy-two) to reflect both the seventy nations of Genesis 10 and the seventy-two elders on whom the Spirit of God was poured out for prophetic witness in Numbers 11.[33] Regarding the latter, Luke interprets Moses's prayer that all God's people would prophesy as finding fulfillment in the events of Pentecost and locates those events in God's concern for the nations. Together the picture emerges of God's reconstituted people, the church, as prophetic witnesses tasked primarily with making God known redemptively among the nations through gospel proclamation.[34] Here again Borgman is instructive, for though he also argues that entering the kingdom lies at the heart

---

[31] Michael W. Goheen, *A Light to the Nations: The Missional Church and the Biblical Story* (Grand Rapids, MI: Baker Academic, 2011), 121.

[32] Paul Borgman, *The Way According to Luke: Hearing the Whole Story of Luke-Acts* (Grand Rapids, MI: Eerdmans, 2006), 1.

[33] On the seventy-two elders, see Robert W. Menzies, *Speaking in Tongues* (Cleveland, TN: CPT, 2016), 32. The lack of clarity as to whether Jesus sent out seventy or seventy-two (in Lk 10:1–16) reflects that the manuscript evidence is divided (ibid., 31).

[34] Borgman, *The Way According to Luke*, 254. See also Conzelmann's observation that the church is to be especially understood in relation to Israel as a "people" whose purpose lies in redemptive history. Hans Conzelmann, *The Theology of St. Luke* (Philadelphia: Fortress, 1961), 162–67.

of Luke's two-part story, he reminds students of Luke-Acts that entering the "'Way' begins with hearing and obeying Jesus's words."[35] Along these same lines Alan J. Thompson argues that "the spread of the word through proclamation, planting and strengthening local churches, in the midst of suffering, therefore dominates Luke's instructions for Christian readers like Theophilus about what is to characterize the people of God in this new stage of salvation history."[36]

Contrary to the trend among Pentecostal scholars toward a loosely defined missional ecclesiology, wherein mission describes all that the church does in its own sociocultural setting, it seems that Luke offers a corrective by articulating a view of missions centering on God's concern for the nations. In other words, even though the practice of *glossolalia* carries ecclesiological implications, as Daniela Augustine has observed,[37] more important, it emphasizes the eschatological orientation of the church to the nations. It is this orientation that reveals the primary mark of the church. This essentially constitutes the argument of evangelical missiologist Ralph Winter in his classic distinction between the modality of the local church (mission in the broad sense) and the sodality of the mission band (mission in the narrow sense), a distinction that also finds expression in Acts 13 and the "setting apart" of Barnabas and Saul for cross-cultural witness. This feature of the Lukan narrative constitutes an important corrective for the holistic mission movement, which largely has failed to recognize the way in which missionary sodalities born of this concern for the nations in Acts differ in purpose and function from the modality of the local church. Such a distinction also lay at the

---

[35] Borgman, *The Way According to Luke*, 7–9.

[36] Alan J. Thompson, *The Acts of the Risen Lord: Luke's Account of God's Unfolding Plan*, ed. D. A. Carson, New Studies in Biblical Theology (Downers Grove, IL: InterVarsity, 2011), 88.

[37] Daniela C. Augustine, *Pentecost, Hospitality, and Transfiguration: Toward a Spirit-Inspired Vision of Social Transformation* (Cleveland, TN: CPT, 2012), 36. Augustine emphasizes the solidarity of the community but neglects the missional role of solidarity in Luke-Acts in favor of a more general focus on hospitality (ibid., 66).

center of the indigenous principles that governed early Pentecostal missiology. In other words, ecclesiology and missiology, though they overlap, are not the same thing—and this is especially evident in Acts in key places where missionary teams are set apart for the church's cross-cultural church-planting efforts.[38]

Regarding many of these holistic Pentecostal theologies, I find the admonition of Simon Chan helpful. He writes, "Pentecostals could become too Pentecostal, that is to say, too divorced from historical existence."[39] This happens by severing Pentecostal theology from historic antecedents and engaging in endless quests for a new Pentecostal paradigm without having made clear that the old paradigm is no longer tenable. This is not to suggest a static view of the Spirit, but simply to note that Luke especially grounds the Spirit's work in the redemptive story of scripture and carefully and frequently links the mission of God's people to the nations.[40] This is where I believe broad approaches to the kingdom of God like those above come up short. Luke's focus on solidarity emphasizes an ecclesiastical ethic meant to cultivate the Spirit's presence for effective mission—defined as taking the gospel across geographic and cultural barriers.[41] As with Israel, implications for social justice in Luke's writings are never divorced from the grand

---

[38] Ralph D. Winter, "Two Structures of God's Redemptive Mission," *Missiology* 2, no. 1 (1974). Also, the clearest text in support of this, as I have argued elsewhere, is Acts 13:2, and the words "set apart for me Barnabas and Saul." Clearly here the work of Barnabas and Saul is distinguished from the much broader mission of the local church. See Jerry M. Ireland, "From Solidarity to Sodality: Compassionate Missions, Local Churches, and the Fostering of Cross-cultural Missionary Bands," in *Churches on Mission: God's Grace Abounding to the Nations*, ed. Geoffrey Hartt et al. (Pasadena, CA: William Carey, 2017), chap. 3. Others have extended this argument to include a number of apostolic bands in Acts; see Edward F. Murphy, "The Missionary Society as an Apostolic Team," *Practical Anthropology* 4, no. 1 (1976): 113.

[39] Simon Chan, *Pentecostal Ecclesiology* (Dorset, UK: Deo, 2011), 69.

[40] Robert P. Menzies, *Empowered for Witness: The Spirit in Luke-Acts* (New York: T & T Clark, 2004).

[41] Cf. Darrell L. Bock, *Acts*, Baker Exegetical Commentary on the New Testament (Grand Rapids, MI: Baker, 2007), 41.

narrative of redemption and in fact find their fullest meaning within that story line. Israel's practice of social justice was always meant both as a response to God's justice and judgment, which made possible Israel's exodus from Egypt, and as a prerequisite for Israel's ongoing participation in God's redemptive activity regarding the nations. Indeed, this has long been the story of Pentecostal missionaries, who practiced social justice primarily in order to facilitate evangelistic ministry precisely because they understood the dialectical relationship between the localized activities of the church and its ultimate trajectory toward the nations.[42]

Pentecostals who adopt a broad understanding of the church's mission, such as Dempster, Lord, Ma and Ma, Macchia, and Vondey, have erred at two points in my opinion. First, they fail to give sufficient attention to the way that Luke orders the Acts narrative around the movement of the gospel to the nations and thereby overlook the orientation of God's people to the nations as the definitive mark of missions. By this I do not deny the importance of social justice, properly defined, as an important and prominent Lukan theme, but I find it more appropriately the work of local congregations or parachurch organizations than of missionaries—a distinction found in Luke and highlighted by references to *glossolalia*. Second, they fail to notice that a biblical and historical case can be made for maintaining both the broad sense of mission and the narrow sense, without contradiction.

One recent work that helps make both points is Michael Goheen's monograph *A Light to the Nations*, in which Goheen shows that fundamental to the identity of God's people both in the Old and New Testaments was their crucial role concerning the redemption of the nations.[43] The above approaches attempt to establish themes like social justice and creation care as equally fundamental to the missional role of Israel and the church in their relation to the nations. Goheen, in much the same way as did

---

[42] Allan Anderson, *Spreading Fires: The Missionary Nature of Early Pentecostalism* (Maryknoll, NY: Orbis Books, 2007), 66.

[43] Goheen, *A Light to the Nations: The Missional Church and the Biblical Story*.

Johann Blauw for a previous generation in his *Missionary Nature of the Church*, brings missiology back to the central point of focusing on the redemptive role of God's people among the nations.[44] Goheen traces this crucial theme in scripture from Israel's calling and election to be a people whose "singular role in history" was to "bring salvation to the nations."[45] While Goheen argues that this salvation includes the restoration of all creation in ways similar to holistic perspectives, he differs in that he clearly articulates concern for the nations as the church's "ultimate horizon."[46]

As his subtitle suggests, the focus of Goheen's study is ecclesiology—the missional church. Importantly, Goheen (cautiously) endorses Lesslie Newbigin's distinction between and support for both the narrow sense of missions (plural) and the broad sense of mission (singular), as well as Wilbert Shenk's distinction between the "organic mode" of missions and the "sending mode," based on Acts 13 and what takes place at the church at Antioch.[47] In this, Goheen suggests the importance of both senses of missions even while acknowledging that the last two centuries have seen an overemphasis on the "sending mode." But for Goheen, as for Newbigin, the difference between mission and missions and the need to maintain both requires not only a distinction between the two, but also understanding "the ends of the earth" as "the ultimate horizon of mission."[48] This is, in my view, the misstep in Pentecostal holistic mission paradigms—in not articulating the manner in which the mission of the church in its own sociocultural setting must always be governed by the narrower *missio Dei* that emphasizes crossing geographic, cultural, and linguistic barriers to take the gospel to those places where Christ is not known.

---

[44] As Wrogemann points out, Blauw, along with George Vicedom, emphasized making disciples as the central task of the *missio Dei*. Henning Wrogemann, *Theologies of Missions,* vol. 2 of *Intercultural Theologies,* trans. Karl E. Böhmer (Downers Grove, IL: IVP Academic, 2018), 89.

[45] Goheen, *A Light to the Nations*, 100.

[46] Ibid., 137.

[47] Ibid., 148–51.

[48] Ibid., 219.

THE SPIRIT AND THE NATIONS IN ACTS

One major theme in the book of Acts, and one that directly challenges many of the broad senses of mission described above, is the growth of the church and the movement of the gospel to the nations by the Spirit. This is evident in passages such as Acts 2:41, 47; 6:1, 7; 9:31; and 12:25, all reporting the success of the gospel in Jerusalem and Judea. Beyond that, Luke also provides numerous reports of the gospel going forward outside of Jerusalem and Judea. Indeed, this latter emphasis constitutes the bulk of Luke's second volume. This is evident, for example in:

- Acts 14:27 and the success of the gospel in the Gentile mission of Saul and Barnabas;
- Acts 16:14–15 and the conversion of a Gentile God-fearer named Lydia and her whole household;
- Acts 16:30–34 and the success of the gospel regarding the Philippian jailer;
- Acts 17:4 and the success of the gospel at Thessalonica among both Jews and Gentiles;
- Acts 17:11 and the success of the gospel among the Bereans; and
- Acts 17:34 and the success of the gospel at Mars Hill.

Each of these passages emphasizes the successful movement of the gospel and thereby the successful movement of the church in the Spirit's power to the nations. However, another major theme in Acts relates to obstacles to this movement of the gospel to the nations. Luke reports, for example, the obstacle of cynicism in Acts 2—the disciples were mocked, but they had power. In Acts 3 he reports the obstacle of poverty—Peter and John were poor but had power. In Acts 4, the disciples encounter the obstacle of persecution. Peter and John were arrested, but upon their release the church "prayed and the place where they had gathered was shaken, and they were all filled with the Holy Spirit and began to speak the word of God with boldness" (4:31). In Acts 5 Luke reports the obstacle of self-centeredness demonstrated by Ananias and Sapphira, the obstacle of martyrdom in Acts 6 (Stephen) and Acts 12 (James), the obstacle of the occult in Acts 8 and Acts 13, and so on.

Yet among all of these obstacles, the two that Luke singles out for special attention are the obstacles of concern about "others" in Acts 10 and the obstacle of being without the Spirit's empowerment in Acts 19. At the very least this seems to suggest that a church (1) that is not concerned with ethnic and religious otherness, and (2) that lacks the Spirit's empowerment, cannot continue successfully in God's mission to the nations. What distinguishes these two obstacles from all of the other obstacles faced by the church is that they are internal to the believers themselves, whereas all the other obstacles Luke mentions are external. It seems then that the greatest threats to the church's mission are not those things outside the church, but the dangers that come from within. These obstacles fundamentally represent matters of the heart and of faith. Apart from these internal qualities—a specific concern for religious and ethnic otherness along with the Spirit's empowerment—there simply can be no successful mission to the nations. And this seems to be a primary function of *glossolalia* in the book of Acts.

GLOSSOLALIA AND THE NATIONS

I therefore propose an understanding of *glossolalia*, or tongues speech, that serves to reorient the church to its cross-cultural mandate while simultaneously serving as "landmarks in the growth of the early church."[49] Each occurrence of tongues speech in the

---

[49] Gerald Hovenden, *Speaking in Tongues: The New Testament Evidence in Context* (London: Sheffield Academic, 2002), 99. I follow Menzies in understanding *glossolalia* as unintelligible utterances based on what he calls "impressive literary parallels" between the Acts references and those in 1 Corinthians 12—14. Menzies notes that "all of these texts (1) associate speaking in tongues with the inspiration of the Holy Spirit; (2) utilize similar vocabulary (*laleo glossais*); and (3) describe inspired speech associated with worship and prophetic pronouncements." With this, though, the possibility of unknown human languages remains. See Menzies, *Speaking in Tongues*, 16; Hovenden, *Speaking in Tongues*, 99.

The Missionary Nature of Tongues in the Book of Acts

book of Acts (2:4; 10:46; and 19:6) represents a unique milestone in the gospel's cross-cultural journey to "the ends of the earth." While classical Pentecostals early on framed their understanding of tongues in terms of "initial evidence" of Spirit baptism, their lived theology rather consistently emphasized the missionary nature of tongues, even if they sometimes erred in what that meant practically.[50]

My proposal here is that Pentecostal missiology can be strengthened by moving toward this missional interpretation of tongues, one that moves beyond the "initial evidence" doctrine of classical Pentecostalism to emphasize tongues as the "enduring evidence" of the church's global missionary task. To arrive at this conclusion, I propose, along with others like Goheen, that the theme of Israel as a light to the nations forms the background to Luke-Acts and that tongues speech in volume two of this work points to the prophetic, verbal, and cross-cultural meaning of mission, thereby establishing the ultimate trajectory of the church. Plus, such a reading makes the best sense of the literary structure of the book. This follows from considering Acts 1:8 as the foundational text for Luke's second volume and from his open-ended telling of Paul's missionary journeys, functioning to invite readers to locate themselves within the story as part of the church's ongoing movement toward the yet-unreached.[51]

Harvey Cox has described the way in which tongues speech among classical Pentecostals has moved from a central doctrine to the periphery because of misconceptions regarding the ability to speak foreign languages in the context of missionary outreach. After many sailed to foreign lands as missionaries, expecting to speak in unknown tongues based on having experienced "the

---

[50] For a helpful description of the notion of missionary tongues in the early church and modern classical Pentecostalism, see Janet Everts Powers, "Missionary Tongues?" *Journal of Pentecostal Theology* 8, no. 17 (2000): 39–55.

[51] Cf. González, who observes that Acts 1:8 forms an outline for the entire book; Justo L. Gonzàlez, *Acts: The Gospel of the Spirit* (Maryknoll, NY: Orbis Books, 2001), 20.

initial physical evidence" of Spirit baptism, they quickly discovered their mistake. As Cox observes, "It did not take long, however, for the gift of tongues . . . to assume a less commanding place in Pentecostal belief."[52] Perhaps this diminished role owes to a missed opportunity among early Pentecostals to specifically articulate the missionary nature of tongues. As Gary B. McGee has observed, this shift in thinking did take place at a practical level as some began to reinterpret tongues as fostering greater love for the lost. For example, J. Roswell Flower wrote in a 1908 edition of *The Pentecost* that Spirit baptism (with which tongues was always associated) "fills our souls with the love of God for lost humanity."[53] William Seymour adopted a similar shift, focusing on the missionary nature of tongues and its importance for reaching the nations, even though "he later regarded love as the primary sign of Spirit baptism."[54] Finally, McGee has also noted that A. G. and Lilian Garr, who had been at Azusa Street, shifted their view of tongues to a broader, more missional understanding shortly after arriving in India in early 1907.[55]

All of these show that tongues had historically been understood within early Pentecostalism as having a fuller meaning than simply initial evidence. Yet, oddly, this emphasis never found its way into doctrinal statements such as the Assemblies of God's Sixteen Fundamental Truths as readily as the doctrine of initial evidence, even though these ideas were clearly being articulated by 1914 when

---

[52] Harvey Cox, *Fire from Heaven* (Cambridge, MA: Da Capo Press, 1995), 87.

[53] Gary B. McGee, "Pentecostals and Their Various Strategies for Global Missions: A Historical Assessment," in Dempster et al., *Called and Empowered*, 205.

[54] Frank D. Macchia, *Baptized in the Spirit: A Global Pentecostal Theology* (Grand Rapids, MI: Zondervan, 2006), 35.

[55] Gary B. McGee, "'Latter Rain' Falling in the East: Early-Twentieth-Century Pentecostalism in India and the Debate over Speaking in Tongues," *Church History* 68 (1999): 648–65. See also Martin William Mittelstadt, "Reimagining Luke-Acts: Amos Yong and the Biblical Foundation of Pentecostal Theology," in *The Theology of Amos Yong and the New Face of Pentecostal Scholarship*, ed. Wolfgang Vondey and Martin William Mittelstadt (Leiden, The Netherlands: Brill, 2013), 28.

these official positions were taking shape. Perhaps this warns the church that it can, at times, be too historically close to the events that shape its theology to notice the need for subtle changes that would place the church in better alignment with scripture. At any rate, we are now in a better position to look back and see clearly the dangers inherent in assuming that the missionary nature of Pentecostalism will always be self-evident.

Robert Menzies has stated well the problems with a limited (that is, initial evidence only) understanding of the gift of tongues. Specifically, such a focus can not only produce an overly individualistic pneumatology but can also function merely as a historic marker in a believer's spiritual journey that has little contemporary and enduring relevance: "An inordinate focus on 'evidence' may result in Christians who, looking back into the distant past, can remember the moment they 'got it,' but for whom the Pentecostal dimension of power for witness is presently unknown."[56] Understanding glossolalia as a sign of the church's missionary mandate can greatly aid in overcoming this problem.

THE ENDURING EVIDENCE OF A GLOBAL MISSION

One of the functions in Luke-Acts of the gift of tongues is to point to the church's global and proclamational mission. As John Michael Penney writes, "Luke's primary and pervasive interest is the work of the Holy Spirit in initiating, empowering and directing the church in its eschatological worldwide mission."[57] This story line can be traced from Acts 1:8 and Jesus telling the disciples that they would receive the power of the Holy Spirit to be his witnesses "both in Jerusalem, and in all Judea and Samaria, and even to the remotest part of the earth." Luke connects this task of global witness to the gift of tongues in that when the Holy Spirit comes and the disciples begin to speak in tongues, he immediately

---

[56] Menzies, *Empowered for Witness*, 253.
[57] John Michael Penney, *The Missionary Emphasis of Lukan Pneumatology* (Sheffield, England: Sheffield Academic, 1997), 15.

describes the multinational crowd of Jews gathered: "Now there were Jews living in Jerusalem, devout men from every nation under heaven" (Acts 2:5). The international makeup of the Jewish community here picks up on the biblical theme of God's people being gathered from the nations at the eschaton (Ps 106:47; Is 11:2). Similarly, it suggests the unfolding mission to the Gentiles and a reconstituted Israel's role as light to the nations.[58]

The relationship between tongues speech and the church's orientation to the nations becomes even clearer as the narrative of Acts progresses. It is in Acts 10 and the conversion of Cornelius and his household that this theme finds its most significant expression. For it is in the event of Cornelius's conversion that the "border" between Jerusalem and the nations is finally breached and the Gentiles explicitly become part of the church. To be sure, no geographic border is crossed here, but the profound symbolism of the border-crossing mandate under way should not be missed. The Cornelius incident demonstrates in the most radical way possible the all-inclusive power of the gospel to break through and gather the nations as equal members in God's covenant people.

Not only does this passage describe the conversion of Cornelius, but as Joel Green says, it also describes the ongoing conversion of Peter to the cross-cultural purposes of God.[59] If I am correct in this connection between tongues and the forward movement of the gospel toward cultural and religious otherness, then the absence of any mention of tongues when the Spirit is given to the Samaritans (Acts 8:17) makes perfect sense. This is because while Samaritans were not religiously identical to Jews, they shared some common ethno-religious traits as well as geographic proximity.[60]

---

[58] Craig Keener, "Tongues as Evidence of the Spirit's Empowerment in Acts," in *A Light to the Nations: Explorations in Ecumenism, Missions, and Pentecostalism*, ed. Stanley M. Burgess and Paul W. Lewis (Eugene, OR: Pickwick, 2017), 231.

[59] Joel B. Green, *Conversion in Luke-Acts* (Grand Rapids, MI: Baker Academic, 2015), 98.

[60] Longenecker observes that "the joining of Judea and Samaria by one article (*te*) in the Greek (*en pase te Ioudaia kai Samareia*, 'in all Judea and Samaria') suggests a single geographical area that can be designated by its

Samaria was the northern district of Judea. Thus, Samaria represents sort of a halfway point between the Jewish disciples and the nations.[61] This event, then, stands as a step in the direction of missions, understood as the church taking up Israel's role as a light to the nations, but falls short of actually crossing the most crucial boundaries required for the church to move toward all *ethne*. Of course, Cornelius too shared geographic proximity, but not the same level of cultural and ethnic proximity.

It seems, based on occurrences of *glossolalia*, that Luke defines missions as the breaking down of the ethnic and religious barriers that separate one people from another in order that all peoples and cultures may come to Christ.[62] This is especially true of those most separated because of culture, religion, and geography. As Larry Hurtado writes, scholars generally agree that "the progress of the gospel from the Jerusalem church, across various cultural, geographical, and ethnic lines, to Rome, the capital city of the Roman empire, forms at least an important part of the intention in Luke-Acts."[63]

Seeing tongues speech in light of the movement of God's people to the nations avoids the awkward notion of trying to force the appearance of tongues on the Samaritan outpouring by instead understanding that Luke's point is that each incident of tongues

---

two ethnological divisions." Richard N. Longenecker, *Acts*, ed. Frank E. Gaebelein and J. D. Douglas, vol. 9 of Expositor's Bible Commentary (Grand Rapids, MI: Zondervan, 1984), Accordance electronic ed.

[61] Bock, *Acts*, 324–25. On the various interpretations of this passage, see Matthias Wenk, *Community Forming Power* (Sheffield, England: Sheffield Academic, 2000), 291–92. Wenk argues that this episode of receiving the Spirit does not represent "empowerment" for missions because the Samaritans do not engage in cross-cultural missions. But this seems to overlook that Luke's concern is to tell the story of the disciples and their cross-cultural mandate as representative of the mandate given to the whole church. Wenk, *Community Forming Power,* 294.

[62] Cf. Boer, who observes the crucial place afforded the conversion of Cornelius in the Acts narrative. Boer, *Pentecost and Missions*, 32.

[63] Larry Hurtado, "Normal But Not a Norm: 'Initial Evidence' in the New Testament," in *Initial Evidence*, ed. Gary B. McGee (Eugene, OR: Wipf and Stock, 2007), 194.

speech in Luke-Acts represents the breaking of a vital ethnic, geographic, and religious barrier, ultimately showing that the Spirit's work and the Father's promise are under way through the church to make Jesus known among the nations.[64] Thus Acts 10 and the conversion of Cornelius serve a pivotal function in the church's missionary enterprise for, from this point on, the mission to the gentiles in Asia takes center stage. This also greatly informs present-day Pentecostal missiology by reminding the church of the inherent danger in calling something mission that more accurately should be classified as near-neighbor evangelism. There is no mention of tongues in the Samaritan Pentecost of Acts 8 because it does not meet the ultimate criteria of cross-cultural evangelism outlined in Acts 1:8. The Cornelius incident does meet that requirement (though not technically) because it symbolizes the beginning of the gospel's movement to "the remotest parts." On the mission-missions spectrum, therefore, Acts 8 would fall into the category of mission, but not of missions. And Luke seems especially concerned with the latter.

Luke makes this point even more clearly in the conversion of Cornelius, wherein "the chief actor in the narrative was not Peter, but God."[65] This is evident in Peter's reluctance to accept the meaning of his vision (Acts 10:14). It was God working in the church by the Spirit to fulfill that which God had earlier promised. The promise, of course, was the movement of the disciples as witnesses to Jesus from Jerusalem to the nations. Yet in none of the broad perspectives on mission above is there any explicit orientation of the church along these lines. But this movement to the nations and the significance of Cornelius's conversion can be seen in that the text emphatically demonstrates not only Cornelius's conversion but also Peter's (re)awakening to this mission: "Opening his

---

[64] Hovenden, *Speaking in Tongues*, 100. Seeing this passage in this light also sets aside the interesting but secondary question about whether the disciples were true converts.

[65] Gerhard Krodel, *Proclamation Commentaries: The New Testament Witness for Preaching* (Philadelphia: Fortress, 1981), 40; Boer, *Pentecost and Missions*, 33.

mouth, Peter said: 'I most certainly understand now that God is not one to show partiality, but in every nation the man who fears Him and does what is right is welcome to Him'" (Acts 10:34–35). Thus, the text carefully underscores the disciples' mission to the nations and the unparalleled significance of the Cornelius pericope.[66] As Craig S. Keener points out, the mention of tongues in Acts 10:46 points back to Acts 2, wherein, "the purpose of the empowerment and of the sign is presumably the same as at Pentecost: empowerment to proclaim Christ cross-culturally."[67] Thus, as Menzies notes, "When Cornelius and his household burst forth in tongues, this act provides demonstrative proof that they are in fact part of the end-time prophetic band of which Joel prophesied."[68] Furthermore, this passage especially shows how the activity of God according to Luke and in relation to the mission of the church functions primarily in a proclamational-redemptive fashion. Against the holistic perspectives described above, nowhere in the Acts narrative does Luke equate anything like social justice with this primary evangelistic purpose of the church in relation to the lost among the nations. This is not to say that Luke is unconcerned about caring for the neediest among us, but that in the book of Acts this concern does not feature as prominently as cross-cultural evangelism.

In Acts 19 Luke introduces a group of "disciples" in Ephesus who were disciples of John the Baptist but uninformed regarding the gift of the Spirit. A great deal of debate exists around this passage over whether or not the disciples were Christians. But as Keener observes, this may be missing the main point of the narrative.[69] If one reads Luke-Acts missiologically, then this story appears to be perhaps the greatest obstacle to the advancement of God's mission through the church. If the gift of the Spirit is

---

[66] Hurtado, "Normal But Not a Norm," 194.
[67] Keener, "Tongues as Evidence of the Spirit's Empowerment in Acts," 231.
[68] Menzies, *Speaking in Tongues*, 20.
[69] Craig Keener, *Acts: 15:1—23:35*, vol. 3 (Grand Rapids, MI: Baker Academic, 2014), 2816.

the sine qua non of effective mission, then a disciple that had not received the Spirit would represent a fatal danger to the global mission under way.[70] Just as Jesus's mission was accomplished in the Spirit's power (Lk 3:21; 4:1, 14), so too must the church's. Furthermore, to not understand the missionary nature of the church in which they are being incorporated could spell disaster for the continuation of the mission. This lack of knowledge, therefore, demanded immediate correction. Thus, it seems highly plausible that in this narrative, tongues functions as a signal that the potential obstacle is overcome and that the mission of the church is moving forward once again toward the nations.

It also seems likely that the giving of the Holy Spirit and the report of tongues at Ephesus play a vital function in the structure of Luke's narrative. The conversion of Cornelius represented the breaking through of the gospel to the Gentiles, and Antioch (Acts 11—13) was an extension of that primary event. This is also exemplified in Acts 19 and the filling of the disciples at Ephesus. Ephesus stood on the far western edge of the Roman province of Asia, and thus it, in the same way that Acts 10 pointed to the coming mission to Gentiles at large, points to the movement of the gospel west toward Rome and then on to Spain. Again, Luke's main concern as it relates to the missionary task seems to be one of trajectory.

The significance of the ethno-religious borders being crossed in Ephesus can be seen in Paul's confrontation with the followers of the Greek god Artemis, who declare "great is Artemis of the Ephesians" (Acts 19:28, 34). This cry was not the cry of triumph, but the last whimper of a religion whose days were numbered, and those who profited from it knew it. As Acts 10 and the conversion of Cornelius symbolized the gospel's movement to the Gentiles, Acts 19 and the Spirit's outpouring at Ephesus symbolize the gospel's inevitable confrontation with pagan religions. Jaroslov Pelikan observes of this event, "The apostles seem, much to the regret of later Christian activists and social reformers, to have been concerned exclusively with the religious rather than with

---

[70] Penney, *The Missionary Emphasis of Lukan Pneumatology*, 109.

The Missionary Nature of Tongues in the Book of Acts 53

the socioeconomic dimension of the situation."[71] Thus, the gift of tongues at Ephesus represents the unavoidable conflict that Jesus's disciples will encounter with the world's religions as the gospel advances. This also coheres with Israel's role as light to the nations, especially in that they continuously confronted the destructive idolatry of the nations through their prophetic witness.[72]

The gift of tongues understood as a sign of missions in the narrow sense points to the reality that a people and language previously unknown to the church have taken up residence in the church and joined in God's mission. But this has not happened accidentally or by happenstance. Tongues signals that the mission of God is advancing and simultaneously declares that it must yet advance further.[73] Occurrences of *glossolalia* also represent, as Keener observes, the translatability of the gospel into all cultures and all languages.[74] It is in a sense the localization of the church's global concerns. As the nations are gathered and incorporated into God's end-times prophetic community, the Spirit works in the church to bring unity among diverse languages and cultures, and tongues represents the enduring evidence that God has accepted as God's people those who once were not God's people. This is the very point that Peter, with the aid of Paul and Barnabas, makes at the Jerusalem Council in Acts 15:7–9 (also 1 Pet 2:10).[75] Tongues declares that God is not linguistically bound to a single culture but speaks the language of all peoples and all nations. Tongues reminds the church that a key part of its mission lies outside its own national borders among those who, as with the Ephesians, are either held captive to idolatry or whose knowledge of Jesus

---

[71] Jaroslav Pelikan, *Acts*, Brazos Theological Commentary on the Bible (Grand Rapids, MI: Brazos, 2005), 214.

[72] Goheen, *A Light to the Nations*, 26.

[73] Craig S. Keener, "Why Does Luke Use Tongues as a Sign of the Spirit's Empowerment?" *Journal of Pentecostal Theology* 15, no. 2 (2007): 181; Menzies, *Speaking in Tongues*, 160–61.

[74] Keener, "Why Does Luke Use Tongues as a Sign of the Spirit's Empowerment?" 178.

[75] Boer, *Pentecost and Missions*, 35; Keener, *Acts: 15:1—23:35*, 2233.

and the Spirit are as of yet incomplete. In the interim they await a herald who can share with them the good news of the gospel.

Pentecostal theologies should maintain an appreciation for both mission and missions, that is, for the broad and narrow senses of mission, as both constitute vital functions of the church. Failure to hold in creative tension the broad and narrow sense of mission without observing that an orientation to the nations constitutes the fundamental mark of the church in the book of Acts is to overlook a longstanding hallmark of Pentecostal missiology. Perhaps it has been a growing discomfort among Pentecostal scholars over the kind of individualistic interpretations of *glossolalia* that characterizes many doctrines of initial evidence that has led to this neglect. If so, rediscovering the corporate function of tongues speech as it relates to the advancement of the gospel should offer some comfort to uneasy consciences, for here the emphasis is purely on the church as a people collectively called to prophetic proclamation among the nations.

3

Language, Missions, and Glossolalia *in Patristic Thought*

Pentecostals and non-Pentecostals alike have long sought after the factors contributing to or causing the demise of tongues speaking in the church. Patristic studies have played a crucial role in this endeavor. The importance of early Christian studies to this issue flows from the question of whether speaking in tongues disappeared following the apostolic age or if it disappeared because of its relationship to Montanism in the mid-second and early-third centuries. New research challenges both of these presuppositions and suggests that tongues had close associations to the valuation of linguistic otherness and imbued the church with a missiological ethos that waned as theological controversies arose in the third and fourth centuries that centered on linguistic specificity. In this, language, and by extension linguo-centrism, became an influential demarcation between schismatic and catholic faith. This chapter explores these various strands of research especially as they relate to a missionary view of tongues among patristic writers.

As already noted, early Pentecostal missionaries went to foreign lands often holding firmly to the mistaken idea that the gift of tongues would enable them to preach the gospel in the local languages. In this, most early Pentecostal missionaries held to a view of tongues speech as *xenolalia* (known languages but unknown to the speaker). So confident were these Pentecostal missionaries in this ability that they often referred not to the "gift of tongues" but rather to the "gift of languages."[1] Not only that but, as Andy Lord observes, "the Spirit was believed to be indicating which countries missionaries were to travel to and even translating the message supernaturally." Plus, "the image of a fire spreading around the world was a common image, the fire of the gospel preached and experienced in the Spirit."[2] Many soon learned that these assumptions were misguided and embarked on the difficult task of language study in order to reach the people to whom they were sent. These chastened Pentecostals continued to uphold a connection between tongues speech and missions and to the present day continue to explore the boundaries of this theological distinction as it relates to the nations.

For over half a century now, most historical studies of speaking in tongues have focused their attention on (1) whether tongues should be understood as ecstatic speech (*glossolalia*) or known languages (*xenolalia*) or both; (2) whether the practice persisted beyond the apostolic age; or (3) whether there is historical and exegetical support for the Pentecostal doctrine of initial evidence. For example, Stagg, Hinson, and Oates conclude in their brief study spanning the disciplines of theology, history, and psychosocial analysis that speaking in tongues is best left to a person's private prayer life and that it has rarely aided the church in its mission.[3] Morton Kelsey, writing as an Episcopal priest and non–tongues speaker, concludes that tongues is "undoubtedly dangerous" and

---

[1] Allan Anderson, *Spreading Fires: The Missionary Nature of Early Pentecostalism* (Maryknoll, NY: Orbis Books, 2007), 57–65. Anderson observes that despite numerous reports of people at Azusa Street receiving the ability to speak foreign languages, the dominant story was the failure of Pentecostal missionaries to communicate in those languages when they arrived on the mission field.

[2] Andy Lord, "Pentecostal Mission through Contextualization," *PentecoStudies* 10, no. 1 (2011): 107.

[3] Frank Stagg, E. Glenn Hinson, and Wayne E. Oates, *Glossolalia: Tongue Speaking in Biblical, Historical, and Psychological Perspective* (Nashville, TN: Abingdon, 1967), 74–75.

"causes conflicts"—while also admitting that a dangerous church is better than a dead one.[4] Methodist clergyman Maurice Barnett writes more favorably, arguing that visions, prophecy, and speaking in tongues constitute important works of the Spirit in both the Old and New Testaments, and that what happened on the day of Pentecost was not that actual languages were spoken but rather ecstatic speech much like that recorded by Paul in 1 Corinthians.[5] He argues though that the gift of the Spirit is not particularly *for* tongues (while not denying its legitimate place among the gifts of the Spirit), but rather for "the New Testament idea of the perfect life" in keeping with the Wesleyan holiness tradition.[6] Writing more specifically about speaking in tongues among patristic writers, Harold Hunter concludes that there exists sufficient evidence for believing in the continuation of *glossolalia* up through the third century, "at which time monasticism probably became the center of such activity."[7] He also observes, contrary to the position of most Pentecostals, that tongues speech was interpreted by the church fathers as primarily *xenolalia*—speaking in known languages one had not learned.[8]

Perhaps the most significant recent study that relates to the concerns of this chapter comes from Yuliya Minets's 2017 doctoral dissertation on the influential role of Christianity regarding views of language diversity in Late Antiquity. She observes that "interaction with speakers of other tongues from the distinctly Christian standpoint expanded the previous monolingual or bilingual worldviews typical of the representatives of the traditional

---

[4] Morton Kelsey, *Speaking in Tongues: An Experiment in Spiritual Experience* (New York: Doubleday, 1964), 228.

[5] Maurice Barnett, *The Living Flame: Being a Study of the Gift of the Spirit in the New Testament with Special Reference to Prophecy, Glossolalia, Montanism, and Perfection* (1953; repr. Eugene, OR: Wipf and Stock, 2014), 94.

[6] Ibid., 137.

[7] Harold Hunter, "Tongues-Speech: A Patristic Analysis," *Journal of the Evangelical Theological Society* 23, no. 2 (1980): 135.

[8] Ibid.

Greek and Roman cultures."[9] She devotes an entire chapter of her study to how Greek, Latin, and Syriac authors in Late Antiquity interpreted the concept of speaking in tongues. She notes the ambiguous nature of tongues references in the New Testament and the various ways that ambiguity played out in different writers.[10] Similarly, Barnett argues concerning Acts 2 and *glossolalia* that "the miracle was left in mystical vagueness."[11]

Minets goes on to show that among Greek writers Eusebius of Caesarea "was one of the first Christian writers who explicitly acknowledged that the apostles must have faced linguistic barriers while preaching to other nations and needed the adequate knowledge of other languages in order to accomplish their mission successfully."[12] Though Eusebius never explicitly says the apostles spoke in foreign languages, he is seen as laying the groundwork for later interpretations of *glossolalia* as speaking in known languages in order to overcome barriers to the church's mission.[13] Minets also observes, though, that in the more ascetically oriented works of Basil of Caesarea, Gregory of Nyssa, and in the *Apostolic Constitution*, tongues seem less likely to refer to known languages but rather as mystical signs whose precise nature remains unclear and that accompany the church's global witness.[14] She concludes, like Hunter, that among Latin writers—including Hilary of Poitiers, Jerome, Augustine, and others—the dominant understanding of tongues was as *xenolalia* (even if, as with Jerome and Augustine, in a

---

[9] Yuliya Minets, "The Slow Fall of Babel: Conceptualization of Languages, Linguistic Diversity, and History in Late Ancient Christianity," PhD diss., Catholic University of America, Washington DC, 2017, i.

[10] Ibid., 229.

[11] Barnett, *The Living Flame*, 79.

[12] Minets, "The Slow Fall of Babel," 233.

[13] Ibid., 235. Minets importantly observes that Eusebius never uses the canonical term *glossais lalein* in his references to Montanism, in order to distance orthodoxy from any hint of the kind of ecstatic speech so often associated with the mystery cults (ibid., 245).

[14] Ibid., 241.

metaphorical rather than historical sense), often related to the church's missionary mandate.[15]

Minets also concludes that the Greek, Latin, and Syriac writers all underwent a transformation in their understanding of tongues so that by the fourth century previous (especially Greek) mystical and mysterious views shifted to a more concrete favoring of tongues as *xenolalia*.[16] She relates this transformation to the reality that Greek, owing to the Greco-Roman mystery religions, had conceptual categories for tongues as ecstatic speech that were less common among Latin speakers and foreign to Syriac writers.[17] In addition, as it relates to missions, seeing tongues as *xenolalia* fit well with the increasingly important universal claims of Christianity.[18] However, that optimistic outlook embodied by early Christian communities toward linguistic otherness would fade as theological controversies arose that often centered on language and its usage. Or, as Tim Denecker observes:

> During its first centuries and afterwards, Christianity encountered opposition from various dissenting voices—generally denoted as "schismatics" or as "heretics" (although these terms cannot be used interchangeably)—and was bound to engage in doctrinal (theological, christological, ecclesiological) debate during, e.g., the Origenist, Arian, Donatist, and (semi-) Pelagian controversies (Kelly 1997). This doctrinal context, too, has important bearings on early Christian approaches of linguistic topics, the more so since several controversies centered exactly on the preferable translation of certain crucial terms or phrases from Greek into Latin.[19]

---

[15] Ibid., 285.
[16] Ibid., 294.
[17] Ibid.
[18] Ibid., 295.
[19] Timothy Denecker, *Ideas on Language in Early Latin Christianity: From Tertullian to Isidore of Seville* (Leiden, The Netherlands: Brill, 2017), 7–8.

The goal of this chapter is to expand on Minets's fascinating study by looking at the question of tongues primarily in light of the church's missionary task. Since the primary concern of Minets's study was not missions per se, missional themes only emerge as interesting sidebars to her main goal of understanding shifting views of alloglotic (linguistic) otherness as it related to Christianity in Late Antiquity. The goal of the present study is to better understand those sporadic hints of a uniformly missional outlook suggested by Minets concerning the gift of tongues, even amid debates about its nature. This chapter furthermore asks how this might inform missiological reflection in the modern era. Therefore, for reasons made clear below, I examine how some select early Christian thinkers in the post-apostolic era interpreted Acts 2:1–12, 10:44–46, and 19:1–7, as well as 1 Corinthians 12—14.

Not only does this study aid in the clarification of Pentecostal and charismatic dogma related to their understanding of the *missio Dei*, but it also offers insight into all Christian traditions increasingly forced to wrestle with the issue of tongues speech in the context of missions.[20] Thus, this issue applies broadly to denominational and missionary agencies and especially those working in majority-world contexts where Pentecostal and charismatic expressions are increasingly common.

Early Pentecostal pioneers like Charles Parham and the students at his Bethel Bible School in Topeka, Kansas, believed speaking in tongues represented the supernatural ability to preach the gospel in unlearned languages.[21] But as early Pentecostal missionaries

---

[20] The North American Missions Board (NAMB) of the Southern Baptist Convention, for example, has shifted away from its 2006 position barring new missionaries from speaking in tongues to their current position that broadly affirms spiritual gifts without providing any specific guidelines regarding *glossolalia*. Deann Alford, "Tongues Tied," *Christianity Today* 50, no. 2 (2006): 21; NAMB, "Baptists and Speaking in Tongues," https://www.namb.net.

[21] Gary B. McGee, "'The New World of Realities in Which We Live': How Speaking in Tongues Empowered Early Pentecostals," *Pneuma* 30, no. 1 (2008): 108–9. Charles Parham claims that Agnes Ozman, the first

went out to foreign lands from various early-twentieth-century revivals in places like Los Angeles, Fargo, North Dakota, Spokane, Chicago, England, and Stockholm, they soon discovered that their confidence in the gift of tongues as known languages was misplaced. Yet, rather than abandoning their belief in Spirit baptism and speaking in tongues as its evidence, they began to reformulate their understanding of tongues in other missiological ways. They began to focus especially on the joy, love for others, and empowerment for witness that Spirit baptism and speaking in tongues signified. Furthermore, in all of these, Pentecostal missionaries often felt an urgency regarding the task of world evangelization and could not imagine another reason why these apostolic gifts so long silent were once again being restored.[22] Thus, the Azusa Street revival led by William Seymour became not only a missions-sending center for early Pentecostalism but also a priority destination for missionaries returning from foreign lands who had been sent out by other organizations. In this, some began to see Los Angeles as the New Jerusalem from which the gospel would spread to the whole world.[23]

THE NEW TESTAMENT DATA

The noun *glossolalia* is not found in the Bible, but rather the verbal phrase "to speak in tongues" (*glossais lalein*). References

---

student at his Bible School to speak in tongues, spoke in Chinese; see Edith L. Blumhofer, *Restoring the Faith: The Assemblies of God, Pentecostalism, and American Culture* (Chicago: University of Illinois Press, 1993), 51. And as Allan Anderson notes, this understanding of tongues as *xenolalia* was nearly universal among early Pentecostals following the beliefs of Parham and Seymour. Anderson, *Spreading Fires*, 46.

[22] McGee, "The New World," 110–35.

[23] Allan Anderson, "The Origins of Pentecostalism and Its Global Spread in the Early Twentieth Century" *Transformation* 22, no. 3 (2005): 181. Importantly, though, as Anderson observes, there were in fact many "Jerusalems" around the world to which similar expectations were attached.

to the practice of *glossolalia* occur explicitly in three books of the New Testament: (1) the longer ending of Mark (16:17); (2) Acts 2:3–4, 11; 10:46; 19:6; and (3) in Paul's discussion of spiritual gifts in 1 Corinthians 12–14 (though some argue for implicit references elsewhere, especially, Lk 10:21; Rom 8:26–27; Eph 5:18–20; Col 3:16; and 1 Thess 5:19–20). Exegetical debates swirl around the nature of tongues speech in 1 Corinthians and Acts, while the longer ending of Mark 16 is sometimes considered evidence that *glossolalia* was valued among early- to mid-second-century Christians.[24] Interestingly, none of the passages that mention *glossolalia* offer much in the way of explanation concerning its nature. As a result, exegetes have found support for seeing tongues as both ecstatic speech in unknown (heavenly?) languages and as known earthly languages the speaker has not learned.[25] In every instance writers connect the gift to the operations of the Spirit, marking it as a *charism*—a work of grace.

At a most fundamental level, Paul in 1 Corinthians expounds on *glossolalia* as it relates to congregational worship and personal

---

[24] Mark Cartledge, *Charismatic Glossolalia: An Empirical-Theological Study* (Burlington, VT: Ashgate, 2002), 62.

[25] The common tendency is to equate Paul's understanding of *glossolalia* with ecstatic speech and Luke's with known languages, but even that point remains highly debated. For Paul's *glossolalia* in 1 Corinthians 12–14 as ecstatic speech, see Johannes van Oort, "The Holy Spirit and the Early Church: The Experience of the Spirit," *HTS Teologiese / Theological Studies* 68, no. 1 (2012): 2. Robert Menzies says that the Pauline use of *lalein glossais* in 1 Corinthians must refer to ecstatic speech due to Paul's insistence on translation (14:6–19) and believes the same should be true of tongues in Acts based on among other reasons: (1) the reality that Luke could have used other terms for known languages as he does in Acts 2:6, 8, where the term *dialectos* is used; and (2) because the phrase "in his own language" modifies the verb of hearing in Acts 2:6 and 2:8. Menzies, *The Language of the Spirit: Interpreting and Translating Charismatic Terms* (Cleveland, TN: CPT, 2020), 98–101. John Michael Penney argues for the distinction between Pauline *glossolalia* and that of Acts based on what he considers the equation of *heterais glossais* in verse 4 with *dialectos* in verse 8. Penney, *The Missionary Emphasis of Lukan Pneumatology* (Sheffield, England: Sheffield Academic, 1997), 82.

edification, while Luke in the book of Acts employs the term missiologically to emphasize the church's cross-cultural mandate accomplished in the Spirit's power.[26] Scholars debate the nature of tongues in both 1 Corinthians and Acts. Concerning Acts, disagreements arise especially over whether there exists a difference between what occurs in Acts 2 and what happens in Acts 10 and 19 and whether or not Luke meant for tongues to be an enduring sign or a temporal one.[27] That said, most agree that at least for the early church, *glossolalia* signaled the universal scope of the gospel, and that the reconstituted people of God under the New Covenant would include not only those within Israel who recognize Jesus as the Messiah, but Gentiles as well. Along these lines Lutheran scholar Richard Bliese has argued that "tongues are a marker of mission to the whole world. The Spirit is missionary in character—moving the church outward from Jerusalem to Judea and Samaria and then to the 'ends of the earth.'"[28] Likewise, Craig Keener argues that *glossolalia* is "not an arbitrary sign, but the one sign, of any Luke might have narrated, which most effectively communicates the purpose of baptism in the Spirit as an empowerment for universal mission."[29] And Frank Macchia observes, "These tongues of Pentecost represent an overabundance of prophetic communion that signals the global reach of the gospel and the renewal of all flesh."[30] While scholars undoubtedly debate

---

[26] Craig S. Keener, "Why Does Luke Use Tongues as a Sign of the Spirit's Empowerment?" *Journal of Pentecostal Theology* 15, no. 2 (2007); Jerry M. Ireland, "The Missionary Nature of Tongues in the Book of Acts," *PentecoStudies* 18, no. 2 (2019): 200–223.

[27] Robert Menzies, *Speaking in Tongues: Jesus and the Apostolic Church as Models for the Church Today* (Cleveland, TN: CPT, 2016); James D. G. Dunn, *Baptism in the Holy Spirit: A Re-examination of the New Testament Teaching on the Gift of Spirit in Relation to Pentecostalism Today*, 2nd ed. (London, UK: SCM, 2010).

[28] Richard H. Bliese, "Speaking in Tongues and the Mission of God *Ad Gentes*," *Journal of Pentecostal Theology* 20, no. 1 (2011): 47.

[29] Keener, "Why Does Luke Use Tongues as a Sign of the Spirit's Empowerment?" 184.

[30] Frank Macchia, *Jesus the Spirit Baptizer: Christology in Light of Pentecost* (Grand Rapids, MI: Eerdmans, 2018), 127.

the ongoing relevance and nature of this gift as it relates to the mission of the church, most do not dispute that it functioned with a clear missiological purpose in Luke's narrative.[31]

MONTANISM AND TERTULLIAN

Luke's emphasis on tongues as an important feature of Christian missions especially raises the question of how this distinctive aspect was expressed by later theologians and missionary thinkers. One of the most historically troubling aspects of *glossolalia* for Pentecostals has surely been the large swath of silence related to tongues that extends from the late second century until about the nineteenth century, with a few notable exceptions.[32] As already observed, many scholars see the longer ending of Mark as evidence that tongues speech persisted into the mid-second century.[33] Piercing silence dominates the centuries that follow, however, causing some to label tongues speech as having a "peculiar" or "strange history."[34] Pentecostals have usually responded to this problematic history by arguing that because *glossolalia* occurred frequently

---

[31] For example, as F. F. Bruce observes, "On the present occasion the content of the ecstatic utterances was 'the mighty deeds of God' (v. 11), and the range of the languages in which these were proclaimed suggests that Luke thought of the coming of the Spirit more particularly as a preparation for the worldwide proclamation of the gospel." F. F. Bruce, *The Book of the Acts*, New International Commentary on the New Testament, Accordance electronic ed. (Grand Rapids, MI: Eerdmans, 1988), 53; cf. also Richard N. Longenecker, *Acts*, ed. Frank E. Gaebelein and J. D. Douglas, vol. 9 of the Expositor's Bible Commentary, Accordance electronic ed. (Grand Rapids, MI: Zondervan, 1984), n.p.; Craig S. Keener, *Acts: An Exegetical Commentary,* vol. 1: *Introduction and 1:1—2:47* (Grand Rapids, MI: Baker Academic, 2012), 780–82.

[32] For brief summaries, see Prudencia Damboriena, *Pentecostalism in Contemporary Christianity: Tongues as of Fire* (Cleveland, OH: Corpus Books, 1969), 101–3; and especially Kelsey, *Speaking in Tongues*, 32–68.

[33] Cartledge, *Charismatic Glossolalia*, 62.

[34] Kelsey, *Speaking in Tongues*, 32; Stagg et al., *Glossolalia*, 54.

among second-century Montanists—a supposition based on a somewhat vague description by Eusebius—the heterodox nature of the sect cast a shadow over the practice, causing it to drop out of favor among orthodox believers until its recent revival. Specifically, Eusebius (in the early fourth century) writes:

> There is said to be in Mysia near Phrygia a certain village called Ardabav. There, they say, first, that a certain one of the recent converts, Montanus by name, when Gratus was proconsul of Asia, in an unrestrained desire of soul for primacy gave to the Adversary access to himself, and became obsessed, and, falling suddenly into a kind of frenzy and distraction, raved and began to babble and utter strange things, prophesying contrary to the custom of the Church according to the tradition and the succession of the Church from the beginning.[35]

Though this statement appears to refer to the practice of *glossolalia* in its reference to those who "babble and utter strange things," it is hard to be certain, given the distance of two centuries between the event and its description. In fact, as Minets observes, it may be noteworthy that Eusebius does not use the term *glossais lalein* but instead chooses more obscure terminology, perhaps in an attempt to distance the Montanists from the narrative of Acts 2 and suggest that their behavior was contrary to scripture.[36] In other words, the lack of a clear reference to tongues could be motivated by ecclesiological concerns rather than historical ones. Those who see here a reference to speaking in tongues also find grounds for the practice's demise, however, since adherents to Montanism could be described "as enthusiastic Christians with questionable theological tendencies."[37] Furthermore, the association Eusebius makes between tongues speech and the demonic (here Adversary) rather than as

---

[35] Eusebius, *Ecclesial History*, 5.16.
[36] Minets, "The Slow Fall of Babel," 236.
[37] Hunter, "Tongues-Speech," 129.

a work of the Spirit has continued well into the modern era.[38] But it is this association that leads Kelsey to declare that "tongues speech was, as it were, filed away" because of its association with Montanism.[39] In the disappearance of tongues Pentecostals have occasionally drawn parallels between their own recovery of *glossolalia* and Luther's revival of the doctrine of salvation by faith and grace alone (*sola fide, sola gratia*).[40] If something as central as the doctrine of salvation could fade away for almost fifteen hundred years, why should it be inconceivable that a less central belief such as speaking in tongues might suffer the same fate?

Tertullian (d. 220) has long been claimed as one of Montanism's most famous adherents.[41] Andrew McGowan, however, has presented a compelling argument against the more traditional schismatic view of Tertullian, denying the supposed distinction between "the early 'orthodox' and late 'Montanist'" Tertullian.[42] While acknowledging the influence of the "New Prophecy" on the development of Tertullian's trinitarianism, he finds little support for the supposition that the Carthaginian theologian ever departed from catholicity, as is evident in his many references to the *regula fidei* even in later works such as *Against Praxeas*.[43]

---

[38] John MacArthur, for example, has referred to modern expressions of *glossolalia* as "a disgraceful jumble of irrational blabber" in his controversial text, *Strange Fire: The Danger of Offending the Holy Spirit with Counterfeit Worship* (Nashville, TN: Thomas Nelson, 2013), 154.

[39] Kelsey, *Speaking in Tongues*, 34.

[40] Jerry Ireland, "Glossolalia," *Brill Encyclopedia of Global Pentecostalism* (London: Brill, 2020), s.v.

[41] Stagg et al., *Glossolalia*, 47–48; Kelsey, *Speaking in Tongues*, 37–38.

[42] Andrew McGowan, "Tertullian and the 'Heretical' Origins of the 'Orthodox' Trinity," *Journal of Early Christian Studies* 14, no. 4 (Winter 2006): 437–57. For a helpful overview of the early and late Tertullian and reasons why some consider the later Tertullian as having converted to Montanism, see Kilian McDonnell, "Communion Ecclesiology and Baptism in the Spirit: Tertullian and the Early Church," *Theological Studies* 49, no. 4 (1988): 684–91.

[43] McGowan, "Tertullian and the 'Heretical' Origins," 439. McGowan particularly notes Tertullian's defense of Trinitarianism in *Against*

McGowan's argument, which I find compelling, not only challenges the theory that tongues disappeared because of its association with the Montanism, but also relocates *glossolalia* closer to the catholic (that is, nonsectarian) faith of Carthage in the early third century. That is, if Tertullian was an advocate of the practice and remained committed to orthodoxy, as the evidence suggests, then perhaps the demise of tongues speech cannot be so readily tied to the Montanist movement.

Furthermore, as Kilian McDonnell has shown, Tertullian generally took a favorable view toward charisms, teaching that baptismal candidates should lift their hands and pray expectantly for charismatic gifts following their emergence from the water.[44] Such charismatic gifts took on an ecclesiastical importance in that "charisms are ministries; [there is] no Christian without a ministry; and each ministry [is] oriented toward the church and world in the work of evangelization."[45] In other words, all of the charisms that catechumens were to seek and that were bestowed were oriented toward the mission of the church in evangelization, "directly or indirectly."[46]

Praxeas, and that this trinitarian thought existed especially among the adherents to the New Prophecy and was rejected by Praxeas, who may or may not have been a historical figure. McGowan argues that the connection between Tertullian's later trinitarian theology and the New Prophecy should not be seen as coincidental but that perhaps the latter informed the former.

[44] McDonnell, "Communion Ecclesiology and Baptism in the Spirit," 681–84. McDonnell's discussion centers on Tertullian's *On Baptism*, where the church father had tremendous influence on North African initiation rites. He notes that Tertullian instructed baptismal candidates to pray, probably the Lord's Prayer, after coming out of the water and that on at least some occasions, those charisms were imparted with visible signs, "observable phenomenon, something experiential," while McDonnell also cites numerous studies giving evidence that "the presence and exercise of the charisms was a fact of ecclesial life in the second and third centuries" (683).

[45] Ibid., 692.

[46] Ibid.

Importantly, Tertullian refers to speaking in tongues as contemporary occurrences, and he uses the presence of spiritual gifts in his *Against Marcion* to distinguish the true community of Christ from those who are only pretenders:

> Let Marcion then exhibit, as gifts of his god, some prophets, such as have not spoken by human sense, but with the Spirit of God, such as have both predicted things to come, and have made manifest the secrets of the heart; let him produce a psalm, a vision, a prayer—only let it be by the Spirit, in an ecstasy, that is, in a rapture [*lit. apart from the mind*], whenever an interpretation of tongues has occurred to him; let him show to me also, that any woman of boastful tongue in his community has ever prophesied from amongst those specially holy sisters of his. Now all these signs (of spiritual gifts) are forthcoming from my side without any difficulty, and they agree, too, with the rules, and the dispensations, and the instructions of the Creator; therefore without doubt the Christ, and the Spirit, and the apostle, belong severally to my God.[47]

Tertullian's argument against Marcion itself may also be seen as missional, if by that term we mean something like what we see from Paul in the book of Acts, who occasionally engages in discourse and demonstrations of the charismata in his encounter with antagonists in order to win them and others to Christ (for example, 13:4–12), as well as in his statement in 1 Corinthians that tongues were for unbelievers (14:26–33).[48]

In *A Treatise on the Soul*, wherein Tertullian argues for the origins of the soul in the acts of God and for the corporeal nature

---

[47] Tertullian, *Against Marcion*, 5.8 (*ANF* 3).

[48] For a helpful summary of Marcion's theology and supposed overlap with Gnosticism, see Justo L. González, *A History of Christian Thought: From the Beginnings to the Council of Chalcedon*, vol. 1, rev. ed. (Nashville, TN: Abingdon, 1984), 137–41.

of the soul (by which he means that the soul is a real thing) against the Platonists, he tells of a woman in the church who

> experiences in the Spirit by ecstatic vision amidst the sacred rites of the Lord's day in the church: she converses with angels, and sometimes even with the Lord; she both sees and hears mysterious communications; some men's hearts she understands, and to them who are in need she distributes remedies.[49]

Likely written after 210 CE, this passage demonstrates not only his valuation of the charismata, but his understanding that they could function apologetically and evangelistically. Moreover, as Barnett observes, prophecy, tongues, and visions constitute a trifecta of end-times charismata, especially in the book of Acts, and all three may be referred to here.[50] It is worth noting as well that much of Tertullian's life and work took on a missionary focus, including his vital role in the creation of Ecclesiastical Latin, in which he coined Latin terms for the church that had previously only been in Greek. These efforts led to his modern reputation as the "Father of Latin Christianity." As Sundkler and Steed point out regarding the missional bent that drove Tertullian's Latin efforts, "The language emerged from a creative personality, dedicated to proclaiming an overwhelming message and reaching out to as many as possible."[51] Thus, Tertullian's understanding of the missional value of tongues fits well with his overall approach to ministry and is rife with echoes of Paul's own missionary ethos (1 Cor 9:19–23).

---

[49] Tertullian, *Treatise*, 9 (*ANF* 3); see also Hunter, "Tongues-Speech," 131.
[50] Barnett, *The Living Flame*.
[51] Bengt Sundkler and Christopher Steed, "The Beginnings," in *A History of the Church in Africa* (Cambridge: Cambridge University Press, 2000), 22.

GREEK FATHERS

As already indicated, Yuliya Minets's study of tongues speech and its interpretation by Greek, Latin, and Syriac Christian writers indicated an understanding among Greek writers that made them particularly relevant to our investigation. Not only did the Greek mystery religions provide a conceptual framework for understanding ecstatic speech as fitting of religious devotion, but Greek Christians also operated from within a highly monolinguistic culture that Christianity would help transform. This was true of Greek culture in a way that was less pronounced in Latin and Syriac cultures. Therefore, the value of Greek thinkers to understanding the transformation of meaning attached to *glossolalia* becomes especially important.[52] As Minets writes, "More often Greek was understood as *the* human language, and speakers of other tongues were virtually non-existent in the public discourse and in the mental universe of ancient Greek intellectuals" (emphasis added).[53] The same was true of Latin speakers, though to a lesser degree in that they at least esteemed and studied Greek language and culture. But generally speaking, rabbinical Judaism after 70 CE continued to emphasize Hebrew as the language of God, or more precisely, as the "the tongue of holiness," and encouraged people to pray in Hebrew, even if this met with little success.[54] It was this mono-linguistic or bi-linguistic milieu that Christianity helped to alter, both positively and negatively:

> Christians were more sensitive to language differences than their predecessors. This growing awareness of the world's linguistic diversity in Late Antiquity was a reason why Christians rethought a number of biblical episodes, such as the Tower of Babel and the Pentecostal gift of tongues, as narratives about linguistic phenomena.[55]

---

[52] Minets, "The Slow Fall of Babel," 134–228.
[53] Ibid., 130.
[54] Ibid., 98, 106.
[55] Ibid., 133.

Irenaeus

Irenaeus (d. 202) was a missionary and theologian who, though a native of Smyrna, served over twelve hundred miles away as bishop of Lyons in southern Gaul.[56] He was appointed bishop not long after the persecution of Christians by Marcus Aurelius there in 177 CE. As Jacob Rodriguez observes, his congregants were mostly "Greek-speaking immigrants from Asia Minor, as well as some Latin-speaking immigrants."[57] But he may also have spoken Gaelic and at the very least refused to denigrate minority languages, as was generally the custom.[58] More important, he championed the translatability of the gospel into the many languages of the world and believed this could happen without loss to the gospel's transforming power. Irenaeus grounded this understanding both in Christology and pneumatology—Christ reconciling all nations to himself as the second Adam, and the Spirit making possible the reception of the gospel message across all cultural-linguistic barriers.[59] Furthermore, Irenaeus has been described as a "mystical theologian" for his deep grounding in God's ineffable nature and consequent need for apophatic approaches to talking about God.[60]

An important difficulty in researching the historical understanding of *glossolalia* in the church is that very early on the term came to be conflated with prophecy, as was the case in Irenaeus's late-second-century discussion of tongues in *Against Heresies*. In this text Irenaeus not only appears to be personally familiar with

---

[56] Jacob Rodriguez, "Irenaeus's Missional Theology: Global Christian Perspectives from an Ancient Missionary and Theologian," *JETS* 59, no. 1 (2016): 132; Ed Smither, *Christian Mission: A Concise Global History* (Bellingham, WA: Lexham, 2019), 16.

[57] Rodriguez, "Irenaeus's Missional Theology," 133.

[58] Ibid., 134. Rodriguez provides a helpful analysis of Irenaeus's more positive view of "barbarians" contra those of contemporaries such as Philostratus as well as later thinkers such as Dio Chrysostom (ibid., 136).

[59] Ibid., 134–38.

[60] Nicholas Gendle, "St. Irenaeus as Mystical Theologian," *Thomist: A Speculative Quarterly Review* 39, no. 2 (1975): 185.

tongues by having witnessed the practice of it, but also indicates its relationship to having received the Spirit. Irenaeus broadly confirms the presence of miracles and spiritual gifts in his day:

> For some do certainly and truly drive out devils, so that those who have thus been cleansed from evil spirits frequently both believe [in Christ], and join themselves to the Church. Others have foreknowledge of things to come: they see visions, and utter prophetic expressions. Others still, heal the sick by laying their hands upon them, and they are made whole. Yea, moreover, as I have said, the dead even have been raised up, and remained among us for many years. And what shall I more say? It is not possible to name the number of the gifts which the Church, [scattered] throughout the whole world, has received from God, in the name of Jesus Christ, who was crucified under Pontius Pilate, and which she exerts day by day for the benefit of the Gentiles, neither practicing deception upon any, nor taking any reward from them [on account of such miraculous interpositions]. For as she has received freely from God, freely also does she minister [to others].[61]

Beyond miracles, he also explicitly notes the missional function of gifts that the church "exerts day by day for the benefit of the Gentiles." Again he writes:

> For this reason does the apostle declare, "We speak wisdom among them that are perfect," terming those persons "perfect" who have received the Spirit of God, and who through the Spirit of God do speak in all languages, as he used Himself also to speak. In like manner we do also hear many brethren in the Church, who possess prophetic gifts, and who through the Spirit speak all kinds of languages, and bring to light for the general benefit the hidden things

---

[61] Irenaeus, *Against Heresies*, 2.32.4.

of men, and declare the mysteries of God, whom also the apostle terms "spiritual," they being spiritual because they partake of the Spirit, and not because their flesh has been stripped off and taken away, and because they have become purely spiritual.[62]

Hunter addresses whether Irenaeus was truly an eyewitness to tongues by pointing out that such questions arise from the later Latin text and not from the earlier Greek in which Irenaeus wrote.[63] Indeed, Hunter notes, both Eusebius's later quotation of Irenaeus and Irenaeus's own distinction between the past tense of what Paul taught and the present tense "we hear" make the non-contemporaneous arguments seem quite strained.

In Irenaeus's citation of Acts 10 and Peter's visit to Cornelius, he observes that Peter would not have known the Holy Spirit had been given "had he not heard them prophesying when the Holy Ghost rested upon them."[64] Interestingly, Irenaeus clearly points to the evidential value of what Peter witnessed, even though he conflates tongues and prophecy. This is of course problematic, given that both Paul (1 Cor 14:4) and Luke (Acts 19:6) apparently understand tongues and prophecy as distinct charisms. This adds to the difficulty in discerning precisely how Irenaeus understood *glossolalia*. Yet Irenaeus in this discussion also observes the missional role of tongues on the day of Pentecost:

> This Spirit did David ask for the human race, saying, "And stablish me with Thine all-governing Spirit;" who also, as Luke says, descended at the day of Pentecost upon the disciples after the Lord's ascension, *having power to admit all nations to the entrance of life*, and to the opening of the new covenant; from whence also, with one accord in all languages, they uttered praise to God, the Spirit bringing

---

[62] Ibid., 5.6.1.
[63] Hunter, "Tongues-Speech," 129.
[64] Irenaeus, *Against Heresies*, 3.12.15; Kelsey, "Speaking in Tongues," 34.

distant tribes to unity, and offering to the Father the first-fruits of all nations. (emphasis added)[65]

Clearly referring to Acts 2, Irenaeus's reference seems to interpret that passage not as speaking in unknown (ecstatic) tongues, but as the supernatural ability to speak in known languages one had not learned. That aside, the emphasis on the missional aspect of tongues is clear—"bringing distant tribes to unity, and offering to the Father the first-fruits of all nations."[66] Furthermore, Irenaeus later describes "many brethren in the Church, who possess prophetic gifts, and who through the Spirit speak all kinds of languages, and bring to light for the general benefit the hidden things of men, and declare the mysteries of God."[67] The reference here to Spirit-inspired speech remains enigmatic and could refer either to speaking unlearned foreign languages or to ecstatic speech, though it seems clear that "he had a positive attitude to the gift."[68] Irenaeus's anti-Gnostic argument centers on both the way in which salvation applies to "the whole nature of man" and that the ability to be used by the Spirit indicates the holistic nature of salvation, uniting body and soul for God's purposes—especially those related to proclamation of the gospel or what he refers to as declaring the mysteries of God. Irenaeus cites Paul's apostolic mission and Paul's declaration in 1 Corinthians 2:6, "We do speak wisdom among them that are perfect," arguing that this Spirit-inspired gift continues in the church as the church fulfills its mission to the nations, speaking all kinds of languages, "even as the apostle himself used to do."[69]

Origen

Hans Urs von Balthasar says of Origen of Alexandria (d. 253/4) that "it is all but impossible to overestimate Origen and his

---

[65] Irenaeus, *Against Heresies*, 3.17.2.
[66] Ibid.
[67] Ibid., 5.6.1.
[68] Minets, "The Slow Fall of Babel," 230.
[69] Ibid.

Language, Missions, and Glossolalia in Patristic Thought 75

importance for the history of Christian thought."[70] Origen—known mostly for his allegorical approach to scripture, reports of self-castration (Eusebius), and his eventual excommunication over theological controversies—was also one of the most prolific writers of the post-apostolic era. His writings include *Against Celsus*, a work in which he deals with Acts 2:2–10, a passage he quoted "at least sixteen times."[71] Origen cites Celsus's incredulous rejection of Christian prophecy, wherein Celsus reasons, "There are many who, although of no name, with the greatest facility and on the slightest occasion, whether within or without temples, assume the motions and gestures of inspired persons."[72] To this, Celsus adds a comment that some have taken as a possible reference to speaking in tongues. Origen observes of Celsus, "Then he goes on to say: 'To these promises are added strange, fanatical, and quite unintelligible words, of which no rational person can find the meaning: for so dark are they, as to have no meaning at all; but they give occasion to every fool or impostor to apply them to suit his own purposes.'"[73] Origen's response, however, suggests that *glossolalia* is not in view as he emphasizes that some of the teachings of Israel's prophets, especially those concerning Christ, were inherently clothed in mystery and intended to be so, especially for those who lacked faith.[74] Thus, Celsus's statement seems directed not at tongues speech as enigmatic but to the teachings of Christ more generally.

Perhaps more important for the continuation of spiritual gifts, Origen observes their diminishing presence, pointing out that this owes more to a lack of holiness than to any sort of dispensational necessity:

---

[70] Hans Urs von Balthasar, ed., *Origen: Spirit and Fire: A Thematic Anthology of His Writing* (Washington, DC: The Catholic University of America Press, 1984), 1; see also Ronald E. Heine, *Origen: Scholarship in the Service of the Church* (Oxford, UK: Oxford University Press, 2011).
[71] Minets, "The Slow Fall of Babel," 230.
[72] Origen, *Against Celsus*, 7.9.
[73] Ibid.; Stagg et al., *Glossolalia*, 51.
[74] Origen, *Against Celsus*, 7.11.

Moreover, the Holy Spirit gave signs of His presence at the beginning of Christ's ministry, and after His ascension He gave still more; but since that time these signs have diminished, although there are still traces of His presence in a few who have had their souls purified by the Gospel, and their actions regulated by its influence. "For the holy Spirit of discipline will flee deceit, and remove from thoughts that are without understanding."[75]

Central to Origen's theology lies his belief that God remains shrouded in darkness apart from God's revelatory word, and many of his writings function as an effort to respond to that reality and to the confusion among those outside the church about the nature and meaning of Christian faith. Especially important for Origen in his *Against Celsus* is the argument from prophecy regarding the life and doctrines concerning Jesus—especially the prophetic connection based on Genesis 49:10 and the reference to "the expectations of the nations" (LXX).[76] Thus, we can conclude that although Origen never links tongues per se to missions, he does describe the works of the Spirit broadly as having evidential value, what he calls "signs of His presence," and as being missiological, especially as it relates to prophecy and Christ's role in redeeming the nations. And, in his exposition of 1 Corinthians 13—14, he considers speaking in tongues not as the vocalization of human languages, but as Spirit-inspired speech that functioned as a countermeasure to an over-rationalized approach to God.[77]

Chrysostom

John Chrysostom (d. 407)—whose name means "golden-mouthed," referring to his homiletical skills—served as archbishop of Constantinople and refers to speaking in tongues on several

---

[75] Ibid., 7.8–11.
[76] Heine, *Origen*, 224.
[77] Minets, "The Slow Fall of Babel," 232.

occasions. In *Homily IV* on Acts 2:1–2 he mentions tongues several times, but without commentary. His focus though in the sermon centers on evangelism and the kind of personal holiness that makes one fit to be used by God. He observes of the Pentecost event in Acts that its chief importance relates to the harvest that comes through the church's missionary efforts: "the time was come to put in the sickle of the word."[78] He connects this to Christ's own words in John 4:35, "Lift up your eyes and look on the fields, for they are white already to harvest."[79] Chrysostom then develops the sermon from this missional perspective to a focus on personal holiness and on the readiness of the disciples who received the Spirit's empowerment. "Observe, how when one is continuing in prayer, when one is in charity, then it is that the Spirit draws near."[80] Perhaps this moralization of the Pentecost outpouring of the Spirit owes to assumptions common then that the gospel had already gone out to the whole world.[81]

In his *Demonstration against the Pagans That Christ Is God*, Chrysostom links the gift of tongues to the early church's missionary success: "Someone might well ask how the apostles drew to themselves all these people. 'How did men who spoke only the language of the Jews win over the Scythian, the Indian, the Sarmatian, and the Thracian?' Because they received the gift of tongues through the Holy Spirit."[82] Though some have questioned the authenticity of this text as genuinely Chrysostom's, good reasons exist to hold to its authenticity merely as an unfinished work.[83] More important, the overtly missional nature of this work directed toward the conversion of "pagans" should not be

---

[78] John Chrysostom, *Homilies on the Acts of the Apostles*, 4 (*Nicene and Post-Nicene Fathers*, 1.11).
[79] Ibid.
[80] Ibid.
[81] Cf. Romans 10:18; Colossians 1:6.
[82] Chrysostom, *Demonstration against the Pagans That Christ Is God*, 7.2; cf. 12.9.
[83] John Chrysostom, *Apologist*, vol. 73 in Margaret A. Schatkin and Paul W. Harkins, *The Fathers of the Church* (Washington, DC: The Catholic University of America Press, 1985), 166.

overlooked, and this holds whether or not the work is authentically Chrysostom's. Heightening the case for authenticity, though, Chrysostom makes a strikingly similar statement in his *Homilies on First Corinthians*. Again, Chrysostom argues that (1) tongues were given preeminently for reaching the nations; and (2) Paul neither denounced nor unduly elevated the gift of tongues. The passage reads:

> At this point he makes a comparison between the gifts, and lowers that of the tongues, showing it to be neither altogether useless, nor very profitable by itself. For in fact they were greatly puffed up on account of this, because the gift was considered to be a great one. And it was thought great because the Apostles received it first, and with so great display; it was not however therefore to be esteemed above all the others. Wherefore then did the Apostles receive it before the rest? Because they were to go abroad every where [sic] and as in the time of building the tower the one tongue was divided into many; so then the many tongues frequently met in one man, and the same person used to discourse both in the Persian, and the Roman, and the Indian, and many other tongues, the Spirit sounding within him: and the gift was called the gift of tongues because he could all at once speak divers languages. See accordingly how he both depresses and elevates it.[84]

Interestingly, Chrysostom's argument proceeds here by suggesting that the gift of tongues outside of a missionary context—that is, apart from those who would actually understand the language being spoken—proves rather useless and this, says Chrysostom, is the thrust of Paul's argument in 1 Corinthians 14. He understands this, though, primarily concerning the work of the apostles among the nations. Chrysostom also conflates the discussion of tongues in 1 Corinthians 12—14 with that of Acts 2 by claiming that those in Corinth spoke Syriac and Persian when they spoke in

---

[84] Chrysostom, *Homily 38.3* (*Nicene and Post-Nicene Fathers*, 1.12).

tongues.[85] As Minets argues, Chrysostom (1) tried to harmonize the accounts of tongues by both Luke and Paul out of his conviction that scripture could not contradict itself, and (2) embodied a typical perspective in which contemporary "speakers of other languages were almost absent from the monolingual mental universe of Greek thinkers."[86]

LANGUAGE, OTHERNESS, AND THE VALUE OF *GLOSSOLALIA*

What are we to make of this "peculiar" history? While some have claimed that tongues speech was only necessary in the church's infancy, the above narrative seems to tell a different story.[87] Well into the fourth century church fathers continued to refer to tongues as indicative of the church's missionary nature, even while differing in their understanding of the precise nature of tongues speech. Whether one understands tongues as ecstatic utterances, as perhaps with Tertullian and Montanus, or as the supernatural ability to speak in a known language one has not learned, there are perhaps a few lessons that can be gleaned from this brief history as it relates to the articulation of a Pentecostal missiology. We have seen that although later writers saw tongues as references to *xenolalia*, this development may reflect a number of nonbiblical factors, including diverse views among Greek, Latin, and Syriac writers regarding the importance and value of language diversity. Additionally, there are some early references to tongues among the Greek fathers that seem to support understanding even the Acts occurrences as ecstatic speech. Plus, many later

---

[85] Minets, "The Slow Fall of Babel," 252.
[86] Ibid., 255.
[87] Benjamin B. Warfield, *Miracles: Yesterday and Today, Real and Counterfeit* (1918; repr., Grand Rapids, MI: Eerdmans, 1965). Warfield famously declared of the miraculous spiritual gifts: "They were part of the credentials of the Apostles as the authoritative agents of God in founding the church. Their function thus confined them to distinctively the apostolic church and they necessarily passed away with it" (6).

writers may have avoided elaborating on tongues due to their own confusion on the matter. It may be, as Minets observes, that the aforementioned ambiguity in Acts especially owes to Luke having had access to diverse sources, one emphasizing ecstatic speech and one emphasizing known languages, and Luke intentionally (as led by the Spirit) embedded that ambiguity in his narrative.[88] But what value would such ambiguity have for the ongoing life of the church on mission?

It is interesting to note alongside the above references that in Pacian of Barcelona's letter to Simpronian the discussion of languages leads to the somewhat random assertion that there were precisely 120 known languages.[89] It is difficult not to imagine, as some have, that this thought traces in some way to the 120 present on the day of Pentecost.[90] The whole issue of language emerges because Simpronian accuses Pacian of quoting Virgil, "a pagan poet after all."[91] Pacian responds by noting that not only does language come from God, but so too do the very letters of the alphabet themselves.[92] This notion though, as Denecker observes, represents one of only a handful of positive appraisals among early Latin Christians regarding language diversity. Others, like Augustine, saw human linguistic diversity as a hindrance to the church's mission. According to Denecker, Augustine "seems to believe that a single, monolingual Bible version might have been preferable for the propagation of faith."[93]

Perhaps as we contemplate this variegated history wherein little clarity emerges from the church fathers regarding the precise nature of tongues, we might consider an alternative to these

---

[88] Minets, "The Slow Fall of Babel," 128–29.
[89] Pacian of Barcelona and Orosius of Braga, "Letter 2," in *Iberian Fathers*, vol. 3, ed. Thomas P. Halton, trans. Craig L. Hanson, The Fathers of the Church (Washington, DC: The Catholic University of America Press, 1999), 31.
[90] Ibid., 14.
[91] Denecker, *Ideas on Language in Early Latin Christianity*, 124.
[92] Ibid., 357.
[93] Ibid., 148.

choices. Perhaps the ambiguity is the point, in that tongues speech in the New Testament represents the invisible barrier between comprehension and obscurity that is overcome only by the Spirit. In this, tongues may be seen as simultaneously bringing the rational aspects of the faith that demand thought and understanding together with that aspect which requires trust and surrender. As Jack Levison observes of tongues in Acts:

> Acts is not about xenolalia (comprehension) versus glossolalia (incomprehension). Acts is not about ecstasy (incomprehension) versus restraint (comprehension). Acts is not about water baptism versus spirit baptism. Luke offers much more: a mode of inspiration that unites the quintessence of ecstasy with intellectual acuity.[94]

Tongues then serves the twofold purpose of reminding the church of its calling (1) to embrace linguistic otherness, to witness to it, to welcome it into the kingdom, and to forever seek out those of other tongues who have no witness; and (2) to embrace the mystery that accompanies God's Spirit wherever the church is found so that we do not become guilty of creating God in our own image or losing sight of Christianity's supernatural character. Regarding the latter, it seems to me that among those who have studied tongues, most have found exactly what they were looking for because their conclusions have often fit very neatly within their own theological tradition. The cessationists have found a friend in Augustine, and Pentecostals have found one in Tertullian. And Paul has been made into a Methodist, a Lutheran, an Episcopalian, and a Pentecostal. Tongues perhaps can *best* serve not as the initial physical evidence of Spirit baptism, but as the enduring evidence that in the church "there is no longer Jew or Greek, there is no longer slave or free, there is no longer male and female; for all of you are one in Christ Jesus" (Gal 3:28).

---

[94] Jack Levison, *Inspired: The Holy Spirit and the Mind of Faith* (Grand Rapids, MI: Eerdmans, 2013), 224.

Furthermore, this oneness in Christ is fundamentally a work of the Spirit and the foundational concept for Christian mission.

In consideration of the above as it relates to a constructive theology of tongues speech, a few helpful guidelines may be suggested. First, contemporary efforts to harmonize tongues in Acts and in 1 Corinthians may be guilty of the same misguided philosophy that led patristic exegetes astray. Pentecostals have long argued that Luke's view of the Spirit should not be interpreted through a Pauline lens in their defense of Spirit baptism as a second (or third) work of grace. True enough. Yet when classical Pentecostal denominations such as the Assemblies of God declare that Luke's reference to speaking in tongues in Acts 2 is the "same in essence" as Paul's description of the gift of tongues, they seem to embrace the very thing previously argued against.[95] It would be helpful, then, to be reminded that *different* does not mean *divergent*, and that harmonization may result in the loss of some of the vital mystery intended by the biblical authors.

Second, the Pentecostal doctrine of initial evidence—indicating that the ability to speak in tongues serves as the primary evidence for having been baptized in the Spirit—never comes up in patristic expositions of the book of Acts, and this ought to be cause for concern.[96] What does appear though is that tongues functions as evidence that the church body has recognized the inclusion in the church of those formerly outside, that those once not a people have been made a people (1 Pet 2:10). Would it not be sorrowfully ironic that the notion of "evidence" would potentially locate Pentecostal theology closer to an Enlightenment paradigm, one not at all consistent with a first-century worldview? In fact, Russell Spittler has argued that "the shift from Wesley's 'assurance'

---

[95] Roger Stronstad, *The Charismatic Theology of St. Luke* (Peabody, MA: Hendrickson, 1984), 9.

[96] That said, Ira Jay Martin has argued that in the apostolic church, at least, *glossolalia* did function as evidence of having received the Spirit. Ira Jay Martin, "Glossolalia in the Apostolic Church," *Journal of Biblical Literature* 63, no. 2 (1944): 123–30.

to the notion of 'evidence' . . . was doubtlessly facilitated by the rise of popular scientism after the Civil War."[97] Could it not be that early Pentecostals in their efforts to defend their experience framed it in ways that minimized the inspired mystery of the text and resulted in precisely the kind of over-rationalization that Origen feared and for which Pentecostals have long claimed to be the antithesis?

Finally, Augustine famously asked regarding tongues, "Who expects in these days that those on whom hands are laid that they may receive the Holy Spirit should forthwith begin to speak with tongues?"[98] Hinson argues that tongues had virtually disappeared by the time of Augustine and Chrysostom, and that though it functioned as a valuable apologetic in the earlier centuries of Christianity, it became increasingly difficult to separate tongues speech from demonic activity. Yet, even Jesus when operating by the Spirit was accused of appropriating the power of demons (Mt 12:24). Thus, Hinson's argument that "the more ecstatic forms" of Christian witness had to disappear fails to take into account the more complex reasons behind the disappearance of *glossolalia*, as well as the ways in which references to *glossolalia* continued to play missional roles in Christian texts, including those by Chrysostom.[99] It may have been the gradual erosion of the appreciation for linguistic otherness that Christianity introduced—but that faded in light of theological controversies that centered on linguistic precision—that functioned as the main culprit in *glossolalia*'s demise. Thus, missions and a missional outlook may be the greatest contribution that *glossolalia* makes in terms of ecclesiology, and this, surely, is worth guarding.

---

[97] Russell Spittler, "Glossolalia," in *Dictionary of Pentecostal and Charismatic Movements*, ed. Stanley Burgess and Gary B. McGee (Grand Rapids, MI: Zondervan, 1988), 339.
[98] Augustine, *On Baptism, Against the Donatists*, 3.17; E. Glenn Hinson, "A Brief History of Glossolalia," in Stagg et al., *Glossolalia*, 52.
[99] Hinson, "A Brief History of Glossolalia," 56.

4

From Solidarity to Sodality

COMPASSIONATE MISSION AND THE LOCAL CHURCH[1]

A colleague recently shared with me a disturbing story. As leader of a group of missionaries working among unreached people groups, he recounted how his team had gathered to plan and strategize on evangelism and church planting. After sitting silently for most of the meeting, one team member spoke up and declared, "I don't need to be here. I'm here to do social justice work, not church planting." The rest of the team sat back in disbelief. Where did this person get the idea that missions, and missions among unreached peoples, no less, could consist of social justice work and *not* church planting and evangelism?

My own conversations with members of the missiology committee within Assemblies of God World Missions suggest that this sort of thinking is increasingly the norm rather than the exception among new missionary candidates. Other evidence suggests a growing trend toward compassion-type work among

---

[1] An earlier version of this chapter appeared as Jerry M. Ireland, "From Solidarity to Sodality: Local Churches, Compassionate Mission, and the Fostering of Cross-cultural Missions Bands," in *Churches on Mission: God's Grace Abounding to the Nations*, ed. Geoffrey Hartt, Christopher R. Little, and John Wang (Pasadena, CA: William Carey Library), 2017. Reprinted with permission.

mission-sending churches. In the United States, missions giving to evangelism and church planting declined by roughly 10 percent between 1998 and 2008, while giving to relief and development work increased by about 5 percent during the same period.[2] This raises the important question of whether there is a way to help those who feel called and gifted in the area of compassion to serve in missions in a way that more directly connects to church planting and evangelism. In this chapter I suggest that compassion *can* serve the primary goal in missions of taking the gospel to the unreached and thereby overcome some of the compartmentalized thinking seen in the story above. My thesis is that solidarity, defined as an essential feature of corporate holiness according to the New Testament, constitutes a vital ingredient in the emergence of indigenous missionary movements, which depend on a movement of the Holy Spirit among God's people. Missionaries can facilitate this vital solidarity by removing themselves as the primary doers of compassion and by focusing on discipleship.

WINTER'S MODALITY AND SODALITY STRUCTURES

In a series of essays and articles in the 1970s Ralph Winter distinguished between what he called "the two structures of God's redemptive mission": modalities and sodalities (wherein the denomination and local church both constitute a modality and the missionary band or mission agency a sodality). According to Winter, it is sodalities that have historically broken through to take the gospel to new frontiers and that have often been the source of renewal within the church. Winter also argues that where sodalities were absent, the church has often lapsed into a dangerous nominalism.[3]

---

[2] Linde J. Weber, *Mission Handbook: US and Canadian Protestant Ministries Overseas*, 21st ed. (Wheaton, IL: EMIS, 2010), 52.

[3] Ralph Winter, "Two Structures of God's Redemptive Mission," *Missiology* 2, no. 1 (1974): 131.

Winter's purpose in making this distinction was to guard the church's missionary mandate by distinguishing between the purpose and function of the missions organization and that of the local church or denomination. Central to this distinction was Winter's belief that church structures (modalities) were too inclusive and democratic for sustained mission to the unreached.[4]

According to these designations, "a modality is a structured fellowship in which there is no distinction of sex or age."[5] That is to say, participation is open to all comers. A sodality, on the other hand, restricts participation based on an adult second decision beyond modality membership. Winter says, "in this use of these terms, both the denomination and the local congregation are modalities, while a mission agency or local men's club are sodalities."[6] Thus, a sodality can be understood as a more specific structure in function that moves beyond the broader structure and function of the local church. Sodalities by definition have a more limited participation and limited scope. For Winter, the primary criterion regarding sodalities is that of a second-level commitment.[7] Also, sodalities tend to be task oriented while modalities are more people oriented.[8]

It is important to note also that Winter believed that modalities and sodalities together form the fabric of the *ecclesia* of the New Testament. He therefore resists any efforts to make one

---

[4] Ralph Winter, "Churches Need Missions Because Modalities Need Sodalities," *Evangelical Missions Quarterly* (1971): 198–99; Winter, "Two Structures of God's Redemptive Mission," 135; Mark I. Fields, "Contours of Local Congregation-Based Mission in the Vineyard Movement, 1982 to 2007," PhD diss., Fuller Theological Seminary, Pasadena, CA, 2011, 49–54.

[5] Winter, "Two Structures of God's Redemptive Mission," 127.

[6] Ibid.

[7] Ibid., 123; Bruce K. Camp, "A Theological Examination of the Two-Structure Theory," *Missiology* 23, no. 2 (1995): 199; Joe L. Wallis, "Church Ministry and the Free Rider Problem: Religious Liberty and Disestablishment," *The American Journal of Economics and Sociology* 50, no. 2 (1991): 187.

[8] Darrell Guder, *The Continuing Conversion of the Church* (Grand Rapids, MI: Eerdmans, 2000), 182–83.

structure more normative—or "more church"—than the other, as is implied in the distinction between "church" and "parachurch."[9] He asks, "Why not call churches para-missions?"[10] Winter intends this to mean that neither can be properly understood apart from the other. "The two are indeed interdependent and the evidences of history do not allow us to understand either of them as complete without the other."[11] In fact, one of Winter's concerns regarding modalities and sodalities lies in the Protestant tendency to foster a "schism" between these two structures.[12] Winter's understanding of the relationship between modalities and sodalities, between churches and mission bands, can be seen in the idea that sodalities "nourish" modalities and thereby breathe life into what otherwise tends toward nominalism due to its broadly inclusive nature.[13]

Following these definitions, Winter argues on historical grounds that modalities and sodalities defined the diocesan and monastic movements up through the Middle Ages, noting that monastic sodalities functioned as a renewing force for the diocesan modality. Winter also argues that early Protestants lost sight of the necessity of sodalities, with Luther explicitly rejecting the idea. Protestantism recovered the importance of sodalities, though only as it rediscovered its missions mandate through individuals such as William Carey.[14] The key to understanding Winter's proposal is that "the New Testament is trying to show us *how to borrow effective patterns.*"[15] By this he means that early Christians borrowed patterns from the surrounding culture, whether Jewish or pagan, and gave them new meaning and significance. What is

---

[9] Ralph Winter, "Protestant Mission Societies: The American Experience," *Missiology* 7, no. 2 (1979): 143.

[10] Ibid.

[11] Ibid., 144.

[12] Ibid., 143.

[13] Winter, "Two Structures of God's Redemptive Mission," 127; Wallis, "Church Ministry and the Free Rider Problem," 186–87.

[14] Winter, "Two Structures of God's Redemptive Mission," 132.

[15] Ibid., 123.

required then is faithfulness to the functions of these patterns or structures, but not necessarily to the forms themselves.[16]

EVALUATING THE MODALITY-SODALITY DISTINCTION

C. Peter Wagner says that while Winter was not the first to observe the modality-sodality distinction, his "unique contribution has been to legitimize the two structures biblically, and to show how they are both needed for God's purposes in the world to be carried out effectively."[17] Whether Wagner is correct and Winter has successfully accomplished this is a matter of some debate.[18]

As Bruce Camp has observed, Roland Allen, Harry Boer, and George Peters are among those who deny that the concept of missions agencies (sodalities) finds support in scripture.[19] Boer, for example, calls them a "blessed abnormality," and Peters argues that the question is not clear enough in scripture to be dogmatic.[20] Camp himself takes issue with the idea that the church and missionary band should both be considered equal expressions of the universal church.[21] In defense, he points out that Paul's missionary bands were never called the "church."[22] He also objects to the notion of limiting participation in sodalities, saying that to

---

[16] Camp, "A Theological Examination of the Two-Structure Theory," 201.

[17] C. Peter Wagner, *Church Growth and the Whole Gospel: A Biblical Mandate* (San Francisco: Harper Row, 1981), 186.

[18] Camp, "A Theological Examination of the Two-Structure Theory"; Fields, "Contours of Local Congregation-Based Mission in the Vineyard Movement," 55–56.

[19] Camp, "A Theological Examination of the Two-Structure Theory," 197.

[20] Ibid., 197–98; Harry R. Boer, *Pentecost and Mission* (Grand Rapids, MI: Eerdmans, 1964), 214; George W. Peters, *A Biblical Theology of Missions* (Chicago: Moody, 1972), 224.

[21] Camp, "A Theological Examination of the Two-Structure Theory," 201.

[22] Ibid.

do so "violates both scriptural teaching (1 Cor. 12:21) and early church practice (Acts 1—2)."[23]

To resolve these questions, some discussion of the biblical marks of the church is needed in order to understand more precisely those things that define the church and those that define the mission band. As Van Zanen has said, much of the disagreement between Winter and Camp likely reflects differing ecclesiologies.[24] Unfortunately, neither Winter nor Camp prove very helpful because neither identifies the marks of the universal church that he believes should be reflected in local churches or in mission bands.

Other critics of the modality-sodality distinction fear that the two-structure system minimizes or negates the obligation of local churches to be involved in mission. Orlando Costas, for example, claims that "there is no ground in the New Testament for a concept of mission apart from the church, just as there is no concept of the church apart from mission."[25] This raises the important question as to whether or not local churches can and should do missions or if that task should be relegated to sodality-type organizations. Before addressing that, it is helpful to determine whether the two-structure system can be defended biblically.

Because Winter's argument is primarily historical (not exegetical, as Wagner suggested), it would be easy to assume that the biblical basis is thin. Fortunately, several others have picked up the argument where Winter left off and have shown that a solid scriptural case can be made. Paramount is Acts 13:2, which says, "While they were ministering to the Lord and fasting, the Holy Spirit said, 'Set apart for Me Barnabas and Saul for the work to which I have called them.'" Edward Murphy refers to this verse and the launching of missionary sodalities using Winston

---

[23] Ibid., 203.

[24] Stephen J. Van Zanen, "Local Churches in Global Missions: Developing a Strategic Plan to Help Christian Reformed Churches to Engage in International Missions," DMin project, Trinity International University, Deerfield, IL, 1991, 14–17.

[25] Orlando Costas, *The Church and Its Mission: A Shattering Critique from the Third World* (Wheaton, IL: Tyndale House, 1974), 168.

Churchill's famous phrase, "a hinge of history."[26] Importantly, this passage is portrayed by Luke as partial fulfillment of the mandate of Acts 1:8.[27] In reference to this passage, given the context of prayer and fasting and the consequent move of the Spirit, Arthur Glasser notes, "From this, we cannot but conclude that both the congregational parish structure and the mobile missionary band are equally valid in God's sight."[28] Indeed, it takes considerable effort to interpret the words "set apart" as anything other than a narrower, task-oriented role unfolding for the missionary band of Barnabas and Saul. Furthermore, this role can be equated with what today is referred to as cross-cultural mission.[29] Beyond this, Murphy has helpfully shown that similar missionary (sodality) structures that functioned differently from church structures soon dominated in carrying out the Great Commission in the remaining chapters of Acts (13:13; 15:22–34; 15:37–39; 15:40;16:1–9; 16:10; 18:2–23; 19; 20:4).[30]

What, though, of the claim that the mission band was born out of church negligence? Costas, arguing along these lines, claims that the formation of missionary sodalities represents only the permissive will of God (not the perfect will), as well as the failure of modalities to be faithful to their calling. Costas fears that the modality-sodality paradigm unbiblically separates church from

---

[26] Edward Murphy, "The Missionary Society as an Apostolic Team," *Practical Anthropology* 4, no. 1 (1976): 113.

[27] Craig Keener, *Acts: An Exegetical Commentary*, vol. 2 (Grand Rapids, MI: Baker Academic, 2013), Kindle edition, under Acts 13:2–3, "The Commission."

[28] Arthur Glasser, "The Apostle Paul and the Missionary Task," in *Perspectives on the World Christian Movement: A Reader*, rev. ed., ed. Ralph Winter and Stephen Hawthorne, A-121–33 (Pasadena, CA: William Carey Library, 1992), A-127–28.

[29] F. F. Bruce, *The Book of the Acts*, New International Commentary on the New Testament (Grand Rapids, MI: Eerdmans, 1988), 246, Accordance electronic ed.; Glasser, "The Apostle Paul and the Missionary Task," A-128; Timothy Tennent, *Invitation to World Missions* (Grand Rapids, MI: Kregel, 2010), 454.

[30] Murphy, "The Missionary Society as an Apostolic Team," 113.

mission.[31] In this, he appears to have overlooked the symbiotic relationship that Winter upheld between modalities and sodalities. Winter never suggests that they can function apart from each other. On the contrary, Winter is quite clear: "It is our attempt here to help church leaders and others to understand the legitimacy of both structures, and the necessity for both structures not only to exist but to work together harmoniously for the fulfillment of the Great Commission."[32] To say that both structures work together harmoniously regarding the Great Commission implies that mission is the prerogative of both modalities and sodalities, but perhaps in different ways. I elaborate more on that below. Nothing, though, in Acts 13:2 implies anything other than that the formation of a mission sodality was by design on the part of God. The church prayed, the Spirit moved, and a new structure for cross-cultural witness was born. One looks to the text in vain for any indication that God was less than pleased with this development.

That said, I agree with Camp on the problematic claim by Winter that both modalities and sodalities are equal expression of the universal church. Without a doubt the modality-sodality structure becomes especially complex at the point of clarifying scripturally the nature of the church and that of the mission band and how they differ. If a sodality, for example, is defined as "task oriented," as Winter says, and that task relates solely to cross-cultural frontier mission, how can Winter claim that both structures are equally "the church?" A church may not do less than mission, but surely it does more.

Some resolution to this tension may be found by looking more closely at Winter's argument. Winter's desire to hold together modalities and sodalities as the fabric of the *ecclesia* constitutes the context for his asking why a parachurch should be less church than a local church. The main issue then, for Winter, is interdependence, and only secondarily whether one structure is more "church" than the other. Winter's main interest, in other words,

---

[31] Costas, "The Church and Its Mission," 169.
[32] Winter, "Two Structures of God's Redemptive Mission," 136.

lies directly in the passage Camp cites in 1 Corinthians 12:21. The body of Christ needs all of its many parts to function properly.

Winter himself seems to define modalities and sodalities differently in terms of their "church-ness" in his well-known E-0 to E-3 evangelism paradigm. Here he rightfully points out that local churches are best suited for E-0 to E-1 evangelism because of cultural proximity. But E-2 and E-3 evangelism require a degree of specialization and commitment that local congregations often lack and of which they are perhaps incapable.[33] Mission bands, because they are not bound to be everything the local church must be, are free to focus on the most urgent task of E-2 and E-3 evangelism and not become bogged down in the many other things that occupy the life of the local church.[34] Given Winter's argument here, it seems wholly unnecessary to the legitimacy of Winter's modality-sodality structure to claim that both the local church and mission band are equal expressions of the universal church. Rather, it is sufficient simply to note that the New Testament supports the idea that cross-cultural mission requires a more specifically mission-oriented structure than what one finds in the local church, as illustrated in the sending of Barnabas and Saul in Acts 13. This does not mean that local churches are excused from the Great Commission, for the church at Antioch plays a vital part, as do many other local congregations with which Paul is associated. Church and mission are inextricably connected.[35]

---

[33] Ralph Winter, "The New Macedonia: A Revolutionary New Era in Mission Begins," in *Perspectives on the World Christian Movement: A Reader*, ed. Ralph D. Winter and Stephen C. Hawthorne, B-157–75 (Pasadena, CA: William Carey Library, 1992), B-169. This scale compares the cultural distances that must be crossed in evangelistic effort and locates them along a spectrum that takes note of greater levels of specialization needed, from same culture (E-0, E-1), to different culture (E-2), and finally to very different culture (E-3).

[34] Ibid.

[35] Timothy C. Carriker, "Missiological Hermeneutic and Pauline Apocalyptic Eschatology," in *The Good News of the Coming Kingdom*, ed. Charles Van Engen, Dean S. Gilliland, and Paul Pierson (Eugene, OR: Wipf and Stock, 1993), 45; Christopher Little, *Mission in the Way of Paul: Biblical Mission for the Church in the 21st Century* (New York:

In Antioch it was that church's fasting and praying that led to the missionary call and sending of Saul and Barnabas in the first place. The church at Antioch thus plays a very different role in mission, though no less important, than those who make up the sodality and are the ones sent to engage in the cross-cultural, church-planting task.

Some may object to this on the grounds that missionaries who go to unreached peoples *are* the local church in that area, at least until an indigenous church is established. Perhaps so. But the very notion of indigeneity requires that missionaries step out of central roles as soon as possible.[36] To the extent that the missionary band considers itself the local church, then it ought to do and be all that a biblical local church should do and be. That would include at least the four marks of the church described by Charles Van Engen in his work *God's Missionary People: Rethinking the Purpose of the Local Church*. He describes the "many-sided" nature of the local church according to the New Testament that includes *koinonia* (community), *kerygma* (proclamation), *diakonia* (service), and *martyria* (witness).[37] It is my contention that the missionary band (sodality) should work to disciple in all of these areas but has no mandate to embody all of these, especially long term. To the extent that it does, the forward momentum of missions grinds to a halt. The goal of the mission band is not ultimately to be the church, but to foster the emergence of an indigenous local congregation. Once this happens, the missionary band ought to either move on or shift its focus to helping foster the emergence of indigenous missions movements. This relates precisely to the value in the modality-sodality distinction. Winter himself seems to recognize this:

Peter Lang, 2005), 119–30; Craig Ott and Stephen J. Strauss, *Encountering Theology of Mission* (Grand Rapids, MI: Baker Academic, 2010), 192–93.

[36] Ott and Strauss, *Encountering Theology of Mission*, 115.

[37] Charles Van Engen, *God's Missionary People: Rethinking the Purpose of the Local Church* (Grand Rapids, MI: Baker Academic, 1991), 89.

It is a tragic perversion of Jesus' strategy if we continue to send missionaries to do the job that local Christians can do better. There is no excuse for a missionary in the pulpit when a national can do the job better. There is no excuse for a missionary to be doing evangelism on an E-3 basis, at an E-3 distance from people, where there are local Christians who are effectively winning the same people as part of their E-1 sphere.[38]

MODALITIES, SODALITIES, AND INDIGENOUS MISSION MOVEMENTS

While affirming compassionate mission, or what Winter refers to as mission "service agencies" that engage in "medical work, orphan work, or radio work, or whatever,"[39] he also argues that these "must be aware of, and concerned about, the interface between that activity and the church-planting function."[40] This interface is what was absent in the story I shared at the beginning of this chapter and what I hope to recover by the conclusion. Winter argues that there must be by mission agencies an intentional effort to plant mission sodalities, by which Winter means non-Western missionary efforts. He points out: "The concept of 'the indigenous church' is widely emphasized today. But how much do we hear about the indigenous mission agency? The task of church planting is fairly well known. But what about the art and science of mission planting?"[41] The distinction between modalities and sodalities for Winter was not only to advance missions among the unreached, but also to see the efforts of missions-sending nations lead to indigenous missionary movements. Winter illustrates this point with the following scenario:

---

[38] Winter, "The New Macedonia," B-164.
[39] Winter, "Two Structures of God's Redemptive Mission," 135.
[40] Ibid.
[41] Winter, "Churches Need Mission Because Modalities Need Sodalities," 193.

Suppose a mission agency goes to Nigeria and establishes fifty indigenous churches among the Yoruba, and those churches then plant even more Yoruba churches. In that case, the initial "missiological breakthrough" would be called mission while the further church planting expansion by the Yoruba churches would be considered evangelism. But if now the Yoruba send missionaries to break through to a cultural group where there is not yet an indigenous church movement, then you can say that the Yoruba believers are not only involved in ordinary evangelism but also in cross-cultural work, in the creation of a new worshipping tradition of Jesus followers. Such efforts classify as a[sic] mission activities.

We can further say that if the initial mission agency is not involved in that further outreach but is content to continue to work with the Yoruba church, then it ceases to be a mission agency but becomes merely what could be called a "foreign evangelism" agency.[42]

Orlando Costas has argued, regarding indigenous sodalities, that "even when they exist apart from modalities, [they] cannot be fabricated from the outside. They emerge naturally and spontaneously as part of concrete historical situations."[43] I agree but would add that the way in which missionaries go about their work, particularly in the area of compassion, can either help or hinder the emergence of indigenous churches and missions movements.

SECOND STAGE MISSIONS

In establishing a means by which to evaluate Protestant mission structures or sodalities such as mission agencies and parachurch organizations, Winter proposes five general questions as a rubric. Of those, the fifth question is particularly relevant for our present discussion. It asks, "For what function is the agency designed?"

---

[42] Ralph Winter, "From Mission to Evangelism to Mission," *International Journal of Frontier Missions* 19, no. 4 (2002): 7.
[43] Costas, "The Church and Its Mission," 172.

In this "agency" refers to the sodality, whether a mission agency or missionary band. In response, Winter notes that there are First Stage Missions, Second Stage Missions, and Consolidation Missions. Winter only clarifies the meaning of the first two of these, stating that First Stage Missions consists in crossing geographic borders to plant the church where it does not exist. Second Stage Missions refers to mission partnerships that ideally strengthen the capacity of established churches through "interchurch aid."[44] This aid or partnership should endeavor especially to strengthen the capacity of indigenous churches toward their own missionary enterprises.[45] Lesslie Newbigin has argued similarly in distinguishing between "fraternal workers," or those who are merely sent from one church to another, and those rightly called "missionaries," who either directly work to plant the church where no Christian witness is present or who "assist another church in its specifically missionary tasks."[46] Winter argues that compassionate service, or social concern, bridges First Stage Missions and Second Stage Missions.

As it concerns the expression of compassion in cross-cultural work, this notion of both modalities and sodalities, along with Second Stage Missions, becomes vital. Missionaries who go to work with other national churches in the area of compassionate ministry must understand their role as not only strengthening the capacity of local churches, but also of doing so with a specific mission agenda in mind. That agenda should be to foster cross-cultural mission bands (sodalities) among the mission-receiving churches (modalities). The ultimate goal in Second Stage Missions, if it is to remain mission, must be to see mission-receiving churches become mission-sending churches. Compassion constitutes a key link in achieving this.

The ability to accomplish this will depend on the manner in which Second Stage Missions proceeds and the ways in which

---

[44] Ralph Winter, "Protestant Missions Societies: The American Experience," *Missiology* 7, no. 2 (1979): 173.

[45] Ibid.

[46] Lesslie Newbigin, "The Future of Missions and Missionaries," *Review and Expositor* 74, no. 2 (1977): 216.

missionaries engage in compassionate work. If missionaries act as the primary "doers" of compassion, then often the result is that local congregations become robbed of their role as salt and light in the community (Mt 5:13–14). It is instructive in this regard to consider Acts 11 and the pattern we find there regarding the ministry of Barnabas and Saul at Antioch. In Acts 11:26 we read that Barnabas and Saul spend a whole year teaching the church. It is also noteworthy that Barnabas and Saul in this passage function as a sodality even before they are sent out in Acts 13. Barnabas was sent from the more mature church in Jerusalem to Antioch, and in turn he went to Tarsus to find Saul. Thus, they were not the local church in Antioch but an extension of the church in Jerusalem sent to aid a fledgling congregation and help it mature. A key point is that Barnabas and Saul were not supposed to be the local church in Antioch; they were there to equip that church. It is also noteworthy that between chapters 11 and 13 of Acts, the Antioch church moves from being a mission-receiving church to becoming a mission-sending church. When their work is finished at Antioch, Barnabas and Saul are called by the Holy Spirit and commissioned by the church to continue moving on toward unreached areas (13:2–3).

What is particularly important in the way Luke has presented the story in Acts 11 is that the teaching/equipping ministry of Barnabas and Saul (11:26) leads directly to the indigenous compassionate response of the local church. In 11:27 we read that a prophet arrives in Antioch proclaiming a coming famine. Acts 11:29 states, "And in the proportion that any of the disciples had means, each of them determined to send a contribution for the relief of the brethren living in Judea." It was not Barnabas and Saul who spearheaded the response; the disciples determined according to their own means how to respond. In fact, this appears to be a consistent pattern in the New Testament, as we read something strikingly similar in 2 Corinthians 8:3, which says of the Macedonian church that "according to their ability, and beyond their ability they gave of their own accord." In both cases the emphasis is on the indigenous compassionate response of the local church to give freely and voluntarily according to its means.

Christopher Little has warned that "when the church engaged in cross-cultural mission ignores Pauline orthopraxy, especially in relation to the proper use of finances, it places unnecessary obstacles in the path of the *missio Dei*."[47] Acts 11 examines precisely this question in relation to compassionate mission. If Barnabas and Saul were part of many missions organizations today, one wonders if any room at all would be given for an indigenous response. It seems to me that the modern tendency would be to start a project— perhaps "The Judean Famine Fund"—and then commission foreign missionaries to head it up, print up some nice JFF tee-shirts, and launch a fundraising campaign with a catchy logo among supporting churches. But such actions become highly problematic precisely because they fundamentally confuse the role of the sodality, in this case the missions band or agency, with that of the local church, the modality. Arguably, this same problem lies at the center of the story I shared in the beginning. This, in fact, underscores the need for Winter's two-structure approach. What ultimately gets neglected in the process of missionaries doing compassion that should be (and could be) done by local believers is the important biblical concept of solidarity. In what follows I explain this concept further to show that solidarity is the key to fostering local expressions of missions—or, indigenous sodalities.

SOLIDARITY IN THE PAULINE EPISTLES

David Horrell, in his book *Solidarity and Difference*, has argued that Pauline ethics consists of two foundational "metanorms," namely, corporate solidarity in Christ regarding the Christian community, and other-regard, or the valuation of those who are socially or culturally different, modeled on Christ's own selfless compassion. Corporate solidarity here focuses on the formation of moral virtue among the believing community, and thereby

---

[47] Little, *Mission in the Way of Paul*, 3.

on an observable distinction between the church and the world. Solidarity therefore refers essentially to oneness in Christ. This oneness, though, as Horrell's title suggests, does not obliterate differences within the community, but it fosters mutual love and concern for one another. That is, differences are not just allowed for but celebrated, so long as they do not impinge upon the solidarity of the community.

According to Horrell, Paul's ethics is concerned not so much with providing specific ethical instructions, though those are present, but rather with declaring the values necessary for the formation of a moral community.[48] The *summum bonum* for Paul is that which contributes to the flourishing of the community and avoids the creation of divisions. This intra-communitarian ethic, however, is not limited to the church but overflows from the church into the world, as believers seek to "do good to all people, but especially to those who are of the household of faith" (Gal 6:10).[49] Furthermore, Paul understands the achievement of this solidarity to depend on the rites of baptism and the Lord's Supper, on the important use of familial language among believers (especially "brothers"), and through the imagery of the church as the body of Christ.[50]

Regarding baptism, Horrell notes that Paul refers to the baptism of believers as incorporation into Christ. Referring especially to 1 Corinthians 12:13 and Galatians 3:26, Horrell notes the emphasis in both passages on baptism, resulting in a profound revaluation of various ethno-social distinctions that existed prior to baptism. For example, in 1 Corinthians 12:13, Paul says, "For by one Spirit we were all baptized into one body, whether Jews or Greeks, whether slaves or free, and we were all made to drink of one Spirit." In Galatians 3:26–29, Paul states the issue even more strongly, declaring: "For you are all sons of God through faith in Christ Jesus. For all of you who were baptized into Christ have

---

[48] David Horrell, *Solidarity and Difference: A Contemporary Reading of Paul's Ethics*, 2nd ed. (London: Bloomsbury, 2015), Kindle edition, chap. 9.1.1.

[49] Ibid., chaps. 4.5 and 9.

[50] Ibid., chap. 4.

clothed yourselves with Christ. There is neither Jew nor Greek, there is neither slave nor free man, there is neither male nor female; for you are all one in Christ Jesus." Thus the rite of baptism "constructs a new form of human solidarity which transcends the lines of previous distinctions."[51]

The Lord's Supper, according to Horrell, also constitutes another important Pauline understanding of corporate solidarity. "While baptism may be defined as a rite of initiation concerned with boundary-crossing and status transformation, the Lord's supper is clearly a ceremony, practiced regularly, which confirms and celebrates the status and identity of community members."[52] Furthermore, the Lord's Supper functions to "confirm and consolidate" the solidarity of oneness in Christ. As Horrell observes, it is important also to note that the primary criticism Paul has of the Corinthians relates to their fractious quarrelling that stands in direct violation of this supreme value of corporate solidarity, as a violation of having been made one body in Christ.[53]

Paul's use of *adelphoi* (or brothers) to refer to fellow believers in several texts is intended "to impress an ethical demand" (especially Rom 14:10–21; 1 Cor 6:5–8; 1 Cor 8:11–12).[54] The designation functions for Paul not merely as a nicety, but as a constant reminder that believers are in a real sense incorporated into a new family. Paul uses this term or some form of it over seventy-five times in his letters, and it is his preferred term for fellow believers. Furthermore, as James Thompson points out, Paul's use of *adelphoi* could refer to men, women, and children, and as such represented a highly inclusive concept of family that crossed both gender and social stratifications in a way that was unknown in that day.[55] Paul's preference for *adelphoi* and his efforts to engender a sense of family belonging and responsibility among

---

[51] Ibid., chap. 4.1.
[52] Ibid., 4.1.2.
[53] Ibid.
[54] Ibid. 4.2.
[55] James W. Thompson, *The Church according to Paul: Rediscovering the Community Conformed to Christ* (Grand Rapids, MI: Baker Academic, 2014), 44.

believers is buttressed by his use of "one another." This includes the instructions to be "devoted to one another" and "give preference to one another" (Rom 12:10), to be "of the same mind with one another" (Rom 12:16), to "love one another" (Rom 13:8), to "build one another up" (Rom 14:19), to "accept one another" (Rom 15:7), and so on.[56] As Thompson says, "Paul's frequent use of 'one another' reflects the family relationship and the solidarity of the community."[57] The significance of this is that those in Christ are to understand their relationship to one another according to obligations such as love and support that are characteristic of obligations toward the members of one's own family.

> The reason why believers should show generous concern for one another is precisely because the other is an *adelphos* and as such belongs with them to the same family group. The mutual love that should characterize the congregations is the love of siblings, a *philadelphia* (Rom 12:10; 1 Thess 4:9). This solidarity, we should note, is explicitly seen to reach beyond the confines of the local congregation to encompass believers everywhere, who also share this family identity (1 Thess 4:10).[58]

Regarding the church as the body of Christ, Horrell observes that "there are two significant texts where Paul presents the notion of the community as a body to engender the idea of a diversity-in-unity, or solidarity and difference: Rom 12.4–8 and 1 Cor 12.12–31."[59] Paul's primary point in these references is to foster mutual care and support among the members of local churches and to regard one another as equally valuable.

Horrell's main point is that, for Paul, the concept of solidarity functions as the key to community formation, and that Paul's ethics is especially concerned with this above all else. The people of

---

[56] Ibid.
[57] Ibid.
[58] Horrell, *Solidarity and Difference*, chap. 4.2.
[59] Ibid., chap. 4.4.

God are to be a transformed people, living in harmonious unity with one another and overcoming former social divisions. This is furthermore meant to stand as a testimony to their participation in Christ. "The basis for solidarity, for the construction of community, as the central Christian rituals show, is found in Paul's Christology: as believers make the story of Christ their own, participating in his death and new life, so they leave behind the old world, and become members of one body, in Christ."[60]

Though much of Paul's ethics is devoted to community formation, he also speaks frequently about the broader role of the church in the community. Furthermore, the nature of concern for others in the larger community stems from the essential character of the community, modeled on the life of Christ who gave himself as a ransom for all. In the same way, the Christian community is to be "for all" in a number of compassionate ways. This compassionate stance of the church should not be conceived as a means to an end, even though there are missional implications that follow, most important the removal of hindrances to gospel proclamation.[61] Rather, the responsibility to be "for others" is a gospel-worthy pursuit in its own right.

A number of important passages in Paul provide a basis for the movement of Christian compassion from the community of faith to the outside world. Among these are three passages in 1 Thessalonians (3:12; 4:12; 5:15). The first, 1 Thessalonians 3:12, states, "May the Lord cause you to increase and abound in love for one another, and *for all people*, just as we also do for you" (emphasis added). Richard Hays rightly points out that this represents not a command by Paul but rather a prayer.[62] Even so, it shows clearly that Paul expected the Thessalonian church to embody agape for one another and for all those whom its members encountered in everyday life. A few chapters later Paul

---

[60] Ibid., chap. 4, "Conclusion."
[61] Ibid., chap. 8.4.
[62] Richard Hays, *The Moral Vision of the New Testament: A Contemporary Introduction to New Testament Ethics* (New York: Harper One, 1996), 22.

expresses a nearly identical idea in more of a command form. In 1 Thessalonians 5:15 he instructs, "See that no one repays another with evil for evil, but always seek after that which is good for one another *and for all people*" (emphasis added). Paul employs strikingly similar language in Galatians 6:10, wherein he instructs "while we have opportunity, let us do good *to all people*, and especially to those who are of the household of the faith" (emphasis added). Other Pauline texts that present a variation on this theme include Philippians 4:8, Romans 12:14–21, and 2 Corinthians 8:21. In each of these passages Paul expresses in various ways a concern for the way in which local believers are perceived by the larger community. Their witness in the community is to be both in word and deed, and there is an inherent expectation that outsiders will take notice. The practice of solidarity within the faith community was to result in radically transformed lives that stood apart from the world and caused believers to "shine like stars in the universe" (Phil 2:15).[63]

SOLIDARITY AND THE SPIRIT

Lesslie Newbigin has said that "the agent of mission is the Holy Spirit who is the living presence of the Kingdom in foretaste."[64] The primary function in both Luke-Acts and in Paul regarding the notion of solidarity is the cultivation of the presence of the Holy Spirit among the people of God. Solidarity leads to holiness, that is, to the people of God being "a people set apart." It is the Spirit's dynamic presence and empowerment that Luke especially demonstrates to be the primary agent in missions.

Whereas it is Paul's Christology that primarily forms the theological basis for believers' oneness in Christ (solidarity), it is his pneumatology that serves especially as the basis for bringing about this reality since the Spirit functions "primarily in the role of motivator and enabler of conduct" as it relates to

---

[63] Horrell, *Solidarity and Difference*, chap. 8.4.
[64] Newbigin, "The Future of Missions and Missionaries," 218.

Christian ethics.[65] When Paul talks about the oneness of believers in Christ (solidarity), he has in mind the cultivation of the Spirit's presences as the ultimate goal. Solidarity is about more than merely treating one another well. Rather, the entire concept is rooted in holiness, and it is holiness that generates the kind of community that makes room for the operation and dynamic presence of the Spirit.

Paul's ethics is especially concerned with not individual transformation, as we are so inclined to conceive of spiritual formation in the West, but corporately and for molding of the gathered saints to conform to Christ as a body and not merely as a collection of individuals.[66] Similarly, as Thompson has explained, Paul's goal in ministry "is a *community* that will be his boast at the day of Christ (2 Cor. 1:14; Phil. 2:16; 1 Thess. 2:19; cf. 2 Cor. 11:3)."[67] Throughout his letters Paul describes his labors as related to primarily the formation of communities whose spiritual progress continues until Christ's coming and who are increasingly conformed to the image of Christ (Rom 8:29; 1 Cor 15:49; 2 Cor 3:18). Furthermore, this community-oriented spiritual formation is a function of the Holy Spirit. Again, as Paul says, "For by one Spirit we were all baptized into one body, whether Jews or Greeks, whether slaves or free, and we were all made to drink of one Spirit" (1 Cor 12:13). Paul's consistent emphasis on the transformation of believers by the Spirit puts the onus on the work of the Spirit among the churches, and not on the will of the individual. "If by the Spirit you are putting to death the deeds of the body, you will live" (Rom 8:13). Thus, Thompson is right in declaring that "ethical transformation is a gift of the Spirit."[68]

It is significant to observe in the book of Acts that there is a dual emphasis both on the role of the Spirit regarding solidarity among the members of the fledgling Jesus movement and concerning the

---

[65] Horrell, *Solidarity and Difference,* "*Solidarity and Difference,* Ten Years On, II."
[66] Thompson, *The Church according to Paul,* 104.
[67] Ibid.
[68] Ibid., 124.

unfolding missionary impulse of church. We see this in that the disciples in Acts are described as being "with one mind" (1:14; 2:46), which certainly bears resemblance to the Pauline notion of solidarity outlined above. But the clearest show of solidarity appears in Acts 4:32–35:

> And the congregation of those who believed were of one heart and soul; and not one of them claimed that anything belonging to him was his own, but all things were common property to them. And with great power the apostles were giving testimony to the resurrection of the Lord Jesus, and abundant grace was upon them all. For there was not a needy person among them, for all who were owners of land or houses would sell them and bring the proceeds of the sales and lay them at the apostles' feet, and they would be distributed to each as any had need.

Later, Ananias and Sapphira are presented as the repudiation of this solidarity, and as such are accused of having "lied to the Holy Spirit" (5:3), who, as we have argued, provides the motivation and power that makes solidarity possible. Thus, not only does the Ananias and Sapphira incident represent a breakdown in solidarity, but also a hindrance to the working of the Holy Spirit within the community. The grievousness of their sins stands on the detrimental nature their actions have toward the whole community and the interference with the vital notion of corporate solidarity, much like in the story of Achan in Joshua 7.

It is not, therefore, incidental to the themes of Luke-Acts that when we come to Acts 13 and the sending of Barnabas and Saul, the context of this sending is the corporate worship of the church. "While they were praying and fasting, the Holy Spirit said, 'Set apart for Me Barnabas and Saul for the work to which I have called them'" (Acts 13:2). Their expression of solidarity and the resulting *koinonia* in which they participate are vital to the proper functioning of the church according to the missional mandate of Acts 1:8. We see this idea of solidarity and community connected to the presence of the Spirit and missions explicitly declared in Acts 9:31: "So the church throughout all Judea and Galilee and Samaria enjoyed peace, being built up; and going on in the fear of the Lord and in the comfort of the Holy Spirit, it continued to increase."

The great challenge in modern missions, in my view, concerns the need for Western missionaries increasingly to step into the background and allow local churches to flourish both in solidarity with one another and in loving their neighbors in the way that Paul envisioned. This means, if we return to Acts 11 as our paradigm, that we follow the model of Barnabas and Saul and disciple for compassion rather than primarily engaging in direct acts of compassion ourselves within the context of missions. For when outsiders function as the primary doers, this interrupts the vital concept of solidarity in which believers show love for one another and concern for the broader needs of the community.

Absent this "metanorm" of Pauline ethics, the important biblical concept of *koinonia* mutates into what C. Peter Wagner calls *"koinonitis,"* that is, a church whose entire activity and attention becomes so inwardly focused that the church no longer functions as it was intended, as a radiant expression of the present and coming kingdom of God.[69] When missionaries engage in compassion in a way that robs local congregations of their role as salt and light in the community, the result will always be churches who have turned inward on themselves and whose missionary impulse is dampened. The remedy is to ensure that missionaries maintain a concern for Second Stage Missions, in which compassion is seen as an essential ingredient in the formation of local missionary sodalities. By stepping away from a central role in compassionate mission, and by instead focusing on teaching and equipping, cross-cultural workers can remove their self-imposed hindrances to the expression of solidarity between the members of local churches and between the churches and the communities

---

[69] C. Peter Wagner, *Your Church Can Be Healthy* (Nashville, TN: Abingdon, 1979), 78.

in which they reside. Because of the broad missional implications for local churches, a focus on discipling for compassion is not only the most compassionate thing that a missionary can do but also the most fruitful.

5

A Pentecostal Approach to Discipleship in Missions[1]

Between April and July of 1994, one of the worst genocides in recent history took place in the nation of Rwanda, where nearly one million Tutsi were slaughtered by their Hutu neighbors. Not only did this massacre take place in a country that was 90 percent Christian at the time of the killing but, alarmingly, *most* of the killings took place in church buildings or on church property.[2] At one Catholic parish over twenty thousand people were killed in just four days.[3] That is almost three times the number of people killed at the battle of Gettysburg during the US Civil War (7,863). The very places that people fled to for safety during the Rwandan crisis became the primary killing grounds. Importantly, in 1991, three years prior to the genocide, a Catholic bishop wrote and published a forty-page document warning of pending disaster.

---

[1] An earlier version of this chapter appeared as Jerry M. Ireland, "A Classical Pentecostal Approach to Discipleship in Missions," *Journal of Pentecostal Theology* 28 (2019): 243–66. Reprinted with permission.

[2] Emmanuel Katongole, *The Sacrifice of Africa: A Political Theology for Africa*, The Eerdmans Ekklesia Series (Grand Rapids, MI: Eerdmans, 2011), 8; Peter Celestine Safari, "Church, State, and the Rwandan Genocide," *Political Theology* 11, no. 6 (2010): 874. According to Safari, the breakdown in denominational affiliation was 62 percent Catholic, 10 percent Protestant, and 8.6 percent Seventh Day Adventist (874–75).

[3] Timothy Longman, *Christianity and Genocide in Rwanda* (Cambridge, UK: Cambridge University Press, 2010), 5.

Among his chief criticisms was that "although the majority of people of Rwanda had over decades converted to Christianity, most people failed to live Christian values."[4]

The reality of Rwanda forces us to ask how it is possible that a faith in which adherents are commanded by Jesus to love not only their neighbor, but also their enemy, could be at the very center of a genocide. The very notion boggles the mind. The bishop's unheeded warning seems to have hit on an important reality. The church's role in the Rwandan genocide demonstrates a deep disconnect between believing faith and obedient living. It points to a discipleship crisis. How else does one understand the fact that the killers "attended mass between the massacres"?[5] Despite over 120 years of missionary activity in Rwanda by the time the massacre occurred, Christians there failed to grasp a fundamental aspect of Christianity, namely, the idea that to follow Jesus means a radical reorientation of the self and a manifest concern for "otherness."[6] Of course, this same crisis of discipleship could readily be documented in the United States, in Europe, and in many other places around the globe. But my concern here relates to the question of compassionate missions, and whether or not our cross-cultural efforts in compassion are producing fruit that endures. My contention in this chapter is that compassionate missions must prioritize disciple making in order to plant churches that are dependent on the Spirit's power for their success. This emphasis on the Spirit's power has been inherent in classical Pentecostal missions from the beginning. But the drift lately toward a project-centered approach to compassion in missions threatens to undermine this crucial focus and thereby trade spiritual power for structural power.

---

[4] Safari, "Church, State, and the Rwandan Genocide," 883.
[5] Leon Saur, "From Kibeho to Medjugorjc: The Catholic Church and Ethno-Nationalist Movements and Regimes," in *Genocide in Rwanda: Complicity of the Churches?* ed. Carol Rittner, John K. Roth, and Wendy Whitworth (St. Paul, MN: Paragon House, 2004), 211–27.
[6] On missionary presence in Rwanda, see Phillip A. Cantrell, "'We Were a Chosen People': The East African Revival and Its Return to Post-Genocide Rwanda," *Church History* 83, no. 2 (2014): 425.

COMPASSION AND THE KINGDOM OF GOD

As noted in Chapter 1, Paul Pomerville argues that the concept of the kingdom of God functions as a central feature of Jesus's ministry, but that contrary to many evangelical approaches, the kingdom advances primarily through (1) preaching the gospel of the kingdom, and (2) charismatic manifestations of the Spirit, with the latter serving to attest to the veracity of the former.[7] This perspective stands very near to that of Roland Allen, who argues that miracles functioned as an important and inherent part of the apostle Paul's preaching.[8]

As Pomerville has observed, advocates of the broad sense of mission often emphasize the equal standing of the church's evangelistic and cultural mandates as the result of a kingdom rubric rooted in dispensational theology. Such perspectives, though, neglect the particular way in which the Third Person of the Trinity works uniquely through the church and denies "the very age of the Spirit itself."[9] Specifically, these approaches tend to minimize the way in which the Spirit works, namely, by indwelling the Christian community in miraculous power in accompanying gospel proclamation.[10] In this approach Pentecostalism offers a corrective to a Western cultural corruption of the gospel that moved away from the experiential aspects of the faith to a more rationalistic approach. Not only ecumenical movements but also evangelical treatments of the kingdom of God, such as the seminal work of George Eldon Ladd, have noticeably been lacking in emphasis on the Spirit's role as it concerns the kingdom.[11] This emphasis has found its way into some Pentecostal approaches to the church's mission, however.

---

[7] Paul Pomerville, *The Third Force in Missions* (1985; repr. Peabody, MA: Hendrickson, 2016), 223.
[8] Roland Allen, *Missionary Methods: St. Paul's or Ours?* (1962; repr. Grand Rapids, MI: Eerdmans, 2009), 42–48.
[9] Pomerville, *The Third Force in Missions*, xviii.
[10] Ibid., 97–105.
[11] Ibid.

Murray Dempster, for example, argues along these lines in asserting that the phrase "the time is fulfilled"—from Mark 1:14–15, in relation to Jesus's declaration about the kingdom of God—emphasizes the liberating aspect of the kingdom, especially where it concerns the neediest in society.[12] This suggestion seems quite strained, however, and appears to overlook the peripatetic nature of Jesus's ministry and the fact that the kingdom arrived when and where Jesus did.[13] It is the King that constitutes the central feature of the kingdom. And in the post-resurrection era of the church, the King is known through proclamation of the gospel and the power of the Spirit. This is quite evident in the Markan passage cited, in which the phrase "the time is fulfilled" is itself is sandwiched between explicit references to gospel proclamation and the need for repentance. Not only that, but the parallel passage to Mark 1:14–15 cited by Dempster (Matthew 4:12–16) explicitly links the movement of Jesus to the later disciples' movement toward the nations by referencing Isaiah's "Galilee of the nations" (*ethnos*). As Leon Morris says of this passage, "While Jesus did not mingle much with Gentiles, the salvation he came to bring was just as much for them as for the Jews."[14] The kingdom, then, has less to do with the social transformation of society (though that may be an indirect result) and more to do with the gathering of the nations at the *parousia*.

In addition, many who base their theology of social justice on the appearance of the kingdom overlook the relationship between the coming kingdom and the last days.[15] The presence of the already-but-not-yet kingdom signified for the first-century church that it was living in the end times, and this understanding

---

[12] Murray W. Dempster, "A Theology of the Kingdom—A Pentecostal Contribution," in *Mission as Transformation*, ed. Vinay Samuel and Chris Sugden (Eugene, OR: Wipf and Stock, 2011), 51.

[13] Samuel and Sugden, *Mission as Transformation*, 13.

[14] Leon Morris, *The Gospel according to Matthew*, Pillar New Testament Commentary, Accordance electronic ed. (Grand Rapids, MI: Eerdmans, 1992), 82.

[15] Pomerville, *The Third Force in Missions*, 228.

was grounded not in human approximations of the kingdom but in the giving of the Spirit as the down payment of the future to which God was leading his people (1 Cor 1:22). This is evident in Peter's Pentecost sermon, which he frames in the context of "these last days." As Craig Keener says, "Peter's 'last days' fits the expectation that the disciples had entered an interim era between the first and second comings of the Messiah . . . called to testify to the nations by the eschatological gift of the Spirit."[16] Any biblical understanding of the kingdom must be oriented, then, toward the end, to the second coming of Christ and thereby to an eschatological urgency to reach the lost among the nations. This was in fact a central feature of early Pentecostal missions.

Vinay Samuel and Chris Sugden, while rightly arguing for an integrated approach to the church's mission, argue for mission as transformation and reject any notion of priorities. For them, and for the holistic mission/mission-as-transformation movement as a whole, mission is something the church does in multiple directions, and all of these directions have equal value. They base this concept on an integrated understanding of the kingdom of God. While this model does not deny Jesus's concern for the nations as part of the *missio Dei*, neither does it make it explicit or in need of special attention.[17] Grant McClung also argues for an "integrated balanced agenda" for Pentecostal missions that operates along four dimensions in order to respond to contemporary challenges related to "an ominous technological revolution, environmental decay, the arms race in a new ethnic tribalism, international

---

[16] Craig Keener, *Acts: Introduction and 1:1—2:47* (Grand Rapids, MI: Baker Academic, 2012), 879. See also Veli-Matti Kärkkäinen, "The Pentecostal Understanding of Mission," in *Pentecostal Mission and Global Christianity*, ed. Wansuk Ma, Veli-Matti Kärkkäinen, and J. Kwabena Asamoah-Gyadu (Oxford, UK: Regnum, 2014), 27.

[17] Samuel and Sugden, *Mission as Transformation*, ix–xviii; Julie C. Ma and Wonsuk Ma, *Mission in the Spirit: Towards a Pentecostal/Charismatic Missiology* (Eugene, OR: Wipf and Stock, 2010), 6; Arthur McPhee, "The Missio Dei and the Transformation of the Church," *Vision* (Winnipeg, Man.) 2, no. 2 (2001).

indebtedness, urban deterioration, plagues, viruses, drugs, and the decline of the traditional family."[18]

The problem with all of these contemporary Pentecostal approaches to missions is that they have moved from a broad understanding of the kingdom of God that is widely agreed upon by scholars to a broad understanding of missions that overlooks the unique way in which scripture links the gospel of the kingdom and the role of the Spirit to the appearance of the kingdom. Such a move also ignores a vast body of literature that addresses the difference between the function and purpose of the local church and that of the missions band discussed in previous chapters. To correct this misunderstanding, I propose an understanding of the primary and secondary aspects of witness and attention to the modality-sodality distinction already described.

THE PRIMARY AND SECONDARY ASPECTS OF WITNESS

Important for understanding the church's task as it relates to compassion is the notion of witnesses found in Acts 1:8. Many within the holistic mission/mission-as-transformation movement tend to define witness broadly and give equal importance to the verbal and nonverbal aspects of witness.[19] Yet, the very notion of nonverbal witness is misleading to the extent that it implies that

---

[18] Grant McClung, "'Try to Get People Saved': Revisiting the Paradigm of Urgent Pentecostal Missiology," in *The Globalization of Pentecostalism: A Religion Made to Travel*, ed. Murray W. Dempster, Byron D. Klaus, and Douglas Petersen (Oxford, UK: Regnum, 1999).

[19] Ma and Ma, *Mission in the Spirit*, 278–80; Bryant Myers, *Walking with the Poor* (Maryknoll, NY: Orbis Books, 2011), 204–44. Even though Chris Wright argues for the "ultimacy" of evangelism, his definition of mission is broad and lacks room for the modality/sodality distinction I am arguing for here. Wright's argument that different people in the church function according to different priorities seems to ignore certain passages (such as 1 Pet 2:9) that suggest the church's entire orientation is toward gospel proclamation. The point here is not to deny many and various giftings within the church but to caution against abandoning priorities on that basis. Christopher J. H. Wright, *The Mission of God: Unlocking*

the verbal aspect might at times be optional. This is never the case. When Jesus told the disciples to wait for the coming of the Holy Spirit, who would empower them for global witness, the notion of witness must be understood, as Keener says, preeminently in a christological manner. That is, the content of their witness is the proclamation of the gospel story.[20] In fact, throughout Luke-Acts the primary emphasis regarding the church's witness centers on the proclamation of the gospel and its impact on individuals for salvation.[21] Support for this idea comes from Isaiah 43:9–12, which almost certainly informed the disciples' understanding of the word *witnesses*.[22]

> All the nations have gathered together
> So that the peoples may be assembled.
> Who among them can declare this
> And proclaim to us the former things?
> Let them present their witnesses that they may
>   be justified,
> Or let them hear and say, "It is true."
> "You are My witnesses," declares the LORD,
> "And My servant whom I have chosen,
> So that you may know and believe Me
> And understand that I am He.
> Before Me there was no God formed,
> And there will be none after Me.
> "I, even I, am the LORD,
> And there is no savior besides Me.
> "It is I who have declared and saved and
>   proclaimed,

---

the Bible's Grand Narrative (Downers Grove, IL: IVP Academic, 2006), 302–23.

[20] Keener, *Acts: Introduction and 1:1—2:47*, 696; James D. G. Dunn, *The Acts of the Apostles* (Grand Rapids, MI: Eerdmans, 1996), 11.

[21] See Acts 2:21; 4:12; 13:47–48; 16:30–31; 28:28. See also Walter Liefeld, *Interpreting the Book of Acts* (Grand Rapids, MI: Baker, 1995), 92–93.

[22] Keener, *Acts: Introduction and 1:1—2:47*, 692.

And there was no strange *god* among you;
So you are My witnesses," declares the LORD,
"And I am God."

Especially important in this passage is the statement that it is God who has "declared and saved and proclaimed." The implication, then, is that salvation through God's witnesses likewise is accomplished mainly through declaration or proclamation of God's revealed will.[23] In addition, "the nations" function as the foundational concept here, with Israel a witness to the one true God over against their many false gods. The knowledge of this comes in the form of revelation and the declaration of that revelation. This means that the fundamental characteristic of the New Testament church as witness is that it is "a speaking, proclaiming church and that she addresses all men and all nations with her message."[24] Thus, as David Peterson says of the Isaiah 43 passage and its implications for Acts 1:8, "Isaiah envisages that the renewed people of God will be witnesses to the nations of the salvation of God when the new age arrives."[25] This prohibits any notion of nonverbal witness apart from proclamation, because the gospel centers on declaring the written word and the living Word.[26] This has important implications for the way that the church thinks about compassion in light of the kingdom. Specifically, there can be no gospel actions apart from gospel articulation. This does not mean that the actions and lives of those who follow Jesus are unimportant, but that witness must be understood in

---

[23] Harry R. Boer, *Pentecost and Missions* (Grand Rapids, MI: Eerdmans, 1961), 118.
[24] Ibid., 102.
[25] David Peterson, *The Acts of the Apostles,* Pillar New Testament Commentary. Accordance electronic ed. (Grand Rapids, MI: Eerdmans, 2009), 110.
[26] This bears some resemblance to Karl Barth's threefold understanding of the word of God: the word preached, written, and revealed. *Church Dogmatics* I/1 and I/2, trans. G. W. Bromiley, G. T. Thompson, and Harold Knight (New York: Continuum, 2010).

terms of *primary witness* referring to gospel proclamation and *secondary witness* describing the inner life of the church. Classical Pentecostalism recovered this emphasis on primary witness by stressing what Pomerville refers to as the two main signs of the kingdom, namely, preaching the gospel and the Spirit's charismatic activity.[27] Thus, "the kingdom is a missions theme; it concerns Great Commission mission! It involves the activity of the Holy Spirit in the world of mission."[28]

The emphasis on verbal proclamation as the primary emphasis in the notion of "witnesses" in Acts likely lies behind the "tongues of fire" seen when the Spirit is poured out in the upper room (Acts 2:3). As Eddie Gibbs writes, "The tongue over their head released the tongue in their head."[29] The point here is that, as important as it is for the church to serve the needy, a cold cup of water cannot tell people that Jesus is God incarnate, or that he died for their sins, or that he rose again on the third day, or that he ascended to heaven and is seated at the right hand of the Father and will one day come again in glory to judge the living and dead, as is stated in the church's ancient creeds. Thus, the primary task of witnesses is to proclaim the gospel, for apart from this there is no salvation. As with the passage in Isaiah, so too with Luke-Acts: witness through the proclamation of God's sovereignty and salvation represents the central calling of God's people. This is further evident in that verbal witness is precisely what happens when the disciples are filled with the Spirit. Peter gets up following the outpouring of the promised Holy Spirit and proclaims to those present, notably from every nation under heaven (Acts 2:5), what Jesus has done on their behalf. The reference to "every nation under heaven," though certainly hyperbolic,

---

[27] Pomerville, "Pentecostalism and Missions," 324.

[28] Ibid., 320.

[29] Eddie Gibbs, "The Launching of Mission: The Outpouring of the Spirit at Pentecost," in *Mission in Acts: Ancient Narratives in Contemporary Context*, ed. Robert L. Gallagher and Paul Hertig (Maryknoll, NY: Orbis Books, 2004), 21.

draws attention to Genesis 10 and 11, to the table of nations after the flood and the dispersing of the nations at Babel.[30] This underscores the missionary nature of the Spirit and the missionary nature of the church.[31] This Spirit-proclamation paradigm in Acts also reflects the pattern of the Spirit-anointed ministry of Jesus, whose public ministry begins in the Spirit's power and with the proclamation of scripture (see Lk 3:22; 4:14–19).

Models of the church emphasizing the broad sense of witness fall short exegetically because scripture prioritizes the proclamational element of witness and links the other elements to that function, especially as they relate to the nations. Again, not only is the mission as witness model problematic because it lacks an explicit concern for the nations, but it is also problematic because the *diakonic* and *koinoniac* functions are not explicitly oriented to the *kerygmatic* function of the church. Even where integration is maintained, there remains the constant danger that some aspect other than proclamation will be emphasized. Church history tells this sordid tale again and again. For example, when Christian service is prioritized over *kerygma*, this produces the social gospel—good deeds done in the name of a nonhistorical, moral Jesus.[32] When community is emphasized at the expense of *kerygma*, the result is liberalism—the fatherhood of God and the brotherhood of man. When the proclamation of the gospel lacks the inclusion of service and community, the result is fundamentalism—a Christianity that seeks the salvation of disembodied souls.

---

[30] Keener, *Acts: Introduction and 1:1—2:47*, 840–51. Even though it is Jews that are from the surrounding nations, the reference points to the "universal sweep" of the gospel. Dunn, *The Acts of the Apostles*, 26.

[31] Johannes Blauw, *The Missionary Nature of the Church* (New York: McGraw-Hill, 1962).

[32] Some social gospel advocates warned against divorcing social teaching from individual salvation. See David O. Moberg, *The Church as a Social Institution* (Englewood Cliffs, NJ: Prenteice-Hall, 1962), 146; C. Norman Kraus, "Introduction," in *Missions, Evangelism, and Church Growth*, ed. C. Norman Kraus (Scottdale, PA: Herald Press, 1980), 21.

All of these are problematic because they make one element of the church's mandate into its entire mandate and result in a truncated gospel.[33] The church-as-witness model falters because it attempts to be everything all at once, and it does this because it lacks a clear end goal. That is, it lacks the teleological orientation that defined the ministries of Jesus and the early church. As a result, the more complex and time-consuming things, in this case, cross-cultural missions and discipleship, tend to be either sacrificed at the altar of expediency or determined according to resources. The tendency of the church throughout history to polarize around one aspect of its calling testifies to this.[34] No one can do everything all at once. Apart from clearly articulated biblical priorities, practical priorities and individual passions will take over. For classical Pentecostals the proper unity of these things comes into view when the church is understood according to its missionary nature. It is missions that gives each of these elements its greatest significance, because they find their ultimate fulfillment only in locating them within the eschatological trajectory of God's redemptive activity. For this reason Noel Perkin, a former leader in Assemblies of God World Missions, refers to literacy programs and clinics as "indirect methods" of evangelism because of the need to connect them to gospel proclamation.[35] This closely relates to what I am here calling primary and secondary witness.

Prioritizing proclamation and making a distinction between primary and secondary witness does not make Christian compassion optional for the task of global missions, as some have suggested. For example, David Bosch has argued that the very notion of priorities must be rejected because to prioritize one thing makes

---

[33] Guder makes this very point as he argues for the church as witness, but witness with a clear missionary trajectory. Thus Guder's model is not too different from what I am proposing. See Darrell L. Guder, *Be My Witnesses* (Grand Rapids, MI: Eerdmans, 1985), 42–44.

[34] David J. Bosch, *Transforming Mission: Paradigm Shifts in the Theology of Mission* (1991; repr. Maryknoll, NY: Orbis Books, 1991, 2004), 181–341; Kraus, "Introduction."

[35] Noel Perkin and John Garlock, *Our World Witness* (Springfield, MO: Gospel Publishing House, 1963), 48.

the second thing optional.[36] In most takes on this, the underlying and false assumption is that integration and priority cannot go together, and this is often chalked up to false dichotomies that are readily resolved by locating everything within a kingdom framework.[37] Yet one can readily call to mind both exegetical and practical reasons for rejecting such a statement. Jesus, the King of the kingdom, clearly prioritized his mission to Israel and did so without making the later mission to the Gentiles optional (Mt 15:24; 29:18–20). To deny prioritization is to deny hierarchy, because these concepts are inseparable, and the Bible frequently endorses various forms of hierarchy. Without prioritization, stealing a loaf of bread would be as serious an offense as human trafficking, and human beings would be no more significant than microbes. Yet, in scripture God does not deal with all human sin as equal; nor does God shy away from establishing a hierarchy that gives priority to people as the apex of creation. This is evident in that the punishment for accidentally killing the neighbor's ox differs from the punishment for killing the neighbor (Ex 21:33; Gen 9:5–6). In the New Testament blasphemy against the Holy Spirit is the sole offense that Jesus describes as unpardonable (Mk 3:28). The point here is not that these Old Testament laws about oxen and so on are binding on New Testament believers, but that priorities and resultant hierarchies consistently make up a biblical worldview. In fact, on a practical level priorities and hierarchies define much of human existence. People prioritize things all the time without making other things optional. If I say, for example, that I have to first deposit my paycheck and then pay my bills, the fact that I have prioritized depositing my check does not make paying my bills optional—no matter how much I may wish it were so. So not only do priorities not render subsequent tasks optional, but such a perspective installs compassion as a

---

[36] David J. Bosch, *Transforming Mission: Paradigm Shifts in the Theology of Mission* (Maryknoll, NY: Orbis Books, 1991), 405. Dempster, "A Theology of the Kingdom—A Pentecostal Contribution," 47.

[37] Dempster, "A Theology of the Kingdom—A Pentecostal Contribution," 48.

fundamental element of the *missio Dei*. In this perspective all of the church's compassion activities from the side of the sending church function missiologically to facilitate gospel proclamation. In addition, it means that compassion must be an inherent part of the disciple-making process in missions.

COMPASSION AND THE CHURCH

Another problem with the mission-as-witness model is that one can live out this approach and neglect both the formation of a set-apart people (discipleship) and a concern for the nations (cross-cultural missions). It is for this reason that the New Testament primarily emphasizes compassion as an aspect of the church's inner life. For example, Paul says, "While we have opportunity, let us do good to all people, and *especially* to those who are of the household of the faith" (Gal 6:10, emphasis added). This perspective runs throughout the Pauline letters, the Gospels, and other epistles; for sake of space I focus on how Luke develops this in the book of Acts. Specifically, one finds in Luke a clear picture of the necessary way in which compassion among fellow believers paves the way for the Spirit's missionary agenda.

Justo González has rightly suggested that the book of Acts might properly be titled "the Acts of the Spirit."[38] It is significant that Jesus's statement regarding the mandate of the church to be his witness to the nations in the power of the Spirit comes on the heels of confusion among the disciples about their mission. In Acts 1:6 the disciples turn to Jesus and ask, "Lord, is it at this time You are restoring the kingdom to Israel?" This question demonstrates that the disciples continued to misunderstand what it was they were called to be and do. I would suggest that in a similar manner there is great confusion within the church today regarding the nature of the church's mission and much of that confusion owes, likewise, to confusion about the kingdom.

---

[38] Justo L. González, *Acts: The Gospel of the Spirit* (Maryknoll, NY: Orbis Books, 2001), 16.

The disciples were waiting and longing for a localized kingdom in which the glory of Israel would be restored. The chief error in their perspective rested not in it being too temporal, but in being too immobile and thereby not sufficiently missionary.[39] The essence of the problem was that their view of the kingdom was not oriented to the nations.[40] Thus, Jesus's response was this: "You will receive power when the Holy Spirit has come upon you; and you shall be My witnesses both in Jerusalem, and in all Judea and Samaria, and even to the remotest part of the earth" (Acts 1:8). Jesus's answer to his disciples' question was to revise their localized interpretation of the kingdom. So, while the disciples longed mainly for the restoration of Israel, Jesus longed for the restoration of Israel, Samaria, Rome, Spain, India, Ethiopia, the Germanic tribes, the Britons, and the restoration of *all nations* as far as the ends of the earth and on to places that the disciples did not yet know existed.[41] The kingdom of God therefore must be understood as the inevitable reign of God over the kingdoms of the world. The point here is that there is no biblical understanding of the kingdom that is not missional in the sense of being oriented toward the redemption of the nations.[42] The very word *kingdom* implies the overthrow of every earthly kingdom—of "every lofty thing raised up against the knowledge of God" (2 Cor 10:5). In the same way that the early church was waiting for Jesus to establish an earthly kingdom and restore Israel to its former glory, I believe that contemporary models of Pentecostal missions also tend to focus on a localized kingdom—a kingdom of our own making that has little to do with the global concerns of the risen Jesus.

That said, we can find comfort in noting, as González says, that when the Holy Spirit comes it "will amend [the] actions and

---

[39] Keener argues that it was primarily an issue of timing that precipitated the question, and I agree, but I would add that Jesus's answer focuses on the geographical element and thus indicates that their question was flawed. Keener, *Acts: Introduction and 1:1—2:47*, 683.

[40] Dunn, *The Acts of the Apostles*, 11.

[41] González, *Acts*, 19. See Keener on the meaning and location of "ends of the earth" (*Acts: Introduction and 1:1—2:47*, 702–8).

[42] Dunn, *The Acts of the Apostles*, 9–12.

decisions" of the confused band of disciples.[43] In the same way, contemporary Pentecostalism can trust the Holy Spirit to amend our missiology and our missionary praxis if we likewise seek the Spirit and submit to the Spirit. Again, González is helpful here, for he points out that the entire book of Acts centers on the disciples discovering and rediscovering, by the Spirit's presence and power, God's concern for the nations.[44] Much of the confusion over the nature of the kingdom as it relates to missiology can be traced to the failure to distinguish the mission of local churches from that of those called to cross-cultural evangelism and church planting. The central idea here is that local churches and missions teams operate under a different mandate—the broad and narrow sense of missions I referred to previously.

In this model the local church engages its own members and its community through prayer, service, fellowship, and proclamation—mission in four dimensions, but with each of them intentionally oriented toward the *kerygma*. Acts 2:42 presents something strikingly similar. Here the early church is said to have devoted itself to "the apostles' teaching" (*kerygma*) and to fellowship (*koinonia*), to the breaking of bread and to prayer (*proseuche*)." The apostolic teaching comes first because it proves determinative for everything else; on this foundation the church is built (Eph 2:20). In Acts 2:44–45 Luke adds that the disciples also shared all they had so that there was no needy person among them. Even though Luke does not use the word *diakonia* (service), he certainly conveys the same concept in that the believers sold their belongings and shared the proceeds with those in need within the believing community. As Dunn notes, this practice was born of "eschatological enthusiasm."[45] As a result, the Lord "was adding to their number day by day those who were being saved" (Acts 2:47). Here, then, we have a picture of the modality, the local church, functioning evangelistically in its own context.

---

[43] González, *Acts,* 19.
[44] Ibid., 20.
[45] Dunn, *The Acts of the Apostles*, 36.

The compassionate ministries of the church certainly involve outreach to the needy in society, but they must start with and emphasize the need to build up the body of believers and equip the saints for ministry in the church and in the world (cf. 1 Cor 8:1; 10:23; 14:4; 14:17). The church's compassionate mandate relates to the local church functioning as a sign of God's coming kingdom, but it can only accomplish this to the extent that the gospel of the kingdom is the church's primary focus. The church demonstrates love and mercy for members of the church, because in doing so it not only gives tangible evidence of God's presence in its midst, but it also points forward to the coming new creation, in which pain, death, and suffering no longer exist (Rev 21:4). Thus, the church functions as a community of healing and wholeness in which righteousness dwells and in which there are no social, racial, or economic divisions (1 Cor 12:13). The care of members within the community is therefore the church's first priority when it comes to compassion.

This emphasis on the centrality of "being a people" also appears in 1 Peter 2:9: "But you are a chosen race, a royal priesthood, a holy nation, a people for God's own possession, so that you may proclaim the excellencies of Him who has called you out of darkness into His marvelous light."[46] The "so that" in this verse clearly indicates that the holy life the church is called to live is teleologically oriented toward gospel proclamation.

I have described this broad sense of mission only to make a point: missionaries are called not to be the local church in the place where they serve, but to plant the church. Any confusion on this point will cause the wheels of missions to grind to a halt and will hinder the development of truly indigenous local churches. Being the church requires broad sensibilities that cannot be sustained by any other than local people. It is important to note here the way in

---

[46] Also Titus 2:14–15. See also Peter Davids's argument that this text runs contrary to Western individual perspectives on faith and instead emphasizes the community of God's people in *The First Epistle of Peter*, New International Commentary on the New Testament, Accordance electronic ed. (Grand Rapids, MI: Eerdmans, 1990), 91.

which missions teams (sodalities) function throughout the book of Acts as a function of the local church, though not identical to it.

In the previous chapter I have shown how the disciple-making efforts of Barnabas and Saul lead to indigenous and missionary expression of compassion in Acts 11. Following that, Acts 13 emphasizes that Barnabas and Saul are "set apart" and commissioned for missionary service. "While they were ministering to the Lord and fasting, the Holy Spirit said, 'Set apart for Me Barnabas and Saul for the work to which I have called them'" (13:2). The words "set apart" clearly show that missionary teams function under a different mandate than the local church. Indeed, all throughout the book of Acts, apostolic teams are set apart for cross-cultural service and supported by the prayer and gifts of local churches.[47] Missionary sodalities consistently operate as the means by which the churches continue to reach out to evangelize those places where Jesus was not yet known (Rom 15:20).

CHRISTIAN UNITY AND THE HOLY SPIRIT

Luke carefully emphasizes not only the spread of the gospel in the Spirit's power, but also the way in which compassion for fellow believers cultivates the Spirit's presence and prepares the church for mission. The Holy Spirit in Christian theology is the Spirit of an impossible future made real and present. This is the point Luke goes to great efforts to demonstrate in the opening chapters of Acts. This book begins with the admonition that the disciples should wait in Jerusalem for an endowment of the Spirit that will enable them to carry out God's mission (Acts 1:8)—from a practical perspective, a complete impossibility.[48] From the moment this takes place, Luke emphasizes the radical fellowship

---

[47] As Murphy points out, we see this in Acts in the apostolic teams of Barnabas, Saul, and Mark (13:4–13); Paul, Barnabas, and "companions" (13:13—15:12); Paul, Barnabas, Judas, and Silas (15:22–34); and so on. See Edward F. Murphy, "The Missionary Society as an Apostolic Team," *Practical Anthropology* 4, no. 1 (1976): 113.

[48] Cf. Dunn, *The Acts of the Apostles*, 11.

among believers and how that unity is both a gift of the Spirit and the means for the ongoing cultivation of the Spirit's power and presence. Luke makes a point of demonstrating the connection between the reception of the Spirit and the unity of the church when he describes believers awaiting the Spirit's coming as being "all together in one place" (Acts 2:1). The use of the repetitive phrases "all together" and "in one place" is undoubtedly emphatic.[49] Otherwise, simply to say they were all together would suffice. But Luke's point is to show that the unified fellowship of the believers was a key to all that would soon take place. Interestingly, this early unity exists prior to the outpouring of the Spirit, such that the emphasis seems to be on the community worshiping and praying together in the context of its amended kingdom vision, after Jesus set it on the right trajectory to the nations. This fellowship among believers is heightened after the outpouring of the Spirit, as is evident in Acts 2:44—"And all those who had believed were together and had all things in common (*koinos*)." The community of believers has here been moved by the Spirit's power and presence from what Luke earlier portrays as a spatial but pregnant unity, full of hopeful anticipation, to an economic, personal, and costly unity that would intensify as the Spirit worked in the church to advance God's global mission (Acts 4:32–35). This notion of personal and costly unity not only characterizes the relationship of Christ to believers but becomes a paradigm for believers' unity with Christ, with each other, and thereby as a witness to the world through their inner life. As Keener observes, "Though Luke *emphasizes* the Spirit's empowerment especially for verbal proclamation, the community *effectively* evangelizes here through its lifestyle (2:47)" (emphasis added).[50] In other words, the lifestyle of the church plays a vital role in paving the way for gospel proclamation. What is in focus here is the ethic of the community and the role of the Spirit in transforming God's

---

[49] David Peterson, *The Acts of the Apostles*, Pillar New Testament Commentary. Accordance electronic ed. (Grand Rapids, MI: Eerdmans, 2009), 131.

[50] Keener, *Acts: Introduction and 1:1—2:47*, 1003.

people, not in the community's ability to transform the world. As Jacques Ellul states, "[The church] does not have to strive and struggle in order that righteousness may reign on earth. We have to be 'just' or 'righteous' ourselves, bearers of righteousness."[51] This happens only when compassionate missions focuses on making compassionate disciples.

In all of this Luke portrays something of a cyclical process in which believers gather together in unity and mutual love and concern, seeking the Spirit's empowerment for global evangelization. When the Spirit is poured out, this empowers the church for greater unity and thereby more effective witness. There is therefore an unmistakable emphasis in Acts on compassion as a means of greater effectiveness in missions because of the link between a holy community and the Spirit's power and presence. For contemporary missions this means, as Melvin Hodges has put it, "that New Testament methods must be accompanied by New Testament power."[52] This power is cultivated by holy living and caring for needy persons in the community. This same emphasis can be found in Jesus's statement to his disciples, when he declares, "By this all men will know that you are My disciples, if you have love for one another" (Jn 13:35). Paul makes a similar declaration regarding the importance of Christian unity in Ephesians 4:1–6:

> Therefore I, the prisoner of the Lord, implore you to walk in a manner worthy of the calling with which you have been called, with all humility and gentleness, with patience, showing tolerance *for one another* in love, being diligent to preserve *the unity of the Spirit in the bond of peace. There is* one body and one Spirit, just as also you were called in one hope of your calling; one Lord, one faith, one baptism, one God and Father of all who is over all and through all and in all. (emphasis added)

---

[51] Jacques Ellul, *The Presence of the Kingdom* (Colorado Springs, CO: Helmers and Howard, 1989), 66.
[52] Melvin Hodges, *The Indigenous Church* (1953; repr. Springfield, MO: Gospel Publishing House, 1971), 126.

THE GOAL OF COMPASSIONATE DISCIPLESHIP: PRACTICING SOLIDARITY

Compassionate missions should primarily be directed at fostering congregations of believers that demonstrate radical unity with one another as they engage in global missions—that is, *a people* set apart for God's purposes. Yet this cannot happen when missionaries function as the primary doers of compassion. This is because, as Melvin Hodges notes, "the true measure of success is not that which the missionary accomplishes while on the field, but the work that still stands after he has gone."[53] Sadly, many compassionate projects in missions fail to meet this standard because instead of focusing on forming a people, they instead focus on starting a project and depend on outside personnel and resources for survival.

The point here is that what one does makes little difference without a focus on who one is. This seems to partly lie behind the church's problem in Rwanda. When people know *who* they are in Christ, their attitudes and actions find their basis only in the Lordship of Jesus, not in tribal identities or social constructs.[54] A focus on making compassionate disciples represents the doable work of compassionate missions and helps missions agencies avoid becoming bogged down in endless efforts to "make the world a better place." This is not to say that Christians should not be concerned about the plight of the suffering. Indeed, they should. But in the context of cross-cultural missions, that concern must prioritize discipleship. This is not only because this fundamentally represents the primary mandate in missions, but because it offers hope for the greatest, lasting impact.

---

[53] Ibid., 15.
[54] Emmanuel Katongole and Jonathan Wilson-Hartgrove, "Postures of Social Engagement: Reflections on Christianity after Rwanda's Genocide," *Review of Faith and International Affairs* 8, no. 1 (2010).

SOLIDARITY AND THE PEOPLE OF GOD: THE PRIORITY OF COMMUNITY

One of the chief results of compassion exercised among God's people is that it brings about solidarity. As González points out, the concept of *koinonia* goes deeper than the English word *fellowship* suggests. Referring to Acts 2:44–45, he says that central here is the notion of solidarity "and the sharing of feelings, goods, and actions."[55] The church's compassionate mandate relates to the church functioning as a sign of God's coming kingdom. Scholars widely agree on this. The church demonstrates love and mercy because in doing so it not only gives tangible evidence of God's presence in its midst but also points forward to the coming New Creation, in which pain, death, and suffering will no longer exist (Rev 21:4). The church functions as a community of healing and wholeness in which righteousness dwells, and in which there are no social, racial, or economic divisions (1 Cor 12:13). Paul describes this goal clearly in Colossians 3:5–11:

> Therefore consider the members of your earthly body as dead to immorality, impurity, passion, evil desire, and greed, which amounts to idolatry. For it is because of these things that the wrath of God will come upon the sons of disobedience, and in them you also once walked, when you were living in them. But now you also, put them all aside: anger, wrath, malice, slander, *and* abusive speech from your mouth. Do not lie to one another, since you laid aside the old self with its *evil* practices, and have put on the new self who is being renewed to a true knowledge according to the image of the One who created him—*a renewal* in which there is no *distinction between* Greek and Jew, circumcised

---

[55] González, *Acts,* 50–51. See also David G. Horrell, *Solidarity and Difference: A Contemporary Reading of Paul's Ethics*, 2nd ed. (New York: Bloomsbury, 2015).

and uncircumcised, barbarian, Scythian, slave and freeman, but Christ is all, and in all. (emphasis added)

The Greek word for "members" is *melos*, which means both body part and musical harmony (it is where we get the modern English word *melody*). Taken together with the fact that elsewhere Paul refers to the body of Christ and its interdependent parts as the focus of Christian unity (1 Cor 12:12–26), it is no stretch to note that there should be a harmonious nature to the church as it discovers its unity in Christ and Christ's mission. Without this inner harmony, the church cannot speak prophetically to a divided world.

The problem is that this intercommunity concern often gets left behind when the church gives the bulk of its attention to social transformation. This is because a focus on social transformation often entails a project-oriented rather than a people-oriented approach. The end goal of a missionary sodality is a people set apart for participation in the *missio Dei*. This means that compassionate missions must also be oriented toward this end. Put simply, compassionate missions must focus on discipleship and the formation of a people, holy and infused with their own concern for the nations. Anything short of this becomes simply benevolence, not missions.

Missions is always about power. Biblically, it is about the power of the Spirit to advance the gospel against impossible odds. But practically, missionaries have often replaced the Spirit's power with secular power, social power, or structural power. To the extent that this happens, missionaries set up future generations of local believers and missionaries alike for failure. The reasons for this are somewhat obvious. Only the Spirit represents power untainted by sin. All other forms of power tend toward corruption and decay. My contention is that Christian discipleship is fundamentally about identity, and that identity is a byproduct of the Spirit's transformational work in the church. Yet, often, the way we engage in compassionate missions by framing it as "kingdom work" sets in place human power structures that prevent local churches from becoming dependent on the power of the Spirit.

In closing, let us return to the question of Rwanda. My opening observations perhaps gave the impression that the fault lies at the feet of Rwandan Christians. To some extent I suppose that is true. But to a larger extent, a good bit of blame lies also at the feet of Christian missionaries who first came to Rwanda. As many have noted of the Rwandan genocide, there was a bit of awful irony in the fact that those committing atrocities needed to see ID cards in order to tell who was a Hutu and who was a Tutsi. In other words, the differences were not racial or even "tribal," and were not discernable without that piece of paper. Prior to colonialism, the Hutu and Tutsi had coexisted as part of the same kingdom under the same king for centuries.[56] Europeans who first came to Rwanda in the nineteenth century declared the Tutsi minority to be superior to the Hutu majority. Christian missionaries fell in line with this paradigm and only allowed Tutsi children to attend Christian schools.[57] This social oppression of the Hutu led eventually to an uprising in 1959, in which twenty thousand Tutsi were killed. So rather than rejecting the colonial system of racial identification and antagonism, Christian missionaries in Rwanda helped the nation to become inscribed with a hatred for otherness. In short, they became part of the secular power structures that led to and produced the disaster. As is so often true, wherever there is despotism and corruption in Africa, colonialism and its legacy are never very far away. As Emmanuel Katongole explains, regarding Rwanda, "Once this imagination and identity had fomented, Christianity made little difference in Rwanda. Christianity seemed little more than an add-on—an inconsequential relish that did not radically affect people's so-called natural identities. Purpose and goals were dictated to Christians and non-Christians alike by radio personalities and political figures."[58]

---

[56] Emmanuel M. Katongole, "The Pattern of This World," *Sojourners Magazine*, January 2009, 33.
[57] Ibid., 34.
[58] Ibid., 35.

The point here is that missionaries sometimes inadvertently communicate a pseudo-gospel that is antithetical to the gospel of the kingdom, and they do this implicitly through the endorsement of worldly power structures. Pointing to the complicity of the churches in the Rwandan genocide, Timothy Longman observes that "the Christian message received in Rwanda was not one of 'love and fellowship,' but one of obedience, division and power."[59] Likewise, compassionate projects that are driven by outsiders almost invariably depend on some sort of power structure that causes fissures within the host culture. For example, John V. Taylor makes this argument regarding missionaries in Ceylon (modern Sri Lanka). He tells the story of how Christianity came to be an object of fear and suspicion in that country because 50 percent of the nation's schools were Christian schools. Thus, Christians controlled 50 percent of the employment opportunities for teachers and 50 percent of the admissions for students. "So," Taylor notes, "the churches became objects of jealousy and the fear of the general community. Now, you cannot evangelize anybody who is jealous of you or anybody who is afraid of you."[60] Taylor cites D. T. Niles's observation of the way in which compassionate structures become power structures and thereby pose a dilemma for missionaries:

> All institutions of service . . . are also sources of secular strength. You just cannot help it. And so you are caught in a dilemma. Here are people who are sick, illiterate, orphans, or widows, and it is the function of Christians to serve where there is need. On the other hand, if, in order to serve need, you build up institutions which are sources of secular strength for the Church, you put unnecessary obstacles in the way of evangelism. In one sense, weakness is the only

---

[59] Longman, *Christianity and Genocide in Rwanda*, 10.
[60] John V. Taylor, *For All the World* (Philadelphia: Westminster, 1966), 57–58.

A Pentecostal Approach to Discipleship in Missions 133

strength we have in presenting the Gospel. And if you rob us of that, we are going to get in real trouble.[61]

Classical Pentecostalism has long embodied the idea that the church's power lies in the manifest presence of the Spirit. Therefore, compassion in missions must point not to whether outsiders see the church transforming society, but to whether they see the church itself as a microcosm of transformation that is completely foreign to society—as a transformation by the Spirit that is oriented to the nations and thereby to otherness. This can only happen if missionaries willingly set aside their own inclinations toward self-aggrandizement and focus on compassion in missions as fundamentally a matter of discipleship.[62] A church caught up in the eschatological urgency of world evangelization will never get embroiled in a genocide, because it is by its very nature defined by more pressing issues.

---

[61] Ibid., 58. See D. T. Niles, transcript of a tape recording of an address given to the headquarters staff of the Church Missionary Society, London, n.d.
[62] Allen, *Missionary Methods*, 6.

6

From Ubuntu *to* Koinonia

THE SPIRIT-FORMED COMMUNITY AND INDIGENOUS AFRICAN COMPASSION[1]

Pentecostal missions has long abided the three "selfs" deemed crucial to indigenous church-planting movements. The notions of self-support, self-governance, and self-propagation have helped Christianity to flourish in places like Africa, now home to roughly one quarter of all Christians in the world.[2]

Yet the rapid numerical growth of Christianity in Africa has raised questions for both missionaries and local pastors regarding the issue of genuine transformation. For example, Emmanuel Katongole has noted that despite African Christianity's numerical growth and compassionate efforts, "Africans in general are 40 percent worse off than they were in the 1980s."[3] One then wonders: have missionaries and local churches engaged in com-

---

[1] An earlier version of this chapter appeared as "From *Ubuntu* to *Koinonia*: The Spirit-formed Community and Indigenous African Compassion," *Missio Africanus: Journal of African Missiology* 4, no. 1 (2019): 1–20. Reprinted with permission.

[2] David McClendon, "Sub-Saharan Africa Will Become Home to a Growing Share of the World's Christians and Muslims," Pew Research Center (2017).

[3] Emmanuel Katongole, *The Sacrifice of Africa: A Political Theology for Africa* (Grand Rapids, MI: Eerdmans, 2011), 40.

passion in Africa in ways that foster the kind of ethical and moral transformation envisioned in scripture for God's people? The thesis of this chapter is that this has largely not happened, and furthermore that this neglect can be traced to the imposition of Western-style, materialistic, and individualistic forms of compassion that bypass the deeply rooted and tightly linked African notions of community and spirituality. Unfortunately, Western missionaries have rarely been able to overcome their paternalistic tendencies when it comes to Africa and continue to think of Africa's compassionate needs in terms of a problem that can only be solved with Western money and ingenuity. Of course, nothing could be further from the truth.

Missionaries and African pastors can overcome some of these challenges by giving greater attention to the ways in which the African concept of *ubuntu* and the biblical concept of *koinonia* intersect. By maximizing the biblical framework of the church as the Spirit-formed people of God, missionaries and local pastors can help foster forms of compassion that are truly indigenous and that therefore offer the greatest hope for lasting change.

NGOS AND COMPASSION IN AFRICA

One of the chief problems with contemporary Christian compassion in Africa is the tendency to follow the pattern of secular NGOs and development agencies without giving sufficient attention to the many problems they embody. For example, Manji and O'Coill argue that NGOs in Africa often operate from a paternalistic, neocolonial stance.[4] They note, for example:

> As with the racist ideologies of the past, the discourse of development continued to define non-Western people in terms of their perceived divergence from the cultural standards of the West, and it reproduced social hierarchies that had

---

[4] Firoze Manji and Carl O'Coill, "The Missionary Position: NGOs and Development in Africa," *International Affairs* 78, no. 3 (2002): 567–83.

prevailed between both groups under colonialism. On this basis, the so-called "developing world" and its inhabitants were (and still are) described only in terms of what they are not. They are chaotic, not ordered, traditional not modern, corrupt not honest, underdeveloped, not developed, irrational not rational, lacking in all of those things the West presumes itself to be.[5]

Along these same lines Hiruy and Eversole point out that NGOs tend to disempower the very people they claim to help. They do this by inserting themselves as mediators between impoverished communities and government authorities. The effect of this has been to prevent the poor from speaking for themselves. Plus, the ability of NGOs effectively to voice the concerns of the poor is often compromised by the fact that they are indebted to local and foreign governments, who often determine who receives funding and how it can be used.[6] The tendency to be donor driven at times subjugates and humiliates those that NGOs aim to serve. Charles Piot's observations of child sponsorship practices in Togo serve as a case in point. He points out that the process of having to write response letters thanking Western donors subjected barely literate Togolese parents to arduous ninety-minute treks on foot (each way) to donor offices to present their thank-you letter, only to have it critiqued by organizational professionals, and at times sent back for revisions. This amounted to a process that "re-inscribes the African subject as aid-dependent, as saved, always saved, by the European—and the African parent as always inadequate and incomplete/impotent."[7]

---

[5] Ibid., 574. See also Afe Adogome, "African Christianities and Politics from Below," *HTS Theological Studies* 72, no. 4 (2016).

[6] Kiros Hiruy and Robyn Eversole, "NGOs and African Grassroots Community Organisations in Australia," *Third Sector Review* 21, no. 1 (2015): 155.

[7] Charles Piot, "Pentecostal and Development Imaginaries," in *Pentecostalism and Development*, ed. Dena Freeman (New York: Palgrave MacMillan, 2012), 127.

Others have pointed out that NGOs can have little impact in places like Africa unless they confront some of the damaging policies coming from the West that have continued to enslave Africa. These would include the neoliberal economic policies that emerged as part of the Washington Consensus in the 1980s and 1990s and its emphasis on economic growth.[8] As Olaniyan explains, policies enforced by institutions such as the World Bank and the International Monetary Fund "imposed harsh austerity measures on African economies, dragged Africa deeper into debt peonage, and under the guise of instituting 'market reforms,' impoverished the vast majority of Africans."[9] This call for NGOs to be a prophetic voice for the poor and needy is unlikely to be realized, however, given the dependence of NGOs on their donors and on the governments that allow them to operate.

Perhaps the chief problem of NGOs and development goals relates to their inability to foster genuine community. This becomes especially problematic in places like Africa, where the concept of community pervades all of life. This is the argument advanced by Hiruy and Eversole based on their study of NGOs serving African communities in Australia. They have shown that from the perspective of African community organizations, NGOs sometimes ignored community concerns out of a fear of losing some of their funding.[10] Thus, the inability of NGOs to effect lasting change can be traced to their being caught between the

---

[8] Tejumola Olaniyan, "The Paddle That Speaks English: Africa, NGOs, and the Archaeology of an Unease," *Research in African Literatures* 42, no. 2 (Summer 2011): 46–59; Afe Adogame, "African Christianities and the Politics of Development from Below," *Hervormde Teologiese Studies* 72, no. 4 (2016); Manji and O'Coill, "The Missionary Position"; Stephen R. Hurt, Karim Knio, and J. Magnus Ryner, "Social Forces and the Effects of (Post)–Washington Consensus Policy in Africa: Comparing Tunisia and South Africa," *Round Table* 98, no. 402 (2009).

[9] Olaniyan, "The Paddle That Speaks English," 47.

[10] Hiruy and Eversole, "NGOs and African Grassroots Community Organisations in Australia," 151. See also Richard Pithouse, "The Complicated Relationship of Global NGOs and Local Popular Movements: Reflections from South Africa," *Progressive Planning* (Spring 2010).

rock of donor accountability and the hard place of international politics.[11] These two poles contribute to the accurate perception of the NGO as an outsider. Despite the rhetoric of empowerment and transformation, NGOs must come to terms with the reality that numerous studies have shown that in Africa little in the way of lasting change or actual "development" has resulted from their efforts, despite their abundant and enduring presence.[12] This shortcoming has not gone unnoticed by African communities. Ebenezer Obadare shows that one African musician, for example, has made a play on the acronym *NGO* using a local dialect and rendering the term *en jiwo*—which means "you are stealing our money."[13]

CHRISTIAN FAITH-BASED ORGANIZATIONS (FBOS)

Christian FBOs operate, generally speaking, in manners similar to their NGO counterparts, but with some key differences that have sometimes helped them to experience greater success. Chief among these differences is the ability of FBOs to maintain broad acceptance at the community level, something that often eludes NGOs.[14] Part of this acceptance flows from the spiritual emphasis

---

[11] Hiruy and Eversole, "NGOs and African Grassroots Community Organisations in Australia," 151; Dena Freeman, "The Pentecostal Ethic and the Spirit of Development," in *Pentecostalism and Development: Churches, NGOs and Social Change in Africa*, ed. Dena Freeman, 1–40 (New York: Palgrave McMillan, 2012), 25.

[12] Cf. Manji and O'Coill, "The Missionary Position," 568; Lisa Bornstein, "Systems of Accountability, Webs of Deceit? South African NGOs and International Aid," *Conference Papers—International Studies Association* (2006); Freeman, "Pentecostal Ethic and the Spirit of Development," 9; Paul Gifford, *Christianity, Politics, and Public Life in Kenya* (London: C. Hurst, 2009), 160.

[13] Ebenezer Obadare, "Religious NGOs, Civil Society, and the Quest for a Public Sphere in Nigeria," *African Identities* 5, no. 1 (2007): 114.

[14] Matthew Clark and Vicki-Anne Ware, "Understanding Faith-Based Organizations: How FBOs Are Contrasted with NGOs in International Development Literature," *Progress in Development Studies* 15, no. 1 (2015): 48.

and community ties that characterize many FBOs. Thus, community and spirituality go hand in hand. Because faith constitutes a central part of the lives of many people in the majority world, FBOs naturally engender trust more easily than NGOs that lack any specific faith commitment.[15] In fact, this reality has led many NGOs who previously viewed religion with scorn and skepticism to begin to take faith more seriously as an essential element in development.[16]

However, FBOs often fall victim to the same hindrances as their NGO counterparts, and they do so to the extent that they allow donors to determine their priorities, which often compromises faith commitments. Erica Bornstein, for example, in a study two decades ago of child-sponsorship programs in Zimbabwe led by an FBO, concluded that they tend to be destructive to families and communities, even though they have a positive impact on individual children.[17] In short, these programs damage the relationships between children and their biological parents, in exchange for a less concrete, less tangible, and less meaningful relationship with an anonymous donor. For example, the father of one sponsored child in Zimbabwe, named Albert, feared that a Westerner was trying to steal his child. In addition, the sponsored child's educational opportunities made Albert's father feel inferior. At the same time, Albert's mother felt that money being given to the sponsored child should be shared equally among all the siblings. Yet sponsorship rules, set by outsiders, did not allow for this. So, while Albert benefited personally from the sponsorship program, the family itself became more fractured and dysfunctional—an inevitable

---

[15] Tanja Winkler, "When God and Poverty Collide: Exploring the Myths of Faith-Sponsored Community Development," *Urban Studies* 45, no. 10 (2008): 2107; Barbara Bompani, "Religion and Development from Below: Independent Christianity in South Africa," *Journal of Religion in Africa* 40, no. 3 (2010): 322.

[16] Jonathan D. Smith, "Positioning Missionaries in Development Studies, Policy, and Practice," *World Development* 90 (2017).

[17] Erica Bornstein, "Child Sponsorship, Evangelism, and Belonging in the Work of World Vision Zimbabwe," *American Ethnologist* 28, no. 3 (2001).

consequence of compassion that is doled out like stale bread for which the recipients are expected to be eternally grateful.[18] This is especially problematic in African culture, where family ties and obligations prove vitally important in the functioning of the society. Moreover, foreign child sponsorship often injects radical individualism into a culture that is highly communal. It does this necessarily, because of the nature of the program. This helps us to see that a compassionate initiative might be helpful in one area (a child's future prospects) but destructive in another (a child's relationship with his or her biological family). Such approaches run contrary to one of Christianity's most transformational resources, ignoring the centrality of community not only among African communities, but also as it relates to Christian spirituality.

DEVELOPMENT AND PENTECOSTAL CHURCHES

Evidence for the connection between community, a vibrant spirituality, and the possibility of genuine transformation can be found in the fact that several observers have noted that Pentecostal churches often succeed in development in ways beyond even that of NGOs and FBOs.[19] Dena Freeman has identified four ways that Pentecostal churches are more successful in producing lasting change; importantly, all of them have to do with the concepts of community and spirituality. The first has to do with the issue of community and the challenges described above as they relate to donors and government agencies. She notes, "Pentecostal churches are almost entirely funded by their followers, through tithes and offerings."[20] This causes Pentecostal churches, according to

---

[18] Ibid., 598–600.

[19] See Bryant L. Myers, "Progressive Pentecostalism, Development, and Christian Development NGOs: A Challenge and an Opportunity," *International Bulletin of Missionary Research* 39, no. 3 (2015); Christine Schliesser, "On a Long Neglected Player: The Religious Factor in Poverty Alleviation," *Exchange* 43, no. 4 (2014): 340.

[20] Freeman, "The Pentecostal Ethic and the Spirit of Development," 24–25.

Freeman, to tend to place the "religious consumer" at the top of its list of those to whom it is accountable. This contrasts sharply with NGOs, who "are often neither responsive nor accountable to the people they supposedly serve, instead having to report back to national and international donors."[21]

The second way that Pentecostal churches tend to be more successful in development has to do with their ability to foster individual transformation. While in some ways this seems to run counter to the idea of community, it is in fact a central component. Communities are made up of individuals, and change within the community must start there.[22] In this, it turns out that the often-lampooned fundamentalists of the early twentieth century who emphasized that social change starts with individual conversion were not as far off the mark as is sometimes claimed.

Closely connected to individual transformation is Freeman's third reason, that of participation. "Pentecostal pastors are adept at getting people involved and helping them feel part of the community."[23] Though Freeman does not point it out, it is worth noting that a key feature of Christian salvation is not only individual transformation, but incorporation of the individual into a community collectively embodying a transformed life as a sign of God's coming kingdom. Finally, Pentecostalism functions as something of an anti-secularizing force, taking seriously the nonmaterial realities that concern many Africans. Not only does Pentecostalism take seriously things such as demonic powers, malevolent spirits, and witchcraft, but it also offers people a genuine alternative regarding how to deal with these things.[24] We will have more to say on this issue of secularization the next chapter,

---

[21] Ibid.
[22] Ibid., 25.
[23] Ibid.
[24] Ibid., 26. See also Ogbu Kalu et al., eds., *The Collected Essays of Ogbu Kalu: Religions in Africa: Conflicts, Politics, and Social Ethics*, vol. 3 (Trenton, NJ: Africa World Press, 2010), 24–25, 169–70; Ogbu Kalu, *African Pentecostalism: An Introduction* (Oxford: Oxford University Press, 2008), 262–63.

but now we turn our attention to community and its centrality in both an African and Christian worldview.

UBUNTU: COMMUNITY IN AFRICAN CULTURE

Many African cultures have traditionally placed a premium on the value of community. This is captured in the concept of *ubuntu* common in Central, Southern, and East Africa—and basically means "a person is a person through other people." Similar notions can be found in most African communities, even if the precise terms differ. *Ubuntu* emphasizes the "interconnectedness of human society, with the implication that people should treat others as part of the extended human family."[25] As Keith Ferdinando explains, "[Africans] see themselves as members of various groups—family, clan and people—and isolation from the community is either one of the greatest evils that can befall or, as with the witch, a sign of utter perversion and dehumanization: 'I am, because we are; and since we are, therefore, I am.'"[26] According to Elechi et al., *ubuntu* "is a prescription for treating others as we would like to be treated" and "a command to care for each other and to embrace the principle of reciprocity and mutual support." As such, it proves foundational for what Elechi et al. refer to as the African indigenous justice system.[27]

However ingrained the concept of community may be in many African cultures, though, it must also be admitted that this idea

---

[25] John L. B. Eliastam, "Exploring Ubuntu Discourse in South Africa: Loss, Liminality, and Hope," *Verbum et Ecclesia* 36, no. 2 (2015): 2; Matsobane Manala, "African Traditional Widowhood Rites and Their Benefits and/or Detrimental Effects on Widows in a Context of African Christianity," *Hervormde Teologiese Studies* 71, no. 3 (2015): 7.

[26] Keith Ferdinando, *The Triumph of Christ in African Perspective: A Study of Demonology and Redemption in the African Context* (Carlisle, UK: Paternoster, 1999), 23.

[27] O. Oko Elechi, Sherill V. C. Morris, and Edward J. Schauer, "Restoring Justice (Ubuntu): An African Perspective," *International Criminal Justice Review* 20, no. 1 (2010): 75.

frequently breaks down. For example, as Ferdinando has observed, traditional African concepts of community tend to extend only as far as family, clan, or tribal affiliations.[28] Thus, *ubuntu* has proven an ineffective instrument in quelling Africa's xenophobic conflicts. Not only has it been an impotent force in this regard, but it also contributes to racial conflict to the extent that *ubuntu* is bound up with tribal identities. Others have pointed out that the concept of *ubuntu* is often vague and patriarchal, and offers little in the way of practical solutions.[29]

The problems described here most likely lie not with the concept of *ubuntu* itself, but with the fact that fallen people act as its guardians. This is true not only for *ubuntu* but for any cultural norm anywhere in the world. Plus, globalism has imported ideas previously foreign to African culture, such as individualism, consumerism, and materialism, all of which have worked together to weaken the concept.[30]

KOINONIA AND THE REDEMPTION OF *UBUNTU*

In the ancient world the Greeks long sought after a source of true and abiding community, as is evident in the writings of Homer, Plato, and Aristotle, among others. But as with the pursuit of *ubuntu* in Africa, the concept often proved elusive, and there was vast disagreement regarding how true social harmony could be achieved. Interestingly, this Hellenistic longing forms the background for Luke's description of the early Christian community as "having all things in common" (Acts 2:44).[31] As previously noted, the Greek word for "common" here is *koinos*, which forms the

---

[28] Ferdinando, *The Triumph of Christ in African Perspective*, 23.
[29] Eliastam, "Exploring Ubuntu Discourse in South Africa," 3.
[30] Ibid., 5.
[31] See "*Koinos*," in *The New International Dictionary of New Testament Theology*, ed. Colin Brown, Accordance electronic ed. (Grand Rapids, MI: Zondervan, 1986).

root for the term *koinonia*, often used to describe Christian fellowship or unity. Luke's point in Acts 2:44 seems to be that this early Christian community, centered on faith in Christ and empowered by the Spirit, had redeemed and actualized what the Greeks often sought, namely, a genuine and practical basis of community that provided for human flourishing. That is, Luke seems to employ the concept apologetically, as if to say to the Hellenistic world, "Look! We have found what you have long searched for! Come, and see for yourself!"

The main idea in this chapter is that in a similar apologetic and redemptive fashion, *koinonia* has the power to set free and redeem both Western individualism and African *ubuntu* by actualizing them through divine presence in the person and work of the Holy Spirit. *Koinonia* in the New Testament essentially describes the notion that believers share in the life of Christ and through Christ share all things with one another. The body of Christ is bound together inextricably with Christ and with one another in sacrificial service (1 Cor 10:16; Phil 2:1). But the interconnectedness of believers, though cultivated through acts of selflessness and compassion, becomes possible only by the work of the Spirit. To be sure, there is a bit of a paradox in this in that shared life appears in Acts as both a product of the Spirit's work and the door through which the Spirit enters. To serve others within the "household of God," to borrow the title of Lesslie Newbigin's book, is to declare in unison, "Welcome, Holy Spirit!"[32]

The concept of the people of God, the church, as a Spirit-formed community that functions as a sign of the kingdom of God pervades much of the New Testament. But one of the clearest declarations of this can be found in Paul's letter to the Philippians, which is worth quoting at length:

> Therefore, if there is any encouragement in Christ, if there is any consolation of love, if there is any fellowship of the

---

[32] Lesslie Newbigin, *The Household of God* (New York: Friendship Press, 1963).

> Spirit, if any affection and compassion, make my joy complete by being of the same mind, maintaining the same love, united in spirit, intent on one purpose. Do nothing from selfishness or empty conceit, but with humility of mind regard one another as more important than yourselves; do not *merely* look out for your own personal interests, but also for the interests of others. Have this attitude in yourselves which was also in Christ Jesus, who, although He existed in the form of God, did not regard equality with God a thing to be grasped, but emptied Himself, taking the form of a bond-servant, *and* being made in the likeness of men. Being found in appearance as a man, He humbled Himself by becoming obedient to the point of death, even death on a cross. (Phil 2:1–8, emphasis added)

Notice that according to the logic of Paul's argument here, the Spirit fosters unity and engenders within the diverse people of God a singular purpose that culminates in the church's evangelistic mandate. Thus, *koinonia* gives direction, purpose, and power to the notion of community by locating all of those things externally in the will of God. By being united with Christ through the Spirit, the body of Christ with all its diverse personalities can be united under the same purpose and values.[33] This concept has the power to help missionaries and pastors in Africa to overcome the broken systems of secular development, Western materialism, hyper-individualism, paternalism, prosperity teaching, and tribalism that have proven so destructive to the flourishing of African societies and to the churches that serve them. The Christian concept of community has great potential because it represents a simultaneous celebration of unity and diversity, sacrifice, and prosperity that defies worldly definitions and categories.

---

[33] Richard R. Melick, *Philippians, Colossians, Philemon*, vol. 32, New American Commentary, Logos electronic ed. (Nashville, TN: Broadman and Holman, 1991), n.p.

KOINONIA IN PAUL

I have already noted the way that *koinonia* functions as a central concept to the church's effectiveness in the book of Acts. Importantly, this same theme appears often in Paul. In Romans 15:26 Paul describes the manner in which Grecian churches in Macedonia and Achaia made a "contribution for the poor among the saints in Jerusalem." Here, again, the word for "contribution" is *koinonia* or "fellowship." This is a concept that Paul elsewhere links to the working of the Spirit, just as Luke does in Acts. For example, in 2 Corinthians 13:14, Paul prays for the divided church at Corinth, saying, "The grace of the Lord Jesus Christ, and the love of God, and the fellowship (*koinonia*) of the Holy Spirit, be with you all." The point in all of this is that the Holy Spirit's presence within the church creates a unity that goes beyond emotional attachment or mere physical presence. Rather, it is a unity that binds the body of Christ together in mutual concern for one another, often expressed in sacrificial care for needy members. As Leon Morris says of Romans 15:26 and the financial gift of the Greek believers to the suffering church in Jerusalem, "The money was not a soulless gift, but the outward expression of the deep love that binds Christian believers in one body, the church."[34]

Later on, we find Paul arguing that this fellowship among believers is meant to spill over into the world as part of the church's witness. In Galatians 6:10, he says, "Let us do good to all people, but especially to the household of faith." He makes a strikingly similar statement in 1 Thessalonians 3:12–13, praying for believers there that the Lord would cause them "to increase and abound in love for one another, and for all people, just as we also do for you; so that He may establish your hearts without blame in holiness before our God and Father at the coming of our Lord Jesus with all His saints." In other words, the church

---

[34] Leon Morris, *The Epistle to the Romans*, Pillar New Testament Commentary, Accordance electronic ed. (Grand Rapids, MI: Eerdmans, 1987), 520.

was tasked to seek and preserve the unity that the Spirit created for it, which was essential to its functioning as the charismatic community needed for the global dissemination of the gospel (Acts 12:24). Thus, while the Spirit-formed community itself is a *charis*, a gift, the church was tasked to be a constant guardian of that gift and to see to it that its expression spilled over into the world (see Acts 5:1–11).

What sets Christian fellowship (*koinonia*) apart is that it is simultaneously transcendent and immanent—it is both spiritual and physical, heavenly and worldly, all at once. Through the giving of the Holy Spirit, believers are united to God both spiritually and practically. In 1 Corinthians 1, Paul describes this in ways similar to Luke, for he emphasizes the unity of believers based on being unified with Christ. The church is "called into fellowship" (*koinonia*) with Jesus Christ (1:9). The effect of this fellowship is unity and the absence of divisions (*schisma*) among God's people for the advancement of the gospel (1 Cor 1:10–17). Paul elaborates the connection between the unification of believers with one another and with Christ through the power of the Holy Spirit throughout chapters 1 and 2 of 1 Corinthians. Without directly mentioning the Spirit, Paul describes the Spirit's work according to power (1:18, 24). Later he admonishes the Corinthians for their divisions and reminds them that this flows from a neglect of the Spirit's power and presence, to which Paul also attributes his own effectiveness in ministry (1 Cor 2:1–16).

My central thesis is that many modern expressions of compassion in Africa by NGOs, FBOs, and missions agencies interrupt this process by hindering the development of genuine fellowship among church members and thereby hindering the church's effectiveness in the community. What Pentecostal churches have long known and NGOs are increasingly becoming aware of is that development has both physical and spiritual causes and therefore requires spiritual and physical responses. Many modern compassionate initiatives, which as we have seen tend to be outside run and financed, interrupt the vital role of unity in ecclesial effectiveness. They do so because they invite discord by setting missionaries in a hierarchical position over local believers and failing properly to respect African cultural values. Without unity, the church tends toward powerlessness as disunity disempowers. As Newbigin has said, "Disunity in the Church is no mere external crack on the surface of a solid reality. It is something that goes down to its very core."[35]

Where discord exists, it drives the people of God backward, hinders that which they are called to be and do, and serves as a constant reminder of the necessity of faith and dependence on the Spirit. As long as discord and a lack of unity exist, the people of God go endlessly in circles, like the Israelites in their wilderness sojourn. But where people act in faith, respond to the Spirit, and cultivate the Spirit's unifying presence, the *ecclesia* enjoys both *koinonia* and missional effectiveness.

GRACE GENERATION MOVEMENT IN TOGO

In 2014, Titus Uwakwe, a Nigerian living in Togo, started Grace Generation Movement (GGM), a ministry that is nondenominational but has close ties with the Assemblées de Dieu in Togo. Uwakwe says of GGM, which is locally run and locally financed, "Our goal is to reach the unreached by all means possible and to perfect the saints."[36] GGM started with musical outreaches focused on attracting young people. "We don't present ourselves as preachers, because music is an easier way to connect with youth." Now, says Uwakwe, the ministry does "pure evangelistic outreach"—meaning its members go to remote, rural areas and conduct door-to-door evangelism, and show Christian films, mostly from Nigeria, that emphasize power encounters. Furthermore, they especially target unreached and hard to reach rural places. Recently Uwakwe and his team visited a village so remote that they had to swim across a river in order to get to

---

[35] Newbigin, *The Household of God*, 83.
[36] Personal interview, November 7, 2017, Lomé, Togo.

the village. When they arrive in a village, someone on the team preaches a sermon, usually followed by an offer to pray for healing and deliverance for any who wish to come forward. But before they make a visit, they work with regional Assemblées de Dieu directors to identify a pastor who, after the visit, will work with new converts and plant a church in that location.

However, GGM does more than plant churches. It is also very engaged in social ministries, especially to vulnerable children and widows. GGM currently supports over one hundred orphans by paying their school fees and providing school supplies. In an average year about twenty widows are given a bag of rice each. This is not extravagant compassion by any means. What it is, though, is local, sustainable, and effective. All of the finances for these things comes from local believers. GGM's board comprises pastors and Christian business people from across denominational lines in Togo who believe in the work and help raise the needed funds. Uwakwe, who himself is a business owner in Lomé, and about ten other individuals, provide most of the financial resources and governance for GGM.

According to Uwakwe, prayer has been the key, and he and his teams spend two weeks in concentrated, focused prayer before doing any outreach. As a result, they have witnessed a number of healings and deliverances. One man who was bedridden and had not left his home for many months attended one of the outreaches and afterward was able to walk without crutches. At another evangelistic campaign, a Muslim Fulani mother and her children came and gave their lives to Christ on the final day of the event. Because the husband was not there, the outreach organizers contacted him by phone to avoid creating any hostilities or problems for the wife and her children. The husband, grateful for the call, gave his assurance that he would allow the conversion of his wife and children and would not cause any trouble. An almost tearful Uwakwe summed up these experiences by declaring: "Miracles still exist. It may take time for us to see them, but they still exist. God honors his word and brings glory to himself."[37]

---

[37] Ibid.

One of the striking features of GGM's work with street kids is its role as an advocate, in order to help children to be integrated back into their families. When GGM first started reaching out to street kids in Lomé, it assumed that many of them were orphans. This proved false, and GGM discovered that the majority had run away from home because they had stolen from their parents and relatives to buy drugs or alcohol. But as Uwakwe explained, in West African culture, because of their offenses against their own families and their own communities, these children are now outcasts. They cannot return home unless an immediate family member advocates on their behalf and pleads their case to the family members and community leaders. But most family members are unwilling to do so, because they have been victims of the child's crimes. So, GGM spends at least two months disciplining these children. Many, according to Uwakwe, are demon-possessed as a result of living on the street and being exposed to voodoo, which is native to this area of Togo and Benin. Uwakwe notes: "Our perception of street kids changed dramatically. We used to think that they were without backgrounds, but we found that many come from good homes." He adds, "Lack of shelter is just a symptom of the real problem, which often has spiritual roots."[38]

As the discipleship process begins to bear fruit and the GGM team members (many of whom are student pastors in Togo) notice genuine changes in the children's attitudes and behavior, they initiate the process of reintegrating them into the child's biological families. Reintegration itself can be a months-long process. Members of GGM travel to the child's village (without the child) to meet with the child's family and verify his or her stories. After doing so, they offer to return with the child and stand in as an advocate, so that the child can return home. The father of one child, a Togolese policeman, recently traveled to Lomé to personally thank Uwakwe for saving his child and helping him be reintegrated to the family. In the process of doing so, the father, too, committed his life to Christ.

---

[38] Ibid.

What is especially poignant about the story of GGM is that it is an indigenous expression of African compassion that is capable of redeeming individuals and communities, as well as traditional notions of both. It does this through practical acts of sacrificial service that are Spirit inspired and Spirit empowered. Furthermore, it is truly integrative, addressing both the physical and spiritual aspects of the lives of those it serves. GGM's approach helps not only the child, but also the child's family, thus upholding rather than destroying the key African value of family and community. When contrasted with many Western or missionary-driven approaches to helping street children, it becomes apparent that such efforts often tend to be ultimately destructive, even if they provide temporary relief. By creating feeding programs for street kids or centers where vulnerable children are housed, fed, or entertained, Western, missionary-driven approaches almost always guarantee that the children will never be reintegrated with their biological families through the creation of systems that ensure a child's perpetual homelessness. The solution lies in indigenous approaches to compassion that maximize African spiritual and community intelligence and that through the agency of the Holy Spirit find genuinely African solutions to uniquely African problems. By focusing on compassionate outreach to foster genuine *koinonia*, missionaries and local pastors alike can, like Luke, declare to the broken communities of Africa, "Look! We have found what you are looking for. Come and see for yourself!"

7

The Secularizing and Anti-Secularizing Potential of African Pentecostalism[1]

Dallas Willard once wrote that "our souls are . . . soaked with secularity."[2] By this he meant that we live in a world permeated by secular notions and that Christians often go about unaware of the secular tendencies to which they normally drift. Willard's comment, though, was largely directed toward Western culture, where secularism has been on the rise and where religion was once expected to disappear entirely as a result. Normally, though, we do not associate secularism with places like Africa. If anything, Africa has proven to be a terrible nuisance for those who had hoped for religion's demise. As J. Kwabena Asamoah-Gyadu points out, this endurable persistence of religion can especially be seen in the shifting perspectives of scholars such as Harvey Cox, who once counted himself among the "death of God" theologians. Reflecting on Pentecostalism, Cox declared that "today it is secularity,

---

[1] An earlier version of this chapter first appeared in Jerry M. Ireland, "The Secularizing and Anti-Secularizing Potential of African Pentecostalism," *Occasional Bulletin* 32, no. 2 (2019): 38–47. Reprinted with permission.
[2] Dallas Willard, *The Divine Conspiracy: Rediscovering Our Hidden Life in God* (New York: HarperOne, 1997), 91.

not spirituality that may be headed for extinction."[3] In 2019 one quarter of all Christians in the world resided in Africa, and by 2030 it will likely be home to one out of three. Pentecostalism is by far the fastest growing form of Christianity in Africa, even though it remains a movement of great diversity.[4] Indeed, it is no exaggeration to speak, as does Asamoah-Gyadu, of "the Pentecostalizaton of Arica."[5]

This chapter explores the ways in which the growth of Pentecostalism in Africa represents both hope and concern in the area of secularization. My thesis is that (1) the prosperity gospel, or *prosperity Pentecostalism*, as I call it, represents a turn away from classical Pentecostalism's historic and theological roots and an embodiment of some of the key elements found in secularism; and that (2) what I refer to as *missional Pentecostalism* describes a stream of African Pentecostalism that has the potential to turn back the secularizing tendencies of prosperity Pentecostalism.

SECULARISM AND AFRICAN PENTECOSTALISM

Secularization describes "a process in which religion diminishes in importance both in society and in the consciousness of individuals."[6] Modern notions of secularism often owe some lineage to, among others, Max Weber's *The Protestant Ethic and*

---

[3] J. Kwabena Asamoah-Gyadu, *Contemporary Pentecostal Christianity: Interpretations from an African Context* (Oxford: Regnum, 2013), 1; Harvey Cox, *Fire from Heaven: The Rise of Pentecostal Spirituality and the Reshaping of Religion in the 21st Century* (Cambridge, MA: Da Capo, 1995), xv.

[4] Ogbu Uke Kalu, "Pentecostalism and Mission in Africa, 1970–2000," *Mission Studies* 24, no. 1 (2007): 9–45; Allan Anderson, "Varieties, Taxonomies, and Definitions," in *Studying Global Pentecostalism*, ed. Allan Anderson et al. (Berkeley and Los Angeles: University of California Press, 2010), 13–29.

[5] Asamoah-Gyadu, *Contemporary Pentecostal Christianity*, 9.

[6] Peter Berger, "Secular and De-Secularization," in *Religions in the Modern World: Traditions and Transformations*, ed. Linda Woodhead, electronic ed. (New York: Routledge, 2002), 384.

the Spirit of Capitalism of 1905. In this work Weber argues for a connection between the "worldly" or practical ethics advocated by the Reformers and the emergence of market capitalism. The Protestant ethic that Weber described and linked to capitalism focused on hard work and delayed gratification, and was set intentionally within a material or, in Weber's terminology, a "disenchanted" framework.[7] Key to understanding the Protestant ethic in Weber's work was a certain irony in which, as Nogueira-Godsey explains, "the rational discipline required of the Calvinist was intrinsically tied to modernization, scientific discovery, maximizing efficiency, and cultivating a rationalistic approach to all areas of life."[8] That is, the very basis of this Protestant ethic would lead to its own demise because it was a system in which belief in God was unnecessary to the achievement of its goals. Weber noted that Calvinism promoted a work ethic that served as evidence of having been part of the elect. In short, "the accumulation of wealth was morally sanctioned in so far as it was combined with a sober, industrious career; wealth was condemned only if employed to support a life of idle luxury or self-indulgence."[9] It is not difficult then to see the inevitable comparison that some contemporary scholars are making between the legitimation of wealth acquisition in Calvinism and that of the modern-day prosperity gospel in places like Africa.[10]

From the mid- to late-twentieth century, American sociologist Peter Berger championed Weber's ideas by proposing (though eventually withdrawing) his own secularization thesis

---

[7] Max Weber, *The Protestant Ethic and the Spirit of Capitalism* (German 1905; repr. New York: Routledge, 2001), 70. Weber's terminology is sometimes translated as the "elimination of magic" or "demagification."

[8] Trad Nogueira-Godsey, "Weberian Sociology and the Study of Pentecostalism: Historical Patterns and Prospects for the Future," *Journal for the Study of Religion* 25, no. 2 (2012): 55.

[9] Anthony Giddens, "Introduction," in Weber, *The Protestant Ethic and the Spirit of Capitalism*, xii.

[10] David Ogungbile, "African Pentecostalism and the Prosperity Gospel," in *Pentecostal Theology in Africa*, ed. Clifton Clarke (Eugene, OR: Pickwick, 2014), 132.

prognosticating the diminishing role of faith.[11] Berger and others specifically attributed their predictions to the growing power of modernity, which they expected to eventually erode the role of faith.[12] Central to this thesis was Weber's notion alluded to earlier of the "disenchantment of the world." As Berger explains, "put simply, the idea has been that the relation between modernity and religion is inverse—the more of the former the less of the latter."[13] Berger's most significant contribution and extension of Weber's theory may be his focus on pluralism as a product of modernity and thereby secularism. Pluralism, made possible by globalization and technology, forced to the forefront a situation in which religious belief exists in a marketplace of competing ideas. "In other words, pluralism forces the religious believer to recognize that their sacred reality is subjective."[14]

It is not uncommon for people to hold contradictory ideas. This is certainly the case regarding religion and elements of secularization in Africa, as both seem to coexist to some degree. It would be shortsighted to assume that Africa's strong and pervasive belief in the supernatural keeps secularism at bay, as the presence of pluralism shows. In Africa, secularism and the attenuating pluralism it produces has proven especially problematic in that it has brought about a resurgent syncretism between Christianity and African Traditional Religions. As T. D. Mashua observes in his study of Traditional Religions and secularism in Africa, "[Pluralism] has promoted a spirit of accommodation and tolerance to the point that it has become almost impossible for one to rebuke the spirit of syncretism without being accused of having a judgmental

---

[11] "Secularism," in *Global Dictionary of Theology*, ed. William Dyrness and Veli-Matti Kärkäinen (Downers Grove, IL: InterVarsity, 2008), 801–4.

[12] Berger, "Secular and De-Secularization," 384–86; Roderick R. Hewitt, "The Changing Landscape of Christianity and the Challenging Context of Secularism," *The Ecumenical Review* 67, no. 4 (2015): 547.

[13] Berger, "Secular and De-Secularization," 284.

[14] Nogueira-Godsey, "Weberian Sociology and the Study of Pentecostalism," 58.

attitude."[15] Mashua's point is that pluralism brings to Africa a subjective perspective on religion and thereby functions as a secularizing agent. And it was a similar secularism and subjectivity that arguably led to the demise of Christianity in Europe.[16]

The rapid growth of Pentecostal Christianity, especially in the Global South, has necessitated a reassessment of those predictions offered by secular theorists, especially concerning the demise of religion.[17] Indeed, some have seen the emergence of Pentecostalism in the early twentieth century as a reaction to modernity, and thereby to secularization, even if the precise nature and classification of that reaction remains the subject of some debate.[18] However, I would add to Mashua's thesis that not only is religious pluralism a secularizing force in Africa, but so too is the prosperity gospel. As Mashua points out, A. Shorter and E. Onyancha have argued that secularism in Africa exists in four ways:

1. Secularism as a worldview—in which theory and practice deny God's presence in the world;
2. Secularism as a division between private sphere of speculative opinion and public truth;
3. Secularism as religious indifference;
4. Secularism as consumer materialism.[19]

---

[15] T. D. Mashua, "A Reformed Mission Perspective on Secularism and Pluralism in Africa: Their Impact on African Christianity and the Revival of Traditional Religion," *Calvin Theological Journal* 44, no. 1 (2009): 120.

[16] Ibid., 108.

[17] Berger, "Secular and De-Secularization," 386; André Droogers, "Essentialist and Normative Approaches," in Anderson et al., *Studying Global Pentecostalism*, 46; Nogueira-Godsey, "Weberian Sociology and the Study of Pentecostalism," 52.

[18] Stephen Hunt, "Sociology of Religion," in Anderson et al., *Studying Global Pentecostalism*, 180–81.

[19] A. Shorter and E. Onyancha, *Secularism in Africa* (Nairobi: Paulines Publications Africa, 1997); Mashua, "A Reformed Mission Perspective on Secularism and Pluralism in Africa," 112.

The prosperity gospel functions as the embodiment of the fourth way and may represent one of the means through which secularism will take hold on a continent long known for its religious devotion. For the purpose of this chapter, then, I define *secularization* as "the presence of certain ideological forces that effectively move religious belief to the periphery of life." Secularization accomplishes this by making religion increasingly irrelevant. As Mashua explains, "Secularization is the process through which everything considered to be secular is detached from the church. When this process takes place, humans rely mainly on their own knowledge and findings, considering God to be redundant."[20] This is precisely what gave rise to liberal theology in the first place. Enlightenment-influenced theologians, such as Friedrich Schleiermacher and those who followed him, sought to "protect God" from the seemingly unstoppable forces of modern thought, embodied especially in higher criticism—and, later on, as contained in evolutionary theory—and they did this by relegating God to the inner realm of subjectivity and values. In doing so, the very idea of "God" became unnecessary.

My main argument in this chapter is that two strands of African Pentecostalism, which I refer to as *prosperity Pentecostalism* and *missional Pentecostalism,* respectively represent secularizing and anti-secularizing forces within the movement. In what follows I articulate the contours of these two opposing strands of African Pentecostalism. In doing so, I hope to build on Ralph Winter's thesis that sodalities—in particular, missions teams in the narrow sense of church planting and evangelism—consistently breathe new life into church structures and keep the church from nominalism and the drift to a disenchanted worldview.

MISSIONAL PENTECOSTALISM

In Chapter 1 I noted the primary expressions of Pentecostalism. Here I examine two strands within those broader categories.

---

[20] Mashua, "A Reformed Mission Perspective on Secularism and Pluralism in Africa," 110–11.

My interest lies particularly with those churches within classical Pentecostalism, which I prefer to call missional Pentecostalism, and on a strand within neo-Pentecostalism, which I refer to as prosperity Pentecostalism.

I begin my discussion by describing missional Pentecostalism because it represents the lesser known of the two. Allan Anderson rightly says that "Pentecostalism is above all else a missionary movement," and that "the fundamental conviction of Pentecostals is that the power they receive through the Spirit is to evangelize all nations and so glorify Jesus Christ."[21] Similarly, Byron Klaus argues that Pentecostalism must be understood "through a lens of mission."[22] Klaus helpfully points out the various historical influences that combined to give birth to modern Pentecostalism and how these contributed to the missional nature of the movement. These included a Wesleyan-Holiness emphasis on the Spirit's power for entire sanctification for service to God, the Keswick emphasis on Holy Spirit empowerment for evangelism, a millennial focus on the imminent return of Christ that empowered and motivated socially marginalized groups, restorationist expectations of a return to the nature and power of the New Testament church, and a multiculturalism that anticipated the new heaven and new earth.[23]

Citing the work of Margaret Paloma, Klaus also notes that Pentecostalism challenges "the sacred/secular dichotomy that characterized modernity" and instead gives rise to "an affirmation of the immediate availability of God's power and presence."[24] For this very reason, and speaking of North American Pentecostalism, Frank Macchia states that "Pentecostals need to rediscover the

---

[21] Allan Anderson, *To the Ends of the Earth: Pentecostalism and the Transformation of World Christianity* (Oxford: Oxford University Press, 2013), 1–2.

[22] Byron Klaus, "Pentecostalism and Mission," *Missiology* 35, no. 1 (2007): 39.

[23] Ibid., 40.

[24] Ibid., 46; David Maxwell, "The Missionary Movement in Africa and World History: Mission Sources and Religious Encounter," *The Historical Journal* 58, no. 4 (2015): 904.

eschatological fervor that allowed them in the early years of the movement to swim against the spirit of the age" and to thereby challenge many social paradigms that were oppressive to women and minorities.[25]

Interestingly, Klaus also shows, citing McClung, that in the developing theology of Pentecostalism there has been a detectable movement away from an early emphasis on evangelism, epitomized in William Seymour's admonition, "Do not go forth from this meeting and talk about tongues, but try to get people saved."[26] This shift does not represent an abandonment of Pentecostalism's missional emphasis, but rather an increased attentiveness to the meaning of the kingdom of God, along with explorations of applying that in a Pentecostal perspective beyond missions. This has, for example, been a dominant theme in the work of preeminent Pentecostal scholar Gordon Fee, and in more recent works such as that by Macchia in *Baptized in the Spirit: A Global Pentecostal Theology*.[27] Similarly, arguing for understanding European Pentecostalism as a reaction to the Enlightenment and to secularism, Anderson says that "for Pentecostals, a rationalistic intellectualism has destroyed the soul of Christianity."[28] This leads to his conclusion that "Pentecostal mission is fundamentally and essentially proclaiming and demonstrating a holistic message."[29]

In ways very similar to Klaus, Anderson says that "Pentecostalism is a mission movement par excellence."[30] He identifies "five

---

[25] Frank Macchia, "The Struggle for Global Witness: Shifting Paradigms in Pentecostal Theology," in *The Globalization of Pentecostalism: A Religion Made to Travel*, ed. Murray W. Dempster et al. (Oxford: Regnum, 1999), 23.

[26] Klaus, "Pentecostalism and Mission," 41.

[27] Frank Macchia, *Baptized in the Spirit: A Global Pentecostal Theology* (Grand Rapids, MI: Zondervan, 2006), 47–49.

[28] Allan Anderson, "Pentecostalism, the Enlightenment, and Christian Mission in Europe," *International Review of Mission* 95, no. 378–79 (2006): 277.

[29] Ibid., 278.

[30] Allan Anderson, "The Significance of Pentecostalism to Mission," in *Mission in Context*, ed. John Corrie and Cathy Ross (Burlington, VT: Ashgate, 2012), 231.

cardinal features" of what I am here referring to as missional Pentecostalism. First, Anderson notes that eschatology and the expectation of an end-times revival proceeding the return of Christ were a driving force in the emergence of the Pentecostal movement. Second, Pentecostalism's beginnings were multicultural. This was true not only of the Azusa Street revival in Los Angeles, led by African American pastor William Seymour, but also of the global revivals that were taking place around that same time in places like India, Korea, and China.[31] Third, Pentecostalism "placed emphasis on missions as a result of the experience of Spirit baptism."[32] That is, many who experienced these Pentecostal revivals went out as missionaries, sensing an urgency to the task and an empowerment for world evangelization. Fourth, Anderson notes that many early Pentecostal missionaries were guilty of colonialism and paternalistic tendencies, often (though not always) failing to recognize the contributions of others, especially indigenous people or women.[33] Finally, Pentecostalism's missionary nature was evident in its extraordinary capacity for contextualization. "Because of its emphasis on the empowering ability of the Spirit to equip ordinary believers for missionary service without requiring prior academic qualifications, Pentecostalism was more dependent on national workers than other missions were at the time."[34]

Further evidence of the missional nature of early Pentecostalism described by Klaus and Anderson can be seen in many of the publications that helped sustain the movement; William Seymour's *The Apostolic Faith* and E. N. Bell's *Word and Witness,* for example, frequently published testimonies of visions, prophecies, and Spirit-inspired songs that underscored the urgency of global evangelization in light of Jesus's imminently expected return. Consider this typical example from Anna Hall, from Houston, Texas, a worker at the Azusa Street revival, who shared a vision that concluded:

---

[31] Ibid., 231–35.
[32] Ibid., 235.
[33] Ibid., 237–38.
[34] Ibid., 240.

> I heard the beautiful warbling of a bird, and thought it was a mocking bird which one might hear there. But no, it seemed away down in my soul. And as that beautiful bird began to sing, I saw a little infant face right before my eyes. And as the song of the bird began to ripple, it began to sound like water running over pebbles. It increased till it sounded like many waters, and the face enlarged till it was a full grown face. I said "Surely this is a messenger from the holy country." The voice answered, "Yes and I have to tell you that Jesus is coming. Go forward in My name, preach the Gospel of the Kingdom, for the King's business demands haste. My people have only time to get on the beautiful garments and prepare for the wedding supper in the Heavens."[35]

Early Pentecostal publications were riddled with similar warnings and admonishments. They served to sustain a sense of urgency created by the dynamic experience of God's presence that accompanied the many global revivals that birthed modern Pentecostalism. The specific focus of that urgency was the task of world missions. Thus, when the Assemblies of God organized in 1914, it did so specifically "for the greatest evangelism the world had ever seen."[36]

This, of course, raises the important question of whether this missionary urgency that defined many of the turn-of-the-century global revivals is also true today of African Pentecostalism. I agree with D. J. Garrard, who says that African Pentecostals do indeed "see themselves as engaged in fulfilling Christ's mandate to go into all the world to teach and evangelise."[37] This missional emphasis was evident in that the success of many Western missionary efforts in Africa was owed to the efforts of indigenous workers and

---

[35] *The Apostolic Faith*, vol. 1, no. 1 (Los Angeles: Apostolic Faith Movement, September 1906), 3.

[36] Combined Minutes of the General Council of the Assemblies of God, Hot Springs, Arkansas, April 2–12, 1914, 12.

[37] D. J. Garrard, "African Pentecostalism," *Journal of Beliefs & Values*, 30, no. 3 (2009): 240.

that the contribution of these workers is often absent in many mission histories.[38] It is therefore far more accurate to speak not of the success of Western missions *to* Africa, but of mission movements from *within* Africa that succeeded in part because of cooperation between mission workers and vast numbers of indigenous peoples. By this I do not mean to minimize the importance played in the overlapping, "enchanted" worldviews of Africans and Pentecostals, for surely this has played a major part. But the need to emphasize that Pentecostal missionaries relied heavily on indigenous workers to spread the gospel must also not be overlooked. Plus, the role played by indigenous people is important not only because it helps to overcome the racial and cultural superiority that often found their way into missionary hagiography, but also because it shows that missional Pentecostalism maintained its evangelistic fervor even as it took root in African soil. Without it, the vibrant African church that we see today would not exist. Plus, many African churches were immediately engaged in cross-cultural work within their own artificially created borders right from the beginning, as local workers engaged in evangelism across the many tribes found within one nation.[39]

Of course contemporary missions among African Pentecostals looks different from that of its Western counterparts. In some ways this difference represents a return to the roots of missional Pentecostalism, which first sent out missionaries with few resources, financial or otherwise. Many early Pentecostal missionaries sent out from Azusa Street, for example, were materially poor themselves and went with scant backing and supplies.[40] Some even packed their belongings in coffins, never expecting to return

---

[38] Anderson, *An Introduction to Pentecostalism*, 2nd ed. (Oxford: Cambridge University Press, 2014), 9; Maxwell, "The Missionary Movement in Africa and World History," 909–10.

[39] Andrew Mkwaila, "Theology of Mission in the Malawi Assemblies of God: An Ecclesial Omission," *Missio Africanus: The Journal of African Missiology* 3, no. 1 (2017): 5.

[40] Anderson, "The Significance of Pentecostalism to Mission," 235.

from the land of their calling.⁴¹ They proceeded in deep faith in the Spirit's leading and empowerment. In a similar manner, many African missionary efforts today also operate on a shoestring and in extreme hardship, and they sometimes struggle against indifference and malaise within their own denomination. What Mkwaila says of the Malawi Assemblies of God holds true for much of Africa when it comes to sending missionaries across geographic borders. He rightly observes that "it is possible, therefore, to concur that far more can and should be done in missionary outreach, while simultaneously acknowledging that great strides have been made towards fostering a critical mass in the church that has been inculcated with a missionary vision."⁴²

African missions has also somewhat reversed the order of the older missions movements that occupied much of the "Great Century" of missions during the nineteenth- and early-twentieth centuries. While the defining ethos of that era was "the West to the rest," Africans are now bringing the gospel and evangelistic fervency back to North American and European nations that are indeed soaked with secularity. As Asamoah-Gyadu points out, "Some of the largest and fastest growing churches in Western Europe today are those set up and run by immigrants from sub-Saharan Africa."⁴³ Granted, many of these focus on diaspora missions and reach mostly those from similar majority world contexts. Nonetheless, there are pockets of exceptions to this, ranging in size from the Sunday Adelaja's massive Embassy of God Church in Ukraine to much smaller congregations like Église evangélique baptiste de Massy in France, which is made up of mostly white French nationals but led by a Togolese pastor. The full impact of diaspora churches among African immigrant

---

⁴¹ Stan Guthrie, *Mission in the Third Millennium: 21 Key Trends for the 21st Century*, rev. ed. (Eugene, OR: Wipf and Stock, 2014), 106.

⁴² Mkwaila, "Theology of Mission in the Malawi Assemblies of God," 6.

⁴³ J. Kwabena Asamoah-Gyadu, "Pentecostalism in Africa and the Changing Face of Christian Mission: Pentecostal/Charismatic Renewal Movements in Ghana," *Mission Studies* 19, no. 2 (2002): 14.

communities in Europe has yet to be seen as it relates to secularism in Europe, and it would be unwise to discount their presence as unimportant.

African Pentecostals are also vigorously pursuing the *missio Dei* regarding unreached people groups. When the Africa Assemblies of God Alliance—a network of over forty Assemblies of God churches from across sub-Saharan Africa—met in Accra, Ghana, in February 2018, it set in writing the goal of sending missionaries and establishing national indigenous churches in Western Sahara, Mauritania, Algeria, Libya, Tunisia, Morocco, Djibouti, Comoros, Eritrea, Somalia, Sudan, and South Sudan—all by the end of 2022. Clearly, missional Pentecostalism is alive and well in sub-Saharan Africa.

PROSPERITY PENTECOSTALISM

I have chosen *prosperity Pentecostlaism* over terms such as *neo-Pentecostalism* because the latter is too broad to depict accurately the movement I have in mind.[44] Specifically, I refer to those forms of African Pentecostalism that promote a "health and wealth" understanding of Pentecostalism, in which proponents preach that faith in Jesus produces wealth and prosperity, and that sickness and suffering reflect a lack of faith. Lovemore Togarasei writes, "According to this Gospel, getting rich is seen as God's will and an outward manifestation of his blessings."[45] Togarasei explains: "The belief is that since God owns everything on earth, those who follow Jesus have a claim in God's riches. Believers therefore have a right to the blessings of health and wealth through positive confession and sowing seeds of prosperity."[46] Additionally, some have seen in the prosperity brand of African Pentecostalism the embodiment of many of the same secular notions articulated by

---

[44] Allan Anderson, "Varieties, Taxonomies, and Definitions," 19.
[45] Lovemore Togarasei, "The Pentecostal Gospel of Prosperity in African Contexts of Poverty: An Appraisal," *Exchange* 40, no. 4 (2011): 339.
[46] Ibid., 341.

Weber and others.[47] Ogungbile says that the prosperity gospel in Africa, almost always associated with Pentecostalism, represents a paradigm shift from the theology of many African Initiated Churches that taught an other-world asceticism. Instead, prosperity Pentecostalism teaches that material prosperity—or an explicit affirmation of this world—"is God's blessing and gift to a successful Christian."[48] Thus, prosperity Pentecostalism represents the very embodiment of secular ideals. In Africa, prosperity Pentecostalism represents a syncretistic combination of Western materialism and individualism with traditional religious beliefs about the spiritual causes and hindrances associated with wealth acquisition. God in this system functions much like the ancestors in the old religion, as a force to be appeased (or manipulated) until one gets the desired results.

Prosperity Pentecostalism has found fertile soil in Africa owing to poverty and to traditional understandings of the interrelatedness of spiritual and material success.[49] Prosperity preachers have cast themselves as the new "Big Man," a role that was first held by local chiefs and later by colonialists and missionaries alike. Their message of the availability of spiritual power for the acquisition of wealth resonates deeply within a culture that has long held that material and spiritual prosperity are inseparable realities, and that malevolent spirits often hinder both. Ogungbile rightly observes, though, that the prosperity gospel contributes to the very things it claims to solve, especially poverty and the oppression of the poor, not to mention bringing disrepute to the Christian faith.[50]

Some claim that prosperity forms of Pentecostalism benefit places like Africa by reducing poverty or at least changing people from a pessimistic, poverty mentality to an optimistic, hopeful

---

[47] Paul Gifford and Trad Nogueira-Godsey, "The Protestant Ethic and African Pentecostalism: A Case Study," *Journal for the Study of Religion* 24, no. 1 (2011); Jean Comaroff, "The Politics of Conviction: Faith on the Neo-liberal Frontier," *Social Analysis: The International Journal of Social and Cultural Practice* 53, no. 1 (2009): 20, 27–28.

[48] Ogungbile, "African Pentecostalism and the Prosperity Gospel," 135.

[49] Ibid., 136–39; Kalu, "Pentecostalism and Mission in Africa," 27.

[50] Ogungbile, "African Pentecostalism and the Prosperity Gospel," 137.

one. This is the argument put forward by Lovemore Togarasei.[51] While acknowledging the work of other African scholars, such as the study done by Nigerian A. O. Dada that concluded that the prosperity gospel peddles false hopes and delusion, enriching only its leaders, Togarasei believes that the prosperity brand of Pentecostalism has contributed to poverty alleviation. Even though he acknowledges its secular bent, evident in its emphasis on market capitalism and materialism, he says that prosperity teaching helps the poor especially through its advocacy of entrepreneurship.[52] Prosperity teachers often emphasize that having a job is tantamount to being just one paycheck away from poverty, and therefore the goal of every believer should be to become an employer rather than an employee. Togarasei says those churches that preach a prosperity gospel often bring in lots of money from their congregants and build large auditoriums, which can create jobs for as many as five hundred workers. But contradictions abound in this logic, especially on the issue of entrepreneurship. For example, one of the lessons learned in the microfinance industry has been that not everyone has the capacity for business, even when given the proper tools.[53] Not only that, but in some African countries, like Zimbabwe, 50 percent of the population belong to Pentecostal churches.[54] It would simply be impossible for all of them to become employers. Beyond these basic sociological and logistical issues, there are the far more pressing theological ones. Specifically, prosperity advocates do not seem to have taken seriously biblical injunctions to defend the poor and weak (Is 1:7, 23), and an argument can readily be made that they take advantage of them by depriving them of the meager income they have. And even though entrepreneurship can be a

---

[51] Togarasei, "The Pentecostal Gospel of Prosperity in African Contexts of Poverty," 339.
[52] Ibid., 345.
[53] Brian Fikkert, "In Pursuit of Holistic Economic Development," in *For the Love of God: Principles and Practice of Compassion in Missions*, ed. Jerry Ireland (Eugene, OR: Wipf and Stock, 2017), 144–49.
[54] Anderson, *An Introduction to Pentecostalism*, 114.

good opportunity for some of Africa's poor, there are far better theological resources for promoting economic independence than the prosperity gospel.

It is not uncommon for Pentecostal churches in West Africa to accept offerings in such a way as to praise those who give more and thus humiliate those who give less. One such offering process, witnessed in Lomé, Togo, at an Assemblies of God church, lasted well over an hour, with the preacher starting at an exorbitant amount—roughly the equivalent of US$1,000—and then slowly working his way down to one of the most common pieces of money available in West Africa, the 100XOF coin, or about 20 cents. Because the person giving must walk to the front of the congregation, everyone knows exactly who gives what. The whole process is designed to put pressure on the congregation to give more than they might otherwise. Congregants are prodded to give more in order to be blessed in greater ways. In this, the worshipful aspect of stewardship is reduced to a purely secular act—an act rooted in worldly values and in materialism.

It's hard to say whether or not the approach is effective as a means of bringing in more funds. By far the largest group to come forward were those in the 500XOF group, roughly US$1. For most, even this amount probably meant a tremendous sacrifice, given that 55 percent of the population in Togo live below the poverty line (about US$2 a day). More interesting regarding the present study was that this practice was witnessed twice in Assemblies of God churches in Lomé, one of those times being during a multi-church Easter service. Given that Assemblies of God churches are generally considered part of classical Pentecostalism, or what I have termed missional Pentecostalism, this suggests that the boundaries between missional Pentecostalism and prosperity Pentecostalism can sometimes become blurred. It also suggests the need to articulate the theological foundations for missional Pentecostalism not only as an anti-secularizing force, but also as a means of helping churches with an historic emphasis on missions to maintain a trajectory toward the *missio Dei*.

CLARIFYING TERMS

When referring to African Pentecostalism, scholars of all disciplines need to distinguish clearly between its prosperity version and its missional version. To equate the prosperity gospel with "most" Pentecostals or with the movement as a whole is grossly inaccurate.[55] Terms such as *classical Pentecostalism* and *neo-Pentecostalism* are useful in defining historic currents regarding Pentecostal origins, but less useful when describing contemporary African Pentecostalism. The terms *missional Pentecostalism* and *prosperity Pentecostalism* more accurately describe precise contemporary approaches to Pentecostalism in that both are alive and well on the continent. This is not to say that they are the only forms or even the most important forms, but they are two expressions of the movement that are worthy of attention, especially regarding the issue of incipient secularization in Africa. Furthermore, the value of these terms lies in the fact that they make explicit the theological motivations behind various strands of Pentecostalism and therefore might also serve as a rubric for African Pentecostal churches in determining who and what they wish to be.

Pentecostalism in Africa has largely succeeded because of its emphasis on the supernatural.[56] Missional Pentecostalism has historically grounded its power in prayer and in contemporary experiences of the Holy Spirit. But experiences of the Holy Spirit were never conceived of as a means to an end; rather, they are both an enacted eschatological event and as empowerment for global witness. Conversely, not only the message but also the tools for the propagation of prosperity Pentecostalism are mostly secular and include especially the use of technology, media, and marketing. As

---

[55] See, for example, Christine Schliesser, "On a Long Neglected Player: The Religious Factor in Poverty Alleviation," *Exchange* 43, no. 4 (2014): 339–59; Tanja Winkler, "When God and Poverty Collide: Exploring the Myths of Faith-Sponsored Community Development," *Urban Studies* 45, no. 10 (2008): 2099–2116.

[56] Ogbu Kalu, "A Discursive Interpretation of African Pentecostalism," *Fides et Historia* 41, no. 1 (2009): 86; Garrard, "African Pentecostalism," 233–34.

Pentecostalism spreads and becomes arguably the dominant form of Christianity in sub-Saharan Africa, missional Pentecostalism should take heed of the dangers of losing its historic dependence on spiritual powers even as it makes use of them. This is not to say that the use of these modern advantages and resources for spreading the gospel are inherently problematic. Rather, as Kalu says, "there is often a thin line between religious and secular techniques in the use of media communication."[57] Attentiveness to this thin line may prove determinative for the future of missional Pentecostalism. I suspect that a lack of attention to this line lies behind the offerings I witnessed in Togo. I do not believe that the pastors who took these offerings had abandoned the missional bent characteristic of most Assemblies of God churches, but rather that they uncritically borrowed from the manipulative practices of the prosperity preachers and lost sight of the more potent and effective power of the Spirit.

Finally, prosperity Pentecostalism represents an abandonment of the very things that drive missional Pentecostalism because mission has historically advanced at great personal sacrifice. Despite the tendency for the boundaries between these two expressions of Pentecostalism to become blurred, it seems unlikely that the two can coexist for very long. When material well-being becomes the high-water mark of the Christian life, then the inevitable consequence is the faltering of missions. Missions will always be a costly enterprise and any understanding of Christianity that exchanges the costly nature of discipleship for wealth acquisition is destined for futility. Of course, this is a lesson that Western Pentecostal missionaries especially need to learn, for we have rarely gone to places around the globe without a treasure chest packed with goodies. We have gone from being missionaries of the one-way ticket to missionaries of the first-class lifestyle in just a couple of generations. As one Nigerian missionary reminded me one day in Togo regarding our relatively big house and our expensive Landcruiser, "You Americans make it very hard for anyone else to do

---

[57] Kalu, "Pentecostalism and Mission in Africa," 23.

missions because you come with all the goodies; and the people look at us Africans and think we are not really missionaries."

Furthermore, an essential feature of missional Pentecostalism is attention to community. Africans have long valued community and viewed with suspicion those who were outsiders or radically individualistic. Yet, prosperity Pentecostalism is individualistic to the core, and thus a betrayal not only of the gospel but of African indigenous identity. James K. A. Smith, in his exposition of Charles Taylor's *A Secular Age*, points out that one of the things that helped secularism overtake the deeply rooted religiosity of the Middle Ages was the loss of community and consequent heightened individualism. "Once individuals become the locus of meaning, the social atomism that results means that disbelief no longer has social consequences. 'We' are not a seamless cloth, a tight-knit social body; instead, 'we' are just a collection of individuals." And, Smith adds, "this diminishes the ripple effect of individual decisions and beliefs. You're free to be a heretic—which means, eventually, that you're free to be an atheist."[58] Missional Pentecostalism in Africa will succeed most when it closely guards its most treasured value, that of a Spirit-formed community. It is through community that missionaries are called and sent, and in community that missions movements emerge. No greater threat exists to undermine African indigenous notions of community than prosperity Pentecostalism and its rampant individualism.

---

[58] James K. A. Smith, *How (Not) to Be Secular: Reading Charles Taylor* (Grand Rapids, MI: Eerdmans, 2014), 31.

Epilogue

Concluding Thoughts on the Missionary Spirit

It is atheistic for the church to pursue a plan that it can accomplish without God's help. Yet many models of Pentecostal missiology tend in this direction by focusing on social agendas that demonstrate no particular dependency on the Spirit and cannot be distinguished in any significant way from their many secular counterparts. The church in every age must be aware of the danger of subtly slipping into a way of being in the world that centers on human agency rather than the agency of the Spirit. Dependence on God's Spirit defined early Pentecostal missions out of both theological and practical concerns, and that, above all else, has been what I have tried to recover in this volume.

Any theology, Pentecostal or otherwise, that seeks to articulate the relationship between evangelism and compassion must acknowledge the need to distinguish between the work of cross-cultural missionaries and that which the local church is called to do in its own community. This crucial argument has long been advanced by scholars like Lesslie Newbigin and Ralph Winter. Rarely, though, has this nuance appeared in contemporary Pentecostal missiologies, and as a result most attempts along these lines function not as missiologies but as ecclesiologies that include little more than a symbolic nod to cross-cultural witness. Missional living, missional churches, missional ethics, and missional worship are all the rage. Yet, usually absent in all of these is any specific reference to God's concern for the nations, to those most separated from the gospel, in any concrete way. Nor is there any distinction made between the church planting and disciple-making ministry of cross-cultural workers, and that which a local church does in its own context. But precision is important in theology, and the church knew this even before Arianism appeared on the scene and heresy was discovered just one Greek letter away from orthodoxy.

Especially important regarding the Pentecostal contribution to the mission/missions discussion has been the recovery of the essential connection among Word, Spirit, and nations. That is, proclamation of the gospel in the power of the Spirit, and how these relate to God's concern for the nations has long constituted the driving force of Pentecostalism. This emphasis emerges clearly in the gospels and Acts and is underscored by speaking in tongues, which serves both as evidence of Spirit baptism and of the unfinished, verbal task of cross-cultural evangelism to which the church is supremely called and which it must carefully guard. This stands in stark contrast to the service-community-proclamation paradigm of holistic missiologies, wherein neither proclamation nor the nations holds a special place. Importantly, the prioritization of evangelism in Pentecostal missions has never in practice meant the neglect of social concern as Pentecostal history clearly shows. Yet, the fear of neglect has often been the basis of any notion of priority. But fear never makes for good theology, and we need look no further than the fundamentalist withdrawal from social concern for evidence of this.

Thomas Oden eloquently frames Jesus's atoning death in a way that seems relevant to Pentecostal views of the relationships between evangelism and compassion. As he reminds us: "Jesus did not come to teach about the cross, but to be nailed to it. He came that there might be a gospel to preach."[1] Notice the subtleties at work here. Jesus was certainly a teacher, and he certainly taught about the cross and what it meant both for himself and for his

---

[1] Thomas Oden, *The Word of Life,* vol. 2 of *Systematic Theology,* (Peabody, MA: Prince Press, 2001), 344.

followers. But that is only part of the story, and not even the main part. Focus on what Jesus did and not why he did it and you lose the gospel. Lose the gospel and you have lost Christ, Christianity, and everything else with it. Likewise, talk about missions in ways that flatten out the kingdom and fail to notice the key connection among Word, Spirit, and the nations, and we subtly slip into our own thinly veiled, well-meaning heterodoxy.

It strikes me as bizarre that skilled theologians like Orlando Costas would call the debate over evangelism and social engagement "a senseless and satanic waste of time, energies, and resources."[2] This could only be true if theological precision were not important, if a proper understanding of the mission of local churches and the work of missionaries were inconsequential. Costas thinks that the church should only be concerned with the integration of these things. But as we have seen, integration by whom and in what way? If integration exists mainly at the level of missionaries doing both evangelism and social justice in places where they should be planting and equipping the church, that church will become malnourished and grow to only a fraction of its potential. Thus, integration improperly applied proves to be the subtle work of the devil, for it creates a weak and ineffective church that knows nothing but dependency.

Discipleship turns out, not surprisingly, to be the key to a church concerned about both evangelism and social justice. The pattern established by Barnabas and Saul in Acts 11—13, as well as numerous other church-planting teams throughout Acts, shows the incalculable value of investing in people so that they know what it means to be God's Spirit-anointed covenant community. But where missionaries invest in social programs and neglect the task of discipleship, they help create churches that have no prophetic voice, for they have become dependent on foreign resources and have been indoctrinated into the language of outsiders. Only by giving their attention to the task of discipleship can missionaries avoid the pitfall of paternalism that so often ensnares them and

---

[2] Orlando Costas, *The Integrity of Mission: The Inner Life and Outreach of the Church* (San Francisco: Harper and Row, 1979), 75.

those they aim to serve. The temptation to "do more" and to build things—feeding programs, schools, hospitals, orphanages, and the like—often flows from insecurities and from the need for significance on the part of missions workers. Anecdotally, I can attest that the major pushback I get from the argument I have laid out here is that it diminishes the importance of those in the church who are not called to cross-cultural church planting by elevating that particular calling. This strikes me as odd at many levels, not the least of which is that the notion of diminishment constitutes a fairly dominant teaching of Jesus as it relates to his followers. John the Baptist's declaration, "He must increase, I must decrease" ought to be the prophetic desire of all Christ followers. That aside, prioritism in many ways adds value to every calling within the church because it prevents them from becoming about a thousand things that have little to do with God's concern for the nations, a concern that runs from Genesis to Revelation.

For Westerners especially, the story of Rwanda reminds us of the dangers inherent in not appreciating the vitality of spiritual power that helps create a church caught up in the purposes of God. What missionaries working in the majority world must realize is that discipleship is always happening, for better or for worse. Our actions, our money, our resources, and the way we use them declare to those we would serve what we believe about true power and where it comes from. Too often, the story we tell through the use of these things is the story of secular and structural power and not the story of the spiritual power that marked the missionary impulse of the early church and that proved definitive for early Pentecostal missions.

Pentecostalism has within its theological and missiological heritage the resources to be a mighty force against the tide of secularism that sweeps across not only the Western world but also has found inroads into places like Africa by way of the prosperity gospel. Yet, too often Western missionaries denounce prosperity teachings out of one side of their mouths and endorse it out of the other by the way we live and the way we serve local and national churches. We cannot have it both ways. Not only that, but the social actions we often take rob local people of the better solutions that would come if we would trust in the Spirit's power to work in and through the church in dynamic ways. We want to help children, and so we create child-sponsorship programs or feeding programs, which may indeed have an immediate benefit to the child. But if in serving a child we wreak havoc on families, destroy the dignity of parents, and decimate the vital bond between siblings, then surely we have failed to be attentive to the Spirit, who cares equally about them all. In the name of social justice we commit a thousand injustices to which we turn a blind eye. We do this because we have forgotten that God's power is made perfect in weakness, and that the Holy Spirit is the greatest resource the church possesses. How we go about missions, and how we define missions, has the potential to hinder or welcome God's transforming presence.

To say the Spirit is the missionary Spirit is to declare that the church is a missionary church and to declare that Pentecostalism is preeminently about missions. To be Spirit led, Spirit filled, and Spirit baptized is to be concerned above all else with taking the gospel to the nations by embracing, even celebrating, our weaknesses, so we can discover what true power is and looks like. That has long been the main storyline in Pentecostal missiology. In this missionary trajectory in which proclamation and discipleship are prioritized, all of the other activities of the church find their greatest significance because we rediscover, or perhaps discover for the first time, our role as a pilgrim people. The missionary Spirit alone can breathe new life into old structures, and creative strategies into local expressions of the church. It really is all about trajectory. It's about the fact that when Spirit moves, God's people become caught up in both purpose and dependence all at the same time. The church discovers simultaneously the impossibility of its task and the limitless power made available when the Spirit is poured out. This has long been the genius of Pentecostal missiology.

Selected Bibliography

Allen, Roland. *Missionary Methods: St. Paul's or Ours?* 1962. Reprint. Grand Rapids, MI: Eerdmans, 2009.
Anderson, Allan. *Spreading Fires: The Missionary Nature of Early Pentecostalism.* Maryknoll, NY: Orbis Books, 2007.
———. *To the Ends of the Earth: Pentecostalism and the Transformation of World Christianity.* Oxford: Oxford University Press, 2013.
Archer, Kenneth. *The Gospel Revisited: Towards a Pentecostal Theology of Word and Witness.* Eugene, OR: Pickwick, 2011.
Asamoah-Gyadu, J. Kwabena. *Contemporary Pentecostal Christianity: Interpretations from an African Context.* Oxford: Regnum, 2013.
Barnett, Maurice. *The Living Flame: Being a Study of the Gift of the Spirit in the New Testament with Special Reference to Prophecy, Glossolalia, Montanism, and Perfection.* 1953. Reprint. Eugene, OR: Wipf and Stock, 2014.
Bauckham, Richard. *Bible and Mission: Christian Witness in a Postmodern World.* Grand Rapids, MI: Baker Academic, 2003.
Blauw, Johannes. *The Missionary Nature of the Church.* New York: McGraw-Hill, 1962.
Bockmuehl, Klaus. *Evangelicals and Social Ethics.* Downers Grove, IL: InterVarsity, 1975.
Boer, Harry R. *Pentecost and Missions.* Grand Rapids, MI: Eerdmans, 1961.
Borgman, Paul. *The Way According to Luke: Hearing the Whole Story of Luke-Acts.* Grand Rapids, MI: Eerdmans, 2006.
Bornstein, Erica. "Child Sponsorship, Evangelism, and Belonging in the Work of World Vision Zimbabwe." *American Ethnologist* 28, no. 3 (2001): 595–622.

Bosch, David J. *Transforming Mission: Paradigm Shifts in the Theology of Mission.* 1991. Reprint. Maryknoll, NY: Orbis Books, 2004.
Cartledge, Mark. *Charismatic Glossolalia: An Empirical-Theological Study.* Burlington, VT: Ashgate, 2002.
Chan, Simon. *Pentecostal Ecclesiology.* Dorset, UK: Deo, 2011.
Costas, Orlando. *The Church and Its Mission: A Shattering Critique from the Third World.* Wheaton, IL: Tyndale House, 1974.
Cox, Harvey. *Fire from Heaven: The Rise of Pentecostal Spirituality and the Reshaping of Religion in the 21st Century.* Cambridge, MA: Da Capo Press, 1995.
Dayton, Donald. *Theological Roots of Pentecostalism.* Metuchen, NJ: The Scarecrow Press, 1987.
Dempster, Murry, et al. *Called and Empowered: Global Mission in Pentecostal Perspective.* Peabody, MA: Hendrickson, 1991.
———. *The Globalization of Pentecostalism: A Religion Made to Travel.* Eugene, OR: Pickwick, 2011.
Denecker, Timothy. *Ideas on Language in Early Latin Christianity: From Tertullian to Isidore of Seville.* Leiden: Brill, 2017.
Douglas, J. D., ed. *Proclaim Christ until He Comes.* Minneapolis, MN: World Wide Publications, 1989.
Dunn, James D. G. *The Acts of the Apostles.* Grand Rapids, MI: Eerdmans, 1996.
———. *Baptism in the Holy Spirit: A Re-examination of the New Testament Teaching on the Gift of Spirit in Relation to Pentecostalism Today.* 2nd ed. London: SCM, 2010.
Elechi, O. Oko, Sherill V. C. Morris, and Edward J. Schauer. "Restoring Justice (Ubuntu): An African Perspective." *International Criminal Justice Review* 20, no. 1 (2010): 73–85.
Faupel, D. William. *The Everlasting Gospel: The Significance of Eschatology in the Development of Pentecostal Thought.* Dorset, UK: Deo, 2009.
Ferdinando, Keith. *The Triumph of Christ in African Perspective: A Study of Demonology and Redemption in the African Context.* Carlisle, UK: Paternoster, 1999.

Ferguson, Everett. *The Church of Christ: A Biblical Ecclesiology*. Grand Rapids, MI: Eerdmans, 1996.
Flett, John. *The Witness of God: The Trinity, Missio Dei, Karl Barth, and the Nature of Christian Community*. Grand Rapids, MI: Eerdmans, 2010.
Freeman, Dena, ed. *Pentecostalism and Development: Churches, NGOs and Social Change in Africa*. New York, Palgrave Macmillan, 2012.
Gifford, Paul, and Trad Nogueira-Godsey. "The Protestant Ethic and African Pentecostalism: A Case Study." *Journal for the Study of Religion* 24 no. 1 (2011): 5–22.
Goheen, Michael. *A Light to the Nations: The Missional Church and the Biblical Story*. Grand Rapids, MI: Baker Academic, 2011.
González, Justo L. *Acts: The Gospel of the Spirit*. Maryknoll, NY: Orbis Books, 2001.
Green, Joel B. *Conversion in Luke-Acts*. Grand Rapids, MI: Baker Academic, 2015.
Guder, Darrell L. *Be My Witnesses*. Grand Rapids, MI: Eerdmans, 1985.
———. *The Continuing Conversion of the Church*. Grand Rapids, MI: Eerdmans, 2000.
Hays, Richard. *The Moral Vision of the New Testament: A Contemporary Introduction to New Testament Ethics*. New York: Harper One, 1996.
Hedlund, Roger E. *The Mission of the Church in the World*. Grand Rapids, MI: Baker, 1991.
Heine, Ronald E. *Origin: Scholarship in Service of the Church*. Oxford: Oxford University Press, 2011.
Henry, Carl F. H. *The Uneasy Conscience of Modern Fundamentalism*. 1947. Reprint. Grand Rapids, MI: Eerdmans, 2003.
Hodges, Melvin. *Growing Young Churches*. Chicago: Moody Bible Institute, 1970.
———. *The Indigenous Church*. 1953. Reprint. Springfield, MO: Gospel Publishing House, 1971, 2009.
———. *A Theology of the Church and Its Mission: A Pentecostal Perspective*. Springfield, MO: Gospel Publishing House, 1977.

Hoekendijk, J. C. *The Church Inside Out*. Philadelphia, PA: Westminster, 1966.

Horrell, David G. *Solidarity and Difference: A Contemporary Reading of Paul's Ethics*. 2nd ed. New York: Bloomsbury, 2015.

Hovenden, Gerald. *Speaking in Tongues: The New Testament Evidence in Context*. London: Sheffield Academic, 2002.

Hunter, Harold. "Tongues-Speech: A Patristic Analysis." *Journal of the Evangelical Theological Society* 23, no. 2 (1980): 125–37.

Ireland, Jerry M. *Evangelism and Social Concern in the Theology of Carl F. H. Henry*. Eugene, OR: Pickwick, 2015.

Johnson, Alan R. *Apostolic Function in 21st Century Missions*. Pasadena, CA: William Carey Library, 2009.

Kalu, Ogbu U. "A Discursive Interpretation of African Pentecostalism." *Fides et Historia* 41, no. 1 (2009): 71–90.

———. "Pentecostalism and Mission in Africa, 1970–2000." *Mission Studies* 24, no. 1 (2007): 9–45.

Kärkkäinen, Veli-Matti. "Mission in Pentecostal Theology." *International Review of Mission* 107, no. 1 (2018): 5–22.

———. "Pentecostal Missiology in Ecumenical Perspective: Contributions, Challenges, Controversies." *International Review of Mission* 88, no. 350 (1999): 207–25.

Katongole, Emmanuel. *The Sacrifice of Africa: A Political Theology for Africa*. Grand Rapids, MI: Eerdmans, 2011.

Keener, Craig S. "Tongues as Evidence of the Spirit's Empowerment in Acts." In *A Light to the Nations*, ed. Stanley M. and Paul Lewis Burgess. Eugene, OR: Pickwick, 2017.

———. "Why Does Luke Use Tongues as a Sign of the Spirit's Empowerment?" *Journal of Pentecostal Theology* 15, no. 2 (2007): 177–84.

Kelsey, Morton. *Speaking in Tongues: An Experiment in Spiritual Experience*. New York: Doubleday, 1964.

Klaus, Byron D. "Pentecostalism and Mission." *Missiology* 35, no. 1 (2007): 39–54.

Levison, Jack. *Inspired: The Holy Spirit and the Mind of Faith*. Grand Rapids, MI: Eerdmans, 2013.

Little, Christopher R. *Mission in the Way of Paul: Biblical Mission for the Church in the 21st Century*. New York: Peter Lang, 2005.
Longman, Timothy. *Christianity and Genocide in Rwanda*. Cambridge, UK: Cambridge University Press, 2010.
Lord, Andrew M. "Good News for All? Reflections on the Pentecostal Full Gospel." *Transformation: An International Journal of Holistic Mission Studies* 30, no. 1 (2013): 17–30.
———. *Network Church: A Pentecostal Ecclesiology Shaped by Mission*. Leiden: Brill, 2012.
———. "Pentecostal Mission through Contextualization." *PentecoStudies* 10, no. 1 (2011): 103–17.
———. *Spirit-Shaped Mission: A Holistic Charismatic Theology*. Bletchley, UK: Paternoster, 2005.
———. "The Voluntary Principle in Pentecostal Missiology." *Journal of Pentecostal Theology* 8, no. 17 (2000): 81–95.
Ma, Julie C., and Wonsuk Ma. *Mission in the Spirit: Towards a Pentecostal/Charismatic Missiology*. Eugene, OR: Wipf and Stock, 2010.
Ma, Wonsuk, et al., eds. *Pentecostal Mission and Global Christianity*, Regnum Edinburgh Centenary Series. Oxford, UK: Regnum, 2014.
Macchia, Frank D. *Baptized in the Spirit: A Global Pentecostal Theology*. Grand Rapids, MI: Zondervan, 2006.
———. *Jesus the Spirit Baptizer: Christology in Light of Pentecost*. Grand Rapids, MI: Eerdmans, 2018.
Manji, Firoze, and Carl O'Coill. "The Missionary Position: NGOs and Development in Africa." *International Affairs* 78, no. 3 (2002): 567–83.
McClendon, David. "Sub-Saharan Africa Will Be Home to Growing Shares of the World's Christians and Muslims." Pew Research, 2017.
McClung, L. Grant, Jr. "Pentecostal/Charismatic Perspectives on a Missiology for the Twenty-First Century." *Pneuma* 16, no. 1 (1994): 11–21.

McDonnell, Killian. "Communion Ecclesiology and Baptism in the Spirit: Tertullian and the Early Church," *Theological Studies* 49, no. 4 (1988): 684–91.

McGee, Gary B. *Initial Evidence: Historical and Biblical Perspectives on the Pentecostal Doctrine of Spirit Baptism.* Eugene, OR: Wipf and Stock, 1991.

———. "Latter Rain Falling in the East: Early-Twentieth-Century Pentecostalism in India and the Debate over Speaking in Tongues." *Church History* 68 (1999): 648.

———. "The New World of Realities in Which We Live: How Speaking in Tongues Empowered Early Pentecostals." *Pneuma* 30, no. 1 (2008): 108–35.

McGowan, Andrew. "Tertullian and the 'Heretical' Origins of the 'Orthodox' Trinity." *Journal of Early Christian Studies* 14, no. 4 (Winter 2006): 437–57.

Menzies, Robert P. *Empowered for Witness: The Spirit in Luke-Acts.* New York: T & T Clark, 2004.

———. *The Language of the Spirit: Interpreting and Translating Charismatic Terms.* Cleveland, TN: CPT Press, 2020.

———. *Speaking in Tongues: Jesus and the Apostolic Church as Models for the Church Today.* Cleveland, TN: CPT Press, 2016.

Minets, Yuliya. "The Slow Fall of Babel: Conceptualization of Languages, Linguistic Diversity, and History in Late Ancient Christianity." PhD diss. Catholic University of America. Washington, DC, 2017.

Mittlestadt, Martin W. *Reading Luke-Acts in the Pentecostal Tradition.* Cleveland, TN: CPT Press, 2010.

———. *The Spirit and Suffering in Luke-Acts: Implications for a Pentecostal Pneumatology.* New York: T & T Clark, 2004.

Moberg, David O. *The Church as a Social Institution.* Englewood Cliffs, NJ: Prentice-Hall, 1962.

Moltmann, Jürgen. *The Church in the Power of the Spirit: A Contribution to Messianic Ecclesiology.* Translated by Margaret Kohl. Minneapolis, MN: Fortress Press, 1993.

Myers, Bryant. "Progressive Pentecostalism, Development, and Christian Development NGOs: A Challenge and an Opportunity." *International Bulletin of Missionary Research* 39, no. 3 (2015): 115–20.

———. *Walking with the Poor*. Maryknoll, NY: Orbis Books, 2011.

Newbigin, Lesslie. "Future of Missions and Missionaries." *Review and Expositor* 74, no. 2 (1977): 209–18.

———. *The Household of God*. New York: Friendship Press, 1954.

Nissen, Johannes. *New Testament and Mission*. Frankfurt: Peter Lang, 2007.

Pelikan, Jaroslav. *Acts*. Grand Rapids, MI: Brazos, 2005.

———. *Light of the World: A Basic Image in Early Christian Thought*. New York: Harper Brothers, 1962.

Penney, John Michael. *The Missionary Emphasis of Lukan Pneumatology*. Sheffield, England: Sheffield Academic, 1997.

Pomerville, Paul. *The Third Force in Missions*. 1985. Reprint. Peabody, MA: Hendrickson, 2016.

Powers, Janet Everts. "Missionary Tongues?" *Journal of Pentecostal Theology* 8, no. 17 (2000): 39–55.

Samuel, Vinay, and Chris Sugden, eds. *Mission as Transformation*. Eugene, OR: Wipf and Stock, 2011.

Snyder, Howard A. *Community of the King*. Downers Grove, IL: InterVarsity, 1977.

Stagg, Frank, et al. *Glossolalia: Tongue Speaking in Biblical, Historical, and Psychological Perspective*. Nashville, TN: Abingdon, 1967.

Stronstad, Roger. *The Charismatic Theology of St. Luke*. Peabody, MA: Hendrickson, 1984.

Studebaker, Steven M. *Defining Issues in Pentecostalism: Classical and Emergent*. Eugene, OR: Pickwick, 2008.

Taylor, John V. *For All the World*. Philadelphia, PA: Westminster, 1966.

———. *The Go-Between God: The Holy Spirit and Christian Mission*. London: SCM Press, 1975.

Tesunao, Donald, and Yamamori Miller. *Global Pentecostalism: The New Face of Christian Social Engagement*. Berkeley and Los Angeles: University of California Press, 2007.

Thompson, Alan J. *The Acts of the Risen Lord: Luke's Account of God's Unfolding Plan.* New Studies in Biblical Theology. Edited by D. A. Carson. Downers Grove, IL: InterVarsity, 2011.

Thompson, James W. *The Church According to Paul: Rediscovering the Community Conformed to Christ.* Grand Rapids, MI: Baker Academic, 2014.

Van Engen, Charles. *God's Missionary People: Rethinking the Purpose of the Local Church.* Grand Rapids, MI: Baker Academic, 1991.

Verkuyl, Johannes. *Contemporary Missiology: An Introduction.* Grand Rapids, MI: Eerdmans, 1978.

Vondey, Wolfgang. *Pentecostal Theology: Living the Full Gospel.* London: T & T Clark, 2018.

Wagner, C. Peter. *Church Growth and the Whole Gospel: A Biblical Mandate.* San Francisco: Harper and Row, 1981.

———. *Your Church Can Be Healthy.* Nashville, TN: Abingdon, 1979.

Wenk, Matthias. *Community Forming Power.* Sheffield, England: Sheffield Academic, 2000.

Winter, Ralph D. "Churches Need Missions Because Modalities Need Sodalities." *Evangelical Missions Quarterly* (1971): 193–200.

———. "From Mission to Evangelism to Mission." *International Journal of Frontier Mission* 19, no. 4 (2002)): 6–8.

———. "Protestant Mission Societies: The American Experience." *Missiology* 7, no. 2 (1979): 139–78.

———. "Two Structures of God's Redemptive Mission." *Missiology* 2, no. 1 (1974): 121–39.

Woolnough, Brian, and Wansuk Ma, eds. *Holistic Mission: God's Plan for God's People.* Regnum Edinburgh Series. Eugene, OR: Wipf and Stock, 2010.

Wright, Christopher J. H. *The Mission of God: Unlocking the Bible's Grand Narrative.* Downers Grove, IL: IVP Academic, 2006.

Wrogemann, Henning. *Theologies of Mission, Intercultural Theology,* vol. 2. Downers Grove, IL: IVP Academic, 2018.

Yong, Amos. *The Missiological Spirit: Christian Mission in the Third Millennium Global Context*. Eugene, OR: Cascade, 2014.
———. *Mission after Pentecost: The Witness of the Spirit from Genesis to Revelation*. Grand Rapids, MI: Baker Academic, 2019.

Index

Abraham, call of, 14–17, 18

Acts, Book of
    Acts 1, 45, 90, 116
        confusion of the disciples, 121
        cross-cultural evangelism, outlining, 50
        endowment of the Spirit, 47, 122, 125
        missional mandate, 91, 106
        witnessing to the nations, 21, 22, 35, 114
    Acts 2, 2, 60, 75
        Assemblies of God interpretation, 82
        Chrysostom on, 77, 78–79
        communal emphasis in, 123, 144–45
        cross-cultural proclamation of Christ, 48, 51
        glossolalia in, 62, 63
        Irenaeus on, 74
        mystical vagueness in, 58
        on obstacle of cynicism, 43
        solidarity, as emphasizing, 129
        Spirit, on the outpouring of, 32, 117, 126
    Acts 4, 43, 106, 126
    Acts 5, 43, 148
    Acts 6, 9, 44
    Acts 8, 32, 44, 48, 50
    Acts 10, 44, 51, 63
        conversion of Cornelius, 32, 48, 50
        Gentiles, solidarity with, 34, 52
        Irenaeus's citation of, 73
    Acts 11
        Barnabas and Saul, pattern set by, 98, 107, 175
        on the compassionate mission, 99, 125
        Gentiles, on the gospel as reaching, 52
    Acts 13, 42, 44, 62
        Barnabas and Saul, on the mission of, 90, 93, 98, 106, 125
        cross-cultural witness, on the call to, 26, 39
        the Great Commission, carrying out, 91
    Acts 19
        gift of the Spirit, on disciples lacking knowledge on, 51–52
        Spirit's empowerment, on being without, 44
        tongues and prophecy as distinct charisms, 73

adelphoi, solidarity of, 101–2

African Pentecostalism, 149, 154, 158
    Faith Based Organizations and, 139–41, 148
    NGOs and compassion in Africa, 136–39, 148
    Pentecostal churches and development, 141–43

Index

Prosperity Pentecostalism in, 155, 165
Ubuntu in African culture, 143–44, 144–46
African Traditional Religions, 156
Against Celsus (Origen), 75, 76
Against Heresies (Irenaeus), 71
Against Marcion (Tertullian), 68
Against Praxeas (Tertullian), 66
agape, 103
Allen, Roland, 89, 111
Ananias and Sapphira, 43–44, 106
Anderson, Allan, 3–4, 5, 13, 159, 160–61
Apostolic Constitution, 58
Apostolic Faith (periodical), 161
Apostolic Faith Mission, 13, 175
Arianism, 59, 174
Asamoah-Gyadu, J. Kwabena, 33, 153, 154, 164
Assemblies of God, 5, 6, 162, 164, 170
    Africa Assemblies of God Alliance, 165
    Assemblées de Dieu of Togo, 149, 150
    Assemblies of God World Missions, 85, 119
    classical Pentecostalism, as part of, 82, 168
    Sixteen Fundamental Truths doctrine, 46–47
Augustine, Daniela, 39
Augustine of Hippo, 58–59, 80, 81, 83
Azusa Street Revival, 3, 46, 61, 161, 163

Balthasar, Hans Urs von, 74–75
Baptized in the Spirit (Macchia), 160
Barnabas and Saul, ministry of
    in Book of Acts, 43, 53, 93, 98–99, 175
    Church of Antioch, as sent from, 94
    as set apart, 39, 90, 91, 106–7, 125
Barnett, Maurice, 57, 58, 69
Barth, Karl, 9
Basil of Caesarea, 58
Bell, E. N., 161
Berger, Peter, 155–56
biblical anthropology, 38
Blauw, Johannes, 14, 15, 18, 19, 21, 42
Bliese, Richard, 63
Bock, Darrell, 22
Boer, Harry, 89
Borgman, Paul, 38–39
Bornstein, Erica, 140
Bosch, David, 119

Called and Empowered (Dempster et al.), 33
Calvinism, 155
Camp, Bruce, 89, 90, 92, 93
Carey, William, 88
Celsus, perspective of, 75
Cerillo, Augustus, 12
Chan, Simon, 40
charisms and charismatics, 2, 60, 67
    charism as a work of grace, 62
    end-times charismata, 69
    in the Kingdom of God, 11, 117
    Spirit-formed community as *charis*, 148
Chrysostom, John, 76–79, 83
church planting
    compartmentalized views on, 85–86
    compassionate missions and, 110
    cross-cultural church planting, 40, 94, 176
    mission planting *vs.*, 95
church-as-witness paradigm, 25, 33, 119
Churchill, Winston, 90–91
compassion, 96, 99, 127, 145, 146
    Christian compassion, 103, 119
    compassion and the church, 121–25

compassionate mission, 95, 99, 130–31, 133
discipling for compassion, 108
evangelism and, 6, 173, 174
in First/Second Stage Missions, 97–98
indigenous African compassion, 135–36, 141, 150, 152
Kingdom of God and, 111–14, 116
missio Dei, as a fundamental element of, 120–21
modern expressions of, 85–86, 148
NGOs and compassion in Africa, 136–39
outsiders, compassionate projects of, 107, 132
project-centered approach to, 110
solidarity and, 128, 129
Consolidation Missions, 97
1 Corinthians, 57, 60, 76, 78, 93
baptism, emphasis on, 100
fellowship of believers, 148
glossolalia for congregational worship, 62–63
harmonizing tongues in Acts and 1 Corinthians, 82
missionary ethos of Paul, 69
nature of tongues in text, scholars debating, 63
on tongues as being for unbelievers, 68
Cornelius, conversion of, 32, 48–51, 52, 73
Costas, Orlando, 90, 91–92, 96, 175
Cox, Harvey, 45–46, 153–54
Dada, A. O., 167
Dayton, Donald, 3–4
Demonstration against the Pagans that Christ Is God (Chrysostom), 77
Dempster, Murray, 9, 11, 41
functional ecclesiology of, 13

holistic mission, calling for, 33, 36, 37
Pentecostal missions, on their coming-of-age, 7–8
"time is fulfilled," phrase, dissecting, 112
Denecker, Tim, 59, 80
diakonia (service), 8, 25, 33
Acts, concept conveyed in, 123
kerygmatic function of the church, not oriented to, 118
of the local church, 94
as table service and service of the world, 9
diaspora churches, 164–65
discipleship, 119, 128, 133, 151, 177
concern for the nations and, 17, 18
continual process of, 176
costly nature of, 170
neglecting the task of, 86, 175
Rwanda, discipleship crisis in, 110
set-apart people, formation of, 121, 130
Teen Challenge discipleship, xxiii
dispensational theology, 7, 111
Dunn, James D. G., 123

Église evangéliue baptiste de Massy, 164
Elechi, O. Oko, 143
Ellul, Jacques, 127
end-times, 4, 5, 51, 53, 69, 112, 161
Europe, 110, 157, 160, 164–65
Eusebius of Caesarea, 58, 65, 73, 75
evangelism, 41, 132, 160, 174, 175
of Assemblies of God, 5, 119, 163
charisms as oriented to, 67, 69
church planting and, 85–86, 96
church-based evangelism model, 26

community evangelism, 126
cross-cultural witness, 26, 39, 92, 123, 173
E-0 to E-3 evangelism paradigm, 93, 95
eschatology, linking to, 36
evangelistic mandate, 1, 6–7, 10, 27, 146
Grace Generation Movement ministry, 149–52
holistic mission of evangelicals, 33
of immigrant populations, 164
for the Kingdom of God, 111
of mission sodalities, 125, 158
missions, distinguishing from, 22
the nations, evangelization of, 12, 18
near-neighbor evangelism vs. mission, 50
personal holiness and, 77
Spirit's empowerment of, 127, 159
urgency in, 4, 34, 61, 93, 113, 133, 161, 162
world evangelism, 13–14
Eversole, Robyn, 137, 138

Faith-Based Organizations (FBOs), 139–41
Faupel, D. William, 4
Fee, Gordon, 160
fellowship, 34, 87, 125–26. See also koinonia
Ferdinando, Keith, 143, 144
Ferguson, Everett, 25
Flett, John, xxxv
Flower, J. Roswell, 46
Freeman, Dena, 141–42
fundamentalism, 118, 142, 174

Garr, Alfred Goodrich, 46
Garr, Lilian, 46
Garrard, D. J., 162
Gibbs, Eddie, 117
Glasser, Arthur, 91
glossolalia, 34, 53, 81

barriers, role in breaking down, 49, 58
continuation of tradition, 57, 63, 64–65
demise of speaking in tongues, 55
ecclesiological implications, 39, 83
foreign tongues, misinterpreting ability to speak, 12, 56
in Greek thought, 70, 75
missional nature of, 31, 41, 46, 56, 73
Montanism, association with, 66–67
the nations and, 44–47
paradigm shift in Pentecostal understanding of, 34–35
receipt of the Spirit and, 71–74, 76, 83, 174
references to practice of, 61–62
God's Missionary People (Van Engen), 94
Goheen, Michael, 41–42, 45
González, Justo, 121, 122–23, 129
Grace Generation Movement (GGM), 149–52
Great Commission, 26, 117
as compelling, 32, 33
imperative of, 11, 17–18
local churches, role in, 23, 93
modalities and sodalities in the fulfillment of, 91, 92
Pentecostal interpretations, 14, 21
Trinity, grounded in the doctrine of, 19–20
Greek language, 69, 70, 79, 174
clarity of understanding in, 73
Greek-speaking immigrants, 71
koinos as Greek word for common, 144–45
melos as Greek word for members, 130
tongues, conceptual understanding of Greek speakers, 59
Greek mystery religions, 59, 70

Green, Joel, 48
Gregory of Nyssa, 58

Hall, Anna, 161
Hartenstein, Karl, xxxv
Hays, Richard, 103
Hebrew as the tongue of holiness, 70
Hedlund, Roger E., 15
Henry, Carl F. H., 7
heresy, 59, 71–72, 171, 174
Hilary of Poitiers, 58
Hinson, E. Glenn, 56, 83
Hiruy, Kiros, 137, 138
Hodges, Melvin, 29, 32, 127, 128
Hoekendijk, Johannes C., xxxvi–xxxvii
holism. *See under* Pentecostalism
Holy Spirit, 110, 117, 120
    in Acts, 32, 34, 43–44, 52, 73, 123
    Africa, Spirit working in, 135–39, 152
    Barnabas and Saul as working with, 90, 98
    Christian community, indwelling within, 111, 145–46
    contemporary expressions of, 169
    empowerment of, 26, 77, 122
    fellowship of/*koinonia*, 147–48
    the future, giving of the Spirit as down payment for, 113
    gifts of, 3, 21, 57, 105, 113, 126
    global witness, as empowering, 115
    initial evidence of Spirit baptism, 34, 45–47, 54, 56, 81, 82
    Keswick, emphasis on, 159
    Kingdom of God, role of Spirit in, 7, 114
    as missionary Spirit, 2, 5–6, 11, 47–48, 86, 118, 177
    otherness, as oriented to, 133
    in Pentecostal theology, 5, 40
    solidarity and the Spirit, 104–8
    Spirit and the nations, 19–22, 31
    Spirit baptism, 37, 45, 46, 61, 81, 82, 161, 174
    unity of believers and, 125–27
    See also glossolalia
Homilies on First Corinthians (Chrysostom), 78
Homily IV (Chrysostom), 77
Horrell, David, 99–100, 101, 102
Hunter, Harold, 57, 58, 73
Hurtado, Larry, 49
Hutu peoples of Rwanda, 109, 131

India, 46, 161
The Indigenous Church (Hodges), xx
indigenous Pentecostalism, xxix, 2
initial evidence, doctrine of, 34, 46, 56
    baptism in the Spirit, 82
    in classical Pentecostalism, 45
    individualistic interpretations, 54
    tongues as evidence of, 81
Irenaeus of Lyons, 71–74

Jerome of Stridon, 58–59
Jerusalem Council, 53
Jesus Christ, 4, 38, 128, 147, 161
    baptism into Christ, 100–101
    body of Christ, 93, 102, 130, 145
    commitment, making to, 150, 151
    corporate solidarity in, 99–100
    cross-cultural proclamation of, 50–51, 53
    demons, accused of appropriating power from, 83
    fellowship in Christ, 148
    Holy Spirit and, 47, 52
    Kingdom of God in the ministry of, 19, 111–12, 113
    "latter rain," return of Christ, 5
    liberation story of Jesus, 34
    on the mandate of the church, 121, 162
    as Messiah, 15, 16, 17–18, 63

the nations, proclamation of Christ among, 22, 26
nonverbal activity of, 9
oneness in Christ, 100, 103, 104–6, 126
otherness, manifest concern for, 110
in Pentecostal Christology, 13, 27
prophetic desire of Christ followers, 176
in prosperity Pentecostalism, 165
sacrifice of, 11, 21, 72, 117, 146, 174–75
as the second Adam, 71
second coming of, 9, 113, 159
Spirit-anointed ministry, 118
teleological orientation of ministries, 119
Joel, Prophet, 51
John the Baptist, 51, 176
Johnson, Alan, 8

Kähler, Martin, 4
Kalu, Ogbu Uke, 170
Katongole, Emmanuel, 131, 135
Keener, Craig, 51, 53, 63, 113, 115, 126
Kelsey, Morton, 56–57, 66
kerygma (proclamation), 8, 25, 33, 94, 118, 123
Kingdom of God, 6, 10, 12
 broad approach to, 33, 35, 36, 40
 compassion and, 111–14, 116
 confusion about, 121–22
 dispensationalism, Kingdom rubric of, 7–8, 11
 Jesus, central role in ministry, 19
 local church as sign of coming Kingdom, 124
 as a missions theme, 117
 Pentecostalism, increasing focus on, 160, 162
 as perpetual, 16
Klaus, Byron, 159, 169–61

koinonia (community), 25, 33, 106, 118, 152
 as fellowship, 123, 129
 koinonitis, danger of mutation into, 107
 in multi-sided ministry of the church, 8, 94
 Paul, in the writings of, 147–49
 Ubuntu concept of redemption and, 136, 144–46
Kuzmic, Peter, 1

Ladd, George Eldon, 7, 111
Latter Rain movement, 5
Latin America, xx, xxii
Latin language, 79, 80
 Ecclesiastical Latin, 69, 73
 Latin writers' understanding of tongues, 58–59
 Latin-speaking immigrants, 71
Lausanne movement, 1, 6, 33
Levison, Jack, 81
liberalism, 118
liberation theologies, xxx, 33, 34
A Light to the Nations (Goheen), 41
linguistic diversity, 57, 70, 79, 80
linguistic otherness, 55, 59–60, 81, 83
Little, Christopher, 99
Longman, Timothy, 132
Lord, Andrew, 9–10, 36, 41, 56
Los Angeles, revival efforts in, 61, 161
Luce, Alice E., xix–xx, xxii
Luke, Apostle, 38, 41, 121, 127, 144
 ambiguity in narrative of, 80
 barriers, on the breaking of, 49–50
 "come and look," inviting communities to, 145, 152
 diakonia concept, conveying, 123
 emphasis on witness, 47, 115
 on empowerment of the Spirit, 21, 104
 fellowship, linking to Spirit, 125–26, 147

Israel in ecclesiology of, 31–32, 45
on the mission to the nations, 39–40
on speaking in tongues, 52, 63–64, 73, 79, 82
on the unity of believers, 126, 148
See also Acts, Book of
Luther, Martin, 88

Ma, Julie C., 10, 35, 37–38, 41
Ma, Wonsuk, 10, 33, 35, 37–38, 41
Macchia, Frank D., 34, 63
broad understanding of, 35, 41
eschatological fervor, on the need for, 159–60
on mission as global justice, 37
Marcus Aurelius, 71
Mark, Apostle, 11, 62, 64, 112
martyria (witness), 94
Mashua, T. D., 156–57, 158
McClung, L. Grant, Jr., 113, 160
McDonnell, Kilian, 67
McGee, Gary B., 46
McGowan, Andrew, 66–67
Menzies, Robert, 47, 51
Minet, Yuliya, 57–59, 60, 65, 70, 79, 80
miracles, 58, 72, 111, 150
missio Dei, 7, 9, 42, 60, 99, 168
the church, remaining oriented to, 24–25
compassion as a fundamental element of, 120–21
concern for the nations as part of, 113
gospel proclamation, defining as, 10
the nations as the proper center of, 14
vigorous pursuit of, 165
Willingen scholars on, 6, 27
Mission in the Spirit (Ma/Ma), 35
Missionary Methods (Allen), xix–xx
Missionary Nature of the Church (Blauw), 42

missions and mission
four dimensions of, 13, 94, 113, 123, 141, 157–58
fraternal cooperation with, 22, 23, 97
global mission, 47–54
holistic mission, 7, 33, 36
creationist motif, argument for, 35
in mission-as-transformation movement, 6, 113, 114
mis-steps in understanding, 31, 39, 42
missional ecclesiology, 35, 39
mission-as-witness model, 121
missions/mission distinction, 22–23, 42, 50, 174
narrow *vs.* broad mission, 10, 14, 30, 31–33, 39, 41–42
Second Stage missions, 96–99, 107
See also missio Dei; Pentecostal missiology; sodalities and modalities
Mkwaila, Andrew, 164
modalities. *See* sodalities and modalities
Moltmann, Jürgen, 4
Montanism, 55, 65–67, 79
Morris, Leon, 112, 147
Murphy, Edward, 90–91

Neill, Stephen, 12–13, 23, 37
Network Church (Lord), 36
Newbigin, Lesslie, 104, 149
fraternal workers/missionaries, distinguishing between, 97
on the household of God, 145
missionaries and local church, distinguishing between, 23, 42, 173
Nigeria, 96, 149, 170
Niles, D. T., 132
Nogueira-Godsey, Trad, 155
nominalism, drift toward, 86, 88, 158

Index

nongovernmental organizations (NGOs), 136–41, 142
nonverbal witness, 114–15, 116

Oates, Wayne E., 56
Obadare, Ebenezer, 139
Oden, Thomas, 174
Ogungbile, David, 166
Olaniyan, Tejumola, 138
Onyancha, E., 157
organic *vs.* sending mode of mission, 42
Origen of Alexandria, 74–76, 83
Overman, Andrew, 19–20

Pacian of Barcelona, 80
Paloma, Margaret, 159
parachurch organizations, 41, 88, 92, 96
Parham, Charles, 60
Parousia, 112
Paul, Apostle, 68, 81, 107, 111, 121
    Artemis, confrontation with followers of, 52
    Christian unity, on the importance of, 127, 130
    on church and mission, 45, 69, 74, 89, 93
    community focus, 105, 129
    on *glossolalia*, 57, 62, 73, 78–79, 82
    Kingdom of God, on the signs of, 145–46
    koinonia in Paul, 147–48
    solidarity in Pauline Epistles, 99–104, 106
Penney, John Michael, 47
Pentecost, day of, 36, 57, 73, 80
The Pentecost (periodical), 46
The Pentecostal Evangel (periodical), xix
Pentecostal missiology, 4, 32, 33, 50, 173
    deeper/wider understanding of, 10, 177
    early missiology, distinctions made in, 39–40
    the nations, keeping central to, 12, 24, 39–41, 54
    Pentecostal Christology and, 13, 27
    on speaking in tongues, 45, 79
Pentecostal Mission and Global Christianity (Ma et al.), 33
Pentecostal World Fellowship, xxi
Pentecostalism
    classical Pentecostalism, 117, 169
        Assemblies of God as representing, 82, 168
        missionary evangelism as focus of, 2, 12, 23, 119, 159
        power of the church and, 110, 133
        Prosperity Pentecostalism as arising from, 154, 168
        speaking in tongues and, 45–46
    corrective approach to the gospel, offering, 111
    missional Pentecostalism, 31–33, 154, 158–65, 169–71
    the nations, reaching, 12–19, 19–22, 37, 39, 40
    neo-Pentecostalism, 2, 159, 165, 169
    Pentecostal ecclesiology, 22–24, 24–27
    Pentecostal holism, 1, 6–12, 24, 33–42, 174
    Pentecostal theology, 34, 36, 40, 47, 54, 82, 160
    prosperity Pentecostalism, 154, 158, 165–68, 169–71
Perkin, Noel, 119
Peter, Apostle, 48, 53, 117
    on the centrality of being a people, 124
    the Great Commission, as compelled by, 33
    Holy Spirit, being filled with, 32, 43

Irenaeus on Peter's visit to Cornelius, 73
reawakening to mission, 50–51
"these last days," sermon in context of, 113
Peters, George, 89
Peterson, David, 116
Peterson, Douglas, xx
Piot, Charles, 137
pluralism as a secularizing force, 156–57
Pomerville, Paul
   on the Great Commission mission, 23, 117
   mission, on the broad sense of, 6–7, 111
   narrower sense of missions, preferring, 9–10, 10–11, 12
primary *vs.* secondary witness, 114–21
proclamational role of the church, 30–31, 47, 118
proseuche (prayer), 123
prosperity gospel
   in Africa, 155, 157, 166, 168
   job creation and, 167
   secularizing tendencies of, 154, 158, 169, 176
The Protestant Ethic and the Spirit of Capitalism (Weber), 154–55

religious otherness, 44, 48
Revelation, Book of, 15, 124, 129
revivals
   Azusa Street, 3, 46, 61, 161, 163
   Second Coming message of, 9
   urgency as accompanying, 5, 162
Rodriguez, Jacob, 71
Rwanda, 128, 176
   Catholic bishop warning on, 109–10
   complicity of the churches in genocide, 132
   otherness, national hatred for, 131

Samuel, Vinay, 113
sanctification, 13, 159
schismatic faith, 55, 59, 66, 148
Schleiermacher, Friedrich, 158
A Secular Age (Taylor), 171
secularism, 136, 146, 153, 165, 171
   African Pentecostalism and, 154–58, 169
   loss of community as tied to rise of, 171
   media communication, secular use of, 170
   Pentecostalism as an anti-secularizing force, 142
   prosperity Pentecostalism, secular bent of, 154, 166, 167, 168
   Rwanda, secular power structures in, 131
   service institutions, secular strength of, 132
   Spirit's power, replacing with secular power, 130, 173
   in Western culture, 153, 159, 160, 164–65
Seymour, William, 46, 61, 160, 161
Shenk, Wilbert, 42
Shorter, A., 157
Simpronian, letter to, 80
Smith, James K. A., 171
Snyder, Howard, 26
social gospel, 118
social justice, 51, 117
   coming kingdom/last days, distinguishing between, 112
   evangelism, doing simultaneously, 85, 175
   narrative of redemption and, 40–41
soda fide, sola gratia doctrine, 66
sodalities and modalities, 125, 130, 158
   cross-cultural church planting, 40, 94, 97, 176
   as indigenous mission movements, 95–96

the mission band, sodalities of, 23, 39
sodality-modality distinction, 23, 89–95, 114
Winter on modality-sodality structures, 86–89, 99
Solidarity and Difference (Horrell), 99
Spirit. *See* Holy Spirit
Spirit-Shaped Mission (Lord), 36
Spittler, Russell, 82–83
Sri Lanka (Ceylon), 132
Stagg, Frank, 56
Steed, Christopher, 69
Stephen, martyrdom of, 32, 44
Sub-Saharan Africa, 164, 165, 170
Sugden, Chris, 113
Sundkler, Bengt, 69
Syriac authors and language, 58, 59, 70, 78, 79

Taylor, Charles, 171
Taylor, John V., 30, 32, 33, 132
Tertullian of Carthage, 66–69, 79, 81
Theophilus the reader, 39
Third Force in Missions (Pomerville), 6
Thompson, Alan J., 39
Thompson, James, 101–2, 105
Togarasei, Lovemore, 165, 167
Togo, 137, 149–52, 168, 170
tongues. *See glossolalia; xenolalia*
Tower of Babel, 70, 78
Transforming Mission (Bosch), xxxiv
Treatise on the Soul (Tertullian), 68–69
Tutsi peoples of Rwanda, 131
Ubuntu in African culture, 143–44, 144–46

Uneasy Conscience of Modern Fundamentalism (Henry), xxiii–xxiv
Uwakwe, Titus, 149–51

Van Engen, Charles, 94
Van Zanen, Stephen J., 90
Verkuyl, Johannes, xxxv
Vondey, Wolfgang, 36–37, 41

Wagner, C. Peter, 89, 90, 107
Weber, Max, 154–56, 166
Welch, John W., 6
Wesleyan Holiness Tradition, 57, 159
Willard, Dallas, 153
Willingen Conference, 6, 20, 27
Winter, Ralph, 97, 99, 158
  Camp, ecclesiological differences with, 90, 92
  on the church *vs.* the mission band, 23, 39, 93, 173
  on indigenous mission movements, 95–96
  on modality and sodality structures, 86–89
  on the value in modality-sodality distinction, 94–95
Word and Witness (periodical), 161
World Council of Churches (WCC), 6

xenolalia (foreign speech), 81
  church fathers on, 57
  missionary understanding of, 55–56
  tongues as references to, 58–59, 79

Yong, Amos, xxi, xxviii–xxix

Zimbabwe, 140, 167

The American Society of Missiology Series

1. *Protestant Pioneers in Korea*, Everett Nichols Hunt Jr.
2. *Catholic Politics in China and Korea*, Eric O. Hanson
3. *From the Rising of the Sun: Christians and Society in Contemporary Japan,* James M. Phillips
4. *Meaning across Cultures*, Eugene A. Nida and William D. Reyburn
5. *The Island Churches of the Pacific*, Charles W. Forman
6. *Henry Venn: Missionary Statesman,* Wilbert R. Shenk
7. *No Other Name? Christianity and Other World Religions,* Paul F. Knitter
8. *Toward a New Age in Christian Theology,* Richard Henry Drummond
9. *The Expectation of the Poor: Latin American Base Ecclesial Communities in Protest,* Guillermo Cook
10. *Eastern Orthodox Mission Theology Today,* James J. Stamoolis
11. *Confucius, the Buddha, and Christ: A History of the Gospel in China,* Ralph R. Covell
12. *The Church and Cultures: New Perspectives in Missiological Anthropology*, Louis J. Luzbetak, SVD
13. *Translating the Message: The Missionary Impact on Culture,* Lamin Sanneh
14. *An African Tree of Life*, Thomas G. Christensen
15. *Missions and Money: Affluence as a Western Missionary Problem . . . Revisited* (second edition), Jonathan J. Bonk
16. *Transforming Mission: Paradigm Shifts in Theology of Mission,* David J. Bosch
17. *Bread for the Journey: The Mission and Transformation of Mission,* Anthony J. Gittins, C.S.Sp.
18. *New Face of the Church in Latin America: Between Tradition and Change,* edited by Guillermo Cook

19. *Mission Legacies: Biographical Studies of Leaders of the Modern Missionary Movement*, edited by Gerald H. Anderson, Robert T. Coote, Norman A. Horner, and James M. Phillips
20. *Classic Texts in Mission and World Christianity*, edited by Norman E. Thomas
21. *Christian Mission: A Case Study Approach*, Alan Neely
22. *Understanding Spiritual Power: A Forgotten Dimension of Cross-Cultural Mission and Ministry*, Marguerite G. Kraft
23. *Missiological Education for the 21st Century: The Book, the Circle, and the Sandals*, edited by J. Dudley Woodberry, Charles Van Engen, and Edgar J. Elliston
24. *Dictionary of Mission: Theology, History, Perspectives*, edited by Karl Müller, SVD, Theo Sundermeier, Stephen B. Bevans, SVD, and Richard H. Bliese
25. *Earthen Vessels and Transcendent Power: American Presbyterians in China, 1837–1952*, G. Thompson Brown
26. *The Missionary Movement in American Catholic History*, Angelyn Dries, OSF
27. *Mission in the New Testament: An Evangelical Approach*, edited by William J. Larkin Jr. and Joel W. Williams
28. *Changing Frontiers of Mission*, Wilbert R. Shenk
29. *In the Light of the Word: Divine Word Missionaries of North America*, Ernest Brandewie
30. *Constants in Context: A Theology of Mission for Today*, Stephen B. Bevans, SVD, and Roger P. Schroeder, SVD
31. *Changing Tides: Latin America and World Mission Today*, Samuel Escobar
32. *Gospel Bearers, Gender Barriers: Missionary Women in the Twentieth Century*, edited by Dana L. Robert
33. *Church: Community for the Kingdom*, John Fuellenbach, SVD
34. *Mission in Acts: Ancient Narratives in Contemporary Context*, edited by Robert L. Gallagher and Paul Hertig
35. *A History of Christianity in Asia: Volume I, Beginnings to 1500*, Samuel Hugh Moffett

36. *A History of Christianity in Asia: Volume II, 1500–1900,* Samuel Hugh Moffett
37. *A Reader's Guide to Transforming Mission,* Stan Nussbaum
38. *The Evangelization of Slaves and Catholic Origins in Eastern Africa,* Paul V. Kollman, CSC
39. *Israel and the Nations: A Mission Theology of the Old Testament,* James Chukwuma Okoye, C.S.Sp.
40. *Women in Mission: From the New Testament to Today,* Susan E. Smith
41. *Reconstructing Christianity in China: K. H. Ting and the Chinese Church,* Philip L. Wickeri
42. *Translating the Message: The Missionary Impact on Culture* (second edition), Lamin Sanneh
43. *Landmark Essays in Mission and World Christianity,* edited by Robert L. Gallagher and Paul Hertig
44. *World Mission in the Wesleyan Spirit,* Darrell L. Whiteman and Gerald H. Anderson (published by Province House, Franklin, TN)
45. *Miracles, Missions, & American Pentecostalism,* Gary B. McGee
46. *The Gospel among the Nations: A Documentary History of Inculturation,* Robert A. Hunt
47. *Missions and Unity: Lessons from History, 1792–2010,* Norman E. Thomas (published by Wipf and Stock, Eugene, OR)
48. *Mission and Culture: The Louis J. Luzbetak Lectures,* edited by Stephen B. Bevans
49. *Comprehending Mission: The Questions, Methods, Themes, Problems, and Prospects of Missiology,* Stanley H. Skreslet
50. *Christian Mission among the Peoples of Asia,* Jonathan Y. Tan
51. *Sent Forth: African Missionary Work in the West,* Harvey C. Kwiyani
52. *Mangoes or Bananas: The Quest for an Authentic Asian Christian Theology,* Hwa Yung

53. *Contemporary Mission Theology: Engaging the Nations: Essays in Honor of Charles E. Van Engen*, edited by Robert L. Gallagher and Paul Hertig
54. *African Christian Leadership: Realities, Opportunities, and Impact*, edited by Kirimi Barine and Robert Priest
55. *Women Leaders in the Student Christian Movement: 1880–1920*, Thomas Russell
56. *Traditional Ritual as Christian Worship: Dangerous Syncretism or Necessary Hybridity?*, R. Daniel Shaw and William R. Burrows
57. *Christian Mission, Contextual Theology, Prophetic Dialogue: Essays in Honor of Stephen B. Bevans, SVD*, edited by Dale T. Irvin and Peter C. Phan
58. *Go Forth: Toward a Community of Missionary Disciples,* Pope Francis, selected with commentary by William P. Gregory
59. *Breaking through the Boundaries: Biblical Perspectives on Mission from the Outside In,* Paul Hertig, Young Lee Hertig, Sarita Gallagher Edwards, and Robert L. Gallagher
60. *A Long Walk, A Gradual Ascent: The Story of the Bolivian Friends Church in Its Context of Conflict,* Nancy J. Thomas. Published by Wipf & Stock, Eugene, OR

www.ingramcontent.com/pod-product-compliance
Lightning Source LLC
Chambersburg PA
CBHW051611230426
43668CB00013B/2061